Ideology

Second Edition

Concepts in the Social Sciences

Series Editor: Frank Parkin

Published Titles

Concepts in the Social Sciences

Ideology

Second Edition

David McLellan

Open University Press
Buckingham

Open University Press
Celtic Court
22 Ballmoor
Buckingham
MK18 1XW

First edition published 1987. Reprinted 1989

First published in this second edition 1995

Reprinted in this edition 1996

A catalogue record of this book is available from the British Library

ISBN 0 335 19466 4 (pb)   0 335 19467 2 (hb)

Typeset by Type Study, Scarborough
Printed in Great Britain by J. W. Arrowsmith Limited, Bristol

For Oliver

Contents

Preface

This small book is intended to be no more than the briefest of introductions to an extremely slippery subject. The topic is as wide as it is fundamental to the social sciences and I am well aware of my being able merely to touch the surface. But I hope at least to stimulate the reader's interest and I have therefore added a detailed list of further reading and an extensive bibliography. I am grateful to Jean Gil, Gabrielle McLellan, Stephanie McLellan, Gay Mitchell, and Keith Webb who have all helped to improve the book.

David McLellan

Preface to the Second Edition

In an effort to keep up with the continuing vagaries of ideology, I have thoroughly revised the text, added a new chapter, and considerably expanded both the Further Reading and the Bibliography.

David McLellan

1
The Career of a Concept

Ideology is the most elusive concept in the whole of social science. For it asks about the bases and validity of our most fundamental ideas. As such, it is an essentially contested concept, that is, a concept about the very definition (and therefore application) of which there is acute controversy.[1]

With significant exceptions, the word ideology comes trailing clouds of pejorative connotation. Ideology is someone *else's* thought, seldom our own. That our thought might be ideological is a suggestion that we almost instinctively reject lest the foundations of our most cherished conceptions turn out to be composed of more shifting sand than we would like. Therefore, the history of the concept of ideology is the history of various attempts to find a firm Archimedean point outside the sphere of ideological discourse, an immoveable spot from which to observe the levers of ideology at work. In the main Marxist tradition this point has consisted in the search for a particular group or class whose representatives would have a peculiar vocation for non-ideological thought. In the Enlightenment, rationalist, empiricist tradition, trust has been placed in an objective science of society which would unmask the irrationality of ideological conceptions. Both traditions envisage the possibility of a society without ideology - whether a Marxist society where ideology seen as a bulwark of class power will no longer be necessary or a capitalist society where the self-evident norms of a rational market economy will impose themselves. But the spectre of the relativism of all claims to truth which has plagued humankind, at least since Plato's Protagoras denied the possibility of objective truth, refuses to be laid. Any examination of ideology makes it difficult to avoid the rueful conclusion that all views about ideology are themselves ideological. But avoided it must be – or at least modified by saying that some views are more ideological than others. For the simple thought that all views are ideological encounters two difficulties: first, that it borders on the vacuous, since it is so all-embracing as to be almost meaningless; second and more damagingly, it contains the same logical absurdity as the declaration of Epimenides the Cretan who declared that all Cretans were liars. A more discriminating approach is therefore necessary not only intellectually but also practically: we are indeed all implicated in ideology which is both real and powerful[2]; but an understanding of this fact can at least prevent us from becoming its unconscious victims.

Unlike many other similarly controversial terms (democracy, say, or liberty), ideology is less than 200 years old. It is the product of the social, political and intellectual upheavals that accompanied the Industrial Revolution: the spread of democratic ideals, the politics of mass movements, the idea that, since we have made the world, we can also remake it. According to the German social philosopher Jurgen Habermas, these new world-views

> emerge from the critique of dogmatism of traditional interpretations of the world and claim a scientific character. Yet they retain legitimating functions, thereby keeping actual power relations inaccessible to analysis and to public consciousness. It is in this way that ideologies in the restricted sense first came into being. They replace traditional legitimations of power by appearing in the mantle of modern science and by deriving their justification from the critique of ideology. Ideologies are coeval with the critique of ideology. In this sense there can be no pre-bourgeois ideologies.[3]

Traditional beliefs, just because they are traditional, tend to be static and to rely on a restricted, hierarchically structured, coherent entities: myths did not compete. Ideologies, on the other hand, were the products of an increasingly pluralist society and were associated with rival groups whose sectional interests they served.[4] Whereas traditional religion concentrated on the interaction between the everyday life of individuals and the sacredness of an other-worldly dimension, the secularized universe of ideology concerned itself with public projects of this-worldly transformation to be legitimized by apparently self-justifying appeals to science and to reason. The organizing myths of past societies were inherited and constituted a given framework that transcended the social world; ideologies are typically our own creation drawn from painstaking investigations of our own societies. This tendency is, in turn, enhanced by the increased democratization of the political process. The industrial revolution involved also a communications revolution in which literacy expended enormously in parallel with the unprecedented cheapness of books and newspapers. The increase in information available and the fact that it issued from highly divergent sources meant that its interpretation became problematic and competing frameworks, reflecting different interests, emerged to make sense of all the new material. But these frameworks, or ideologies, in spite of their inevitably partial origin, had to have a universal appeal. For with the increased participation of the masses in politics, persuasion rather than mere command was the order of the day. In the age of liberty, fraternity and equality, the only approaches that could even aspire to universal acceptance were those based on the apparently universal ideas of reason and science, of which Francis Fukayama's work is but the latest example.[5]

Like so many other enticing things, the word ideology is of French origin. But although directly a product of the French Enlightenment, the notion obviously has its roots in the general philosophical questions about meaning and direction with which the breakdown of the medieval world view confronted Western European intellectuals. These questions were encouraged by the impact of Protestantism with its insistence on the individual, on liberty of conscience, and on the transformative power of the word rather than the reassuring presence of ritual. More direct precursors, however, of the original discussants of ideology, were thinkers such as Francis Bacon and Thomas Hobbes. In his *Novum Organon* (1620) Bacon attempted to outline an approach to the study of society based on observation. Hitherto, human understanding had been obscured by what he called idols – mistaken, irrational conceptions. There were four sorts of idol: idols of the tribe, idols of the cave, idols of the market place, and idols of the theatre. The first idols, those of the tribe, include the tendency to accept what has been hallowed by tradition or to let the passions interfere with the acquisition of rational knowledge. The idols of the cave are those which arise from the particular viewpoint of the individual which often precludes a more general perspective. The idols of the market place are linguistic, the market place being the symbol for social interaction which is often at variance with reality and thus, again, an obstruction to rational understanding. The idols of the theatre are the dogmatic conceptions of former times which, given the absence of any empirical foundation, are no better than dramatic fictions.

The Baconian theory of idols lies at the origin of modern social science. It strongly influenced both the English empirical tradition in Hobbes and Locke and the French Enlightenment which eventually produced the concept of ideology. Unlike their predecessors in England, where the power of throne and altar had been considerably curtailed in the previous century, the philosophers of the French Enlightenment had to contend with an absolutist monarchy in alliance with an autocratic church. Consequently, whereas for Machiavelli and Bacon religion had been a potentially integrating force, for the leading Enlightenment thinkers in France it was the chief obstacle to a rational ordering of society. The keys to this social reformation lay in reason and nature. As Holbach, one of their leading spokesmen, wrote:

> The source of man's unhappiness is his ignorance of nature. . . . The most important of our duties, then, is to seek means by which we may destroy delusions than can never do more than mislead us. The remedies for these evils must be sought for in Nature herself; it is only in the abundance of her resources, that we can rationally expect to find antidotes to the mischiefs brought upon us by an ill-directed, by an overpowering enthusiasm. . . . For this purpose reason must be restored to its proper rank. . . . It must no longer be held down by the massive chains of prejudice.[6]

The solution to the prejudices and lies fostered by priests and kings to bolster their own power lay in the omnipotence of education. Occasionally, Enlightenment thinkers admitted the social determinants of knowledge, as when Helvetius pointed out that insects living on grass eaten by sheep were liable to look on the sheep as ferocious predators but on the wolves, who preyed on the sheep, as entirely beneficent. But in general they had little defence against Marx's subsequent complaint that 'the materialist doctrine concerning the changing of circumstances and upbringing forgets that circumstances are changed by men and that it is essential to educate the educator himself'.[7] Their only reply was to place unlimited confidence in the power of reason to discredit prejudice.

The Enlightenment thinkers were the intellectual precursors of the French Revolution of 1789; and it was in the immediate aftermath of the French Revolution that the term ideology was first coined. Its originator, in 1797, was Antoine Destutt de Tracy, one of a group of philosophers whom the revolutionary Convention had put in charge of the newly founded Institut de France specifically to spread the ideas of the Enlightenment. The Institut briefly enjoyed the patronage of Napoleon, who became an honorary member before his Concordat with the Church and his growing personal despotism caused a breach. In his *Elements d'Ideologie*, written between 1801 and 1815, de Tracy proposed a new science of ideas, an idea-logy, which would be the ground of all other sciences. Rejecting the concept of innate ideas, de Tracy explained how all our ideas are based on physical sensations. A rational investigation of the origin of ideas, free from religious or metaphysical prejudice, would be the foundation of a just and happy society. For the investigation of individual ideas would show their common origin in universal human needs and desires. Those needs would form the framework of laws regulating society on a natural basis and promoting the harmonious fulfilment of the relevant desires. For the natural and the social coincided. And this coincidence would be laid bare by the rational assessment of the origin of ideas, by ideology.

Thus, in its origin, the notion of ideology was positive and progressive. In the eyes of Napoleon, however, it quickly became pejorative. As his government evolved towards an empire supported by established religion, criticism from the liberal and republican ideologues (as they came to be called) became inevitable. And it was partly them that Napoleon blamed after his retreat from Moscow:

> It is to ideology, this cloudy metaphysics which, by subtly searching for first causes, wishes to establish on this basis the legislation of peoples, instead of obtaining its laws from knowledge of the human heart and from the lessons of history, that we must attribute all the misfortunes of our fair France.[8]

This oscillation between a positive and a negative connotation will be characteristic of the whole history of the concept of ideology.

Ideology has a German, as well as a French, origin – though here, too, the French Revolution was a crucial event. For the Enlightenment philosophers, the principles on which they criticized the *ancien régime* and in the name of which the French Revolution was made, were self-evident. However, the aftermath of the French Revolution – Napoleon's rise to power and the cataclysmic events in Europe during the following two decades – seemed neither particularly natural nor rational. Moreover, the gathering pace of the Industrial Revolution put change and development at the very centre of the age. The Romantic movement, particularly strong in Germany, laid emphasis on the way in which we invest the world with our own meanings. Unlike de Tracy, for whom the natural and social worlds were pellucid to the rational mind, the German romantics considered that human beings collectively and individually created their own reality in response to changing circumstances. For Hegel, who tried to give these ideas a systematic intellectual basis, the ideas of a particular age could not claim absolute validity in themselves for they were evidently relative to changing historical situations. If there *were* a rationality, a meaning, to history, it would have to be found in the whole process rather than in the partial aims of particular individuals and epochs. For the projects of individuals and epochs were the means by which the famous 'cunning of Reason' produced a result often far different from that intended by the original thinkers. These Hegelian ideas strongly influenced Marx, and it was Marxism, uniting both the French and the German trends, that put the concept of ideology in the forefront of political discourse. The young Marx, as a disciple of Hegel, sought to explain the changes in social and political ideas in terms of the social divisions occasioned by the different ways in which historically human beings had organized their productive labour. Later on, particularly with Engels, the positivistic tradition of de Tracy, the attempt at an objective science of society, was more prominent. At any rate, until the last few decades, the study of ideology, however conceived, was largely the preserve of those who related themselves in some way to the Marxist tradition.

However, the would-be objective scientific study of ideology in the manner of de Tracy has enjoyed a strong revival in the West after the Second World War, particularly in the United States. The catastrophe visited upon the world by the Nazi movement, the disillusionment of many as the excesses of Stalinism became known, and the perception of Soviet Communism as a monolithic threat to Western-style democracy prompted a concern to explain the origin and power of these ideas. And this concern was reinforced by the startling impact of Mao-tse Tung's 'thought' on Chinese society, particularly in the Great Leap Forward and the Cultural Revolution, as also by the evident power of ideals of national liberation in so many Third World countries. With these writers, the term 'ideology' took on a distinctly pejorative sense associated intellectually with irrationality and politically with the concept of totalitarianism. This antipathy was reinforced by the dominance of behaviourism in American political science and of analytical, linguistic philosophy in Britain, both of which had a strongly pragmatic, empirical approach aimed at debunking large-scale speculation by asking more mundane questions about what were regarded as matters of fact or of linguistic usage. On this view, the 'Age of Ideology' was past.[9] It belonged to the specific period of industrialization which, following the breakdown of traditional societies, had given rise to much intellectual ferment among rival groups. Nazism, and more particularly Communism, were nineteenth century hangovers with no relevance to advanced post-industrial societies, where technical problems with technical solutions were to the fore. Ironically, the term which Marx and his followers had done so much to popularize was now used as a weapon *against* Marxism. This 'end of ideology' approach, has obviously been severely challenged by the more troubled nature of the last three decades. The claim to objectivity has come increasingly under attack. The suspicion that a claim to an objective science of ideology may itself be ideological has gained ground. Feminists have cogently pointed out that our traditional ways of thinking about society are dominated by concepts that are very male-orientated[10]; the green movement has questioned the whole notion of technological progress[11]; the idea of the universal individual of the Enlightenment as a source of valid moral judgements has been put in doubt by those who see particular communities as the only plausible ground for moral agreement[12]; and, finally, the more radical forms of postmodernism reflect a society where ideas of truth, value and reality have been dissolved by a mixture of advertising, consumer choice and information technology.[13]

However varied the uses to which the term 'ideology' has been put over the last two centuries, two main lines have already been discerned. One is the French rationalist view of de Tracy and his colleagues from whom the term originated – though their optimistic rationalism was modified in the Anglo Saxon world with a heavy dose of empiricism. From its inception in the Enlightenment, through Durkheim to recent structuralist and empiricist revisions, it lays emphasis on the consensual nature of society and adopts a contemplative account of truth: truth is a correspondence with reality which observation and reason should enable all people of good will to recognize through the application, in the social sciences, of methods not radically different from those obtaining in the natural sciences. The second, and contrasting, line has Germanic roots, being originally associated with Hegel and Marx, and goes through Mannheim to Habermas. Here the emphasis is on the making of truth rather than on observation. Societies are seen rather as changing entities riven by conflict than held together by a stable consensus. Suspicious of any 'objective' way of deciding what is true, adherents of this view tend to adopt a coherence theory of truth. And this is particularly so in social questions to whose solution the methods of natural science are held to be alien. Of course, there is an infinite variety of positions between these two stark poles. To take but the most obvious example, both are fully represented within the Marxist tradition. It is to outlining the various ways in which these poles have been combined and distinguished that the following chapters are devoted.

Marx

Marx deserves a whole chapter to himself as it was the influence of his writings that gave the concept of ideology the wide currency that it now enjoys. Marx was familiar with the favourable view of ideology as a beneficial science of ideas in the works of de Tracy; but he preferred to give it the critical edge popularized by Napoleon's scorn of 'cloudy metaphysics'. It is the conservation of this critical edge and the different reasons for justifying it that gives to the Marxist tradition its interest. In Marx himself the pejorative sense of 'ideology' comprised two main elements: first, ideology was connected with idealism which, as a philosophical outlook, was unfavourably contrasted with materialism: any correct view of the world had to be, in some sense, a materialist view. Second, ideology was connected with the uneven distribution of resources and power in society: if the social and economic arrangements were suspect then so was the ideology that was a part of them.

It took Marx some time to work out an appropriate materialist theory of society and thus construct a framework for his concept of ideology; and it took him even longer to discuss how and why the social and economic foundation of society was essentially conflictual and the role that ideology played in this conflict. Indeed, as with so many of his central concepts, that of ideology is far from completely clear in Marx: his comments on ideology tend to be *obiter dicta* and he never produced a coherent account. Nevertheless, the main outlines are clear.

In his early writings, Marx established the background from which his treatment of ideology was to emerge. Initially he was interested in unmasking certain religious conceptions of the world and the high-flown conception of the state elaborated by his former master Hegel. In both these areas, two cognate processes were at work: first there was a movement from ideas to material reality instead of the other way round; and second, this inverted process not unnaturally obscured the real nature of things. Religion failed to realize that 'man makes religion, religion does not make man'. The idea of God, Marx claimed, following Feuerbach, is nothing but a projection of human aspirations. As long as God was conceived of as the creator of the world on whose designs humanity was dependent, then the true nature of human beings – to be in control of their own destiny, to be self-producing – would be frustrated. But it was not just that religion was idealist: it had its roots in a deficient reality which, at the same time, it helped to conceal. Therefore,

> the abolition of religion as the illusory happiness of the people is a demand for their real happiness. The demand to give up the illusions about their condition is a demand to give up a condition that requires illusion. The criticism of religion is therefore the germ of the criticism of the valley of tears whose halo is religion.[1]

This same dual process of idealist preconceptions and consequent concealment of reality was at work in Hegel's conception of the state. Since, according to Marx, Hegel started from the *idea* and regarded empirical reality as its manifestation, it was possible for Hegel to gloss over real and intractable conflicts in society by seeing them as ultimately parts of one harmonious ideal whole.

Thus Marx had set the scene for his conception of ideology. The mistaken conception of religion and politics that he criticized were not mere errors: these inverted conceptions had their basis in a real social world that was so misconstructed as to generate these compensatory illusions. So the next step was to investigate this social world, and the result of this investigation was what Marx called 'the materialist conception of history'. He elaborated this in a major work which criticized his idealist German contemporaries, and the prominent place allotted to ideology is indicated by the title – *The German Ideology*, the only work of Marx which contains his general ideas on society and history set out at length.

In *The German Ideology*, Marx sought to clarify the idea of inversion that he had got from his criticism of religion and of Hegel's political philosophy: it was a mistake to start from human consciousness and to proceed from this to an investigation of material reality. The correct approach was the other way round. The origin of the problem was not mistaken ideas but the misshapen nature of social reality which generated mistaken ideas: 'consciousness can never be anything else than conscious existence, and the existence of men is their actual life process. . . . Life is not determined by consciousness but consciousness by life.'[2] The materialist conception of history held that it was the way in which human beings responded to their *material* needs that determined the rest of society. The basic social process was the satisfaction of the material needs for food, clothing and shelter. Human beings satisfied these material needs in the natural world that surrounded them, a world which they transformed for their own ends through the process of labour. It was this labouring process – which Marx sometimes called 'material practice' – that was the fundamental human activity, and it was the starting point for any valid social science. Marx summed this up as follows:

> The production of ideas, of conceptions, of consciousness, is at first directly interwoven with the material activity and the material intercourse of men, the language of real life. Conceiving, thinking, the mental intercourse of men, appear at this stage as the direct efflux of their material behaviour. The same applies to mental production as expressed in the language of politics, laws, morality, religion, metaphysics, etc., of a people. . . . Men, developing their material production and their material intercourse, alter, along with this their actual world, also their thinking and the products of their thinking.[3]

Thus ideology had to be explained from material practice. But not all ideas were ideology and Marx did not wish simply to produce a more dynamic version of de Tracy's science of ideas. What made ideas into ideology was their connection with the conflictual nature of social and economic relationships which characterized the labour process. These conflicts were due, at bottom, to two factors. The first was the division of labour, beginning with the division between mental and manual labour, which implied the unequal distribution – both qualitatively and quantitatively – of both labour and its products. This entailed, second, the existence of private property and a situation in which the interest of the individual no longer coincided with that of the community. 'Out of this very contradiction', Marx continued:

> between the interest of the individual and that of the community the latter takes an independent form as the State, divorced from the real

interests of individual and community, and at the same time as an
illusory communal life, always based, however, on the real ties.

The consequence of all this was that

all struggles within the State, the struggle between democracy,
aristocracy, and monarchy, the struggle for the franchise, etc. etc.
are merely the illusory forms in which the real struggles of the
different classes are fought out among one another.[4]

It was their connection with this class struggle and its social and
economic basis that gave certain ideas their ideological force.
Society was in fact riven by conflicts of interest, but in order for it
not to fall apart these oppositions were covered up by ideas which
represented attempts to portray society as cohesive rather than
conflictual by justifying the asymmetrical distribution of social and
economic power. Hence Marx's famous statement that 'the ideas of
the ruling class are in every epoch the ruling ideas',[5] since those who
controlled economic production and distribution could also regu-
late the production and distribution of ideas. The example Marx
chose to illustrate this was the period in Europe following the
breakdown of the feudal system when the declining aristocracy and
the growing bourgeoisie were struggling for mastery. Here power
was, for a time, shared between monarchy, aristocracy and bourgeoisie and the doctrine of the separation of powers was elaborated
by such as Locke and Montesquieu and proclaimed as an 'eternal
law' of good government, though in reality it merely reflected the
dispositions of the classes contending for power. What made ideas
ideological, therefore, was that they concealed the real nature of
social and economic relationships and thus served to justify the
unequal distribution of social and economic resources in society. It
followed that not all ideas were ideological but only those which
served to conceal social contradictions. Hence, while all classes,
including the working class, could produce ideology, it was only
ideology in so far as it served to further the interest of the ruling
class. And since society and its class structure was constantly
changing, the same ideas could begin or cease to be ideological.

Although *The German Ideology* was Marx's most extended
treatment of ideology, he did also mention it in his more mature
works and some have claimed to see a crucial change of emphasis
between the two. *The German Ideology* was written while Marx was
still evolving his ideas and thus does not contain the specific analyses

of capitalist society that Marx later produced. Its tone is polemical, it is unfinished and was never published by Marx. Moreover, certain of Marx's statements in *The German Ideology* have been thought too simplistic. The statement that 'if in all ideology men and their circumstances appear upside down as in a *camera obscura*, this phenomenon arises just as much from their historical life process as the inversion of objects on the retina does from their physical life process'[6] could give the impression that ideology was little more than an epiphenomenal illusion in which each idea was a distorted representation of some real 'thing'.[7] It is certainly true that Marx refines his concept of ideology in his later writings. In his earlier conceptions, as evidenced by his *camera obscura* reference, Marx thought of ideas as distorting or inverting reality because that reality was itself distorted or inverted. In his later writings, and particularly in *Capital*, Marx was keen to stress the distinction between the phenomenal forms of capitalist society and the essential relations of production that underlay them. In the famous passage on the 'Fetishism of Commodities', Marx writes:

> A commodity is a mysterious thing, simply because in it the social character of men's labour appears to them as an objective character stamped upon the product of that labour; because the relation of the producers to the sum total of their labour is presented to them as a social relation, existing not between themselves, but between the products of their labour.... It is a definite social relation between men which assumes, in their eyes, the form of a relation between things. In order to find an analogy, we must have recourse to the mist-enveloped regions of the religious world. In that world the productions of the human brain appear as independent beings endowed with life, and entering into relation both with one another and the human race. So it is in the world of commodities with the products of men's hands.[8]

Thus the social character of labour was concealed by the inter-change of individual objects in a market which appeared thereby to be natural and unalterable. Ideology was here seen as deriving from the (real) surface relations of capitalist society which served to conceal the fundamental relations of production. Marx wrote:

> *everything appears reversed in competition*. The final pattern of economic relations as seen on the surface, in their real existence and consequently in the conceptions by which the bearers and agents of these relations seek to understand them, is very much different from,

and indeed quite the reverse of, their inner but concealed essential pattern and the conception corresponding to it.[9]

Here ideology still served, as in the earlier conception, to conceal and invert real relationships between people. But in addition Marx now concentrated on the way in which ideology was produced by the form in which people related together in the ordinary everyday transactions of capitalist society – in contrast to *The German Ideology* where he was considering the production of German intellectuals.[10] There was also less emphasis on illusion since ideology was seen here as reflecting something real, if decidedly partial, and also as being itself a real force. Marx's most striking example of this was the ideological power of concentrating simply on the labour market which was

> in fact a very Eden of the innate rights of man. There alone rule Freedom, Equality, Property and Bentham. Freedom, because both buyer and seller of a commodity, say of labour power, are constrained only by their own free will. They contract as free agents, and the agreement they come to is but the form in which they give legal expression to their common will. Equality, because each enters into relation with the other, as with a simple owner of commodities, and they exchange equivalent for equivalent. Property, because each disposes only of what is his own. And Bentham, because each looks only to himself.[11]

Here we have encapsulated Marx's account of ideology in capitalist society: the exploitation and inequality which were inherent in the relations of production were concealed by the appearance of free exchange in the sphere of circulation, concentration on which gave rise to the typically capitalist ideology of freedom, equality and so forth.

Before considering the difficulties in Marx's account, it may help to pose two questions which go to the heart of his ideas. First, in what sense, if any, does the working class have an ideology? Indeed, could Marx's own ideas constitute an ideology? Marx did occasionally give this impression by conflating the ideological nature of thought with the view that all thought was socially determined. In *The German Ideology*, for example, he said that

> Men are the producers of their conceptions, ideas, etc. – real, active men as they are conditioned by a definite development of their productive forces and of the intercourse corresponding to these, up

to its furthest forms. Consciousness can never be anything else than conscious existence, and the existence of men is their actual life-process.[12]

Although the general context might indicate that the sense of the word 'ideology' was meant to be fairly specific, the most obvious meaning is to equate ideology with consciousness in general. Again, in the famous summary of the materialist conception of history in the 1859 *Preface* to his *Critique of Political Economy*, Marx said that in considering social and economic transformations of society

> a distinction should always be made between the material transform-
> ation of the economic conditions of production, which can be
> determined with the precision of natural science, and the legal,
> political, religious, aesthetic, or philosophic – in short, ideological
> forms in which men become conscious of this conflict and fight it
> out.[13]

Here again, the implication seems to be that all practical ideas, including socialism, are ideological. It is true that there was no clear distinction drawn by Marx between the social determination of ideas and ideology in that he did not clearly indicate what kind of social determination led to ideological thinking. Nevertheless, it is equally clear that Marx would not have described his own ideas as ideological: he described the aim of writing *The German Ideology* as 'to work out in common the opposition of our view to the ideological view of German philosophy'.[14] Nor did he believe that all socially-determined consciousness was ideological: even in the passage quoted from the *Preface* he contrasts the study of 'the material transformation of the economic conditions of production' which 'can be determined with the precision of natural science' with the 'ideological forms in which these become conscious of this conflict and fight it out'.[15] Although this might mean that all non-science was ideological, the pejorative sense of ideology, which is by far the most common in Marx, must rule this out. Ideology, for Marx, was not coterminous with the superstructure of ideas, because the superstructure contained both ideological and non-ideological elements; for example, in the *Theories of Surplus Value* when discussing the relation of spiritual to material production, Marx drew a distinction between the 'ideological component parts of the ruling class' and the 'free spiritual production of this particular social formation'.[16] An instance of this latter would be art and poetry to which capitalist production was hostile.

In general, then, for Marx, only those elements in the superstructure of ideas were ideological which served to perpetuate relations of denomination. It follows that any class can produce ideology, but, in so far as the working class generates ideology, it is bourgeois ideology; in so far as it is a genuinely socialist consciousness, it is not ideology being neither illusory nor confined to the surface appearance of bourgeois society.

The second question involves the common equation of Marx's concept of ideology with that of false consciousness.[17] The first point to be made is that Marx never used the expression 'false consciousness': the originator of this expression was Engels, whose rather jejune views on ideology will be discussed in the next chapter. Neither did Engels use it much, but the *locus classicus* is his letter to Mehring:

> Ideology is a process accomplished by the so-called thinker consciously, it is true, but with a false consciousness. The real motive forces impelling him remain unknown to him; otherwise it simply would not be an ideological process. Hence he imagines false or seeming motive forces. Because it is a process of thought he derives its form as well as its content from pure thought, either his own or that of his predecessors.[18]

Second, any attempt to equate ideology and false consciousness in Marx must rely heavily on *The German Ideology* as opposed to Marx's later writings on ideology as illusion as opposed to ideology as functional for everyday life. Third, it is evident that the notion of false consciousness is both too clear-cut and too general to encompass Marx's meaning. It is too clear-cut in that Marx does not operate with a true/false dichotomy; too vague because it is vital to know what kind of falsity is involved and, indeed, Marx's point is often that ideology is not a question of logical or empirical falsity but of the superficial or misleading way in which truth is asserted.[19]

Marx's conception of ideology contains several important difficulties. First, many of the main constituents of his concept are not clearly defined and thus leave room for ambiguity. For example, the debate surrounding the exact meaning of the *camera obscura* simile shows how unclear is Marx's attempt to explicate ideology by talking of inversion. For in order to solve the problem of ideology it is evidently necessary to do more than simply put things the right way up. Marx claimed to have found Hegel standing on his head and put him back on his feet – but what exactly *that* amounted to has given rise to as much disputation as anything else in Marx.

The ideas of reflection and echo in *The German Ideology* are too mechanically determinist and amount to little more than an inverted empiricism which continues the approach of de Tracy and the Enlightenment. In the same work, however, Marx claims that ideas are constitutive of the social world and not simply reflections of it.[20] The same ambiguity is true of the notion of contradiction which ideology is said to conceal and reproduce: the problem of how the concept of a contradiction, which is *prima facie* a logical concept, could apply to the real world is also extremely controversial.[21] First, this conceptual imprecision is partly due to the fact that Marx talked about ideology most extensively in *The German Ideology*, a work written while his thought was in rapid development and which was also left in untidy manuscript form which he would have wanted to revise considerably for publication. The other two places where ideology figures prominently – the *Preface* of 1859 and the beginning of *Capital* – are much briefer and written from different perspectives – not to say problematics. Thus Marx's treatment of ideology amount much more to 'a cluster of brilliant insights'[22] than to a fully worked out theory.

Second, Marx's concept of ideology is part of his general materialist conception of history which, again, is notoriously difficult to describe precisely. The socio-economic cannot be the only form of determination for the same socio-economic circumstances determine differently different things. How to privilege the socio-economic – and it must be privileged for the conception of history to be *materialist* – without lapsing into a crude reductionism is the major problem in Marxism. The traditional spatial metaphor employed by Marx of base and superstructure has been profoundly misleading and many later Marxists have been at pains to correct it – as we shall see in the next chapter.

Third, Marx's materialist conception of history and, inside it, his conception of ideology were conceived of as a critical tool to uncover the illusory conceptions of others. But how can he show that his own conceptions are not themselves ideological? Although Marx is not as open to this *tu quoque* as, say, Mannheim, it is evident that the distinction between science and ideology is not as neat as he does sometimes imply. He can claim to have avoided relativism by firmly adopting that standpoint of the proletariat, but it is at least arguable that this standpoint itself has proved illusory at several points. More potentially damaging, however, is the claim not that Marx was too proletarian but that he was too bourgeois. His optimistic rationalism, his strong emphasis on technology, his Eurocentrism are all the products of high Victorian capitalism, and it is to the ways in which twentieth century Marxists have sought to modify and refine many of his emphases that we now turn.

The Marxist Tradition

As the nineteenth century turned into the twentieth, Marx's ideas became systematized into the doctrine of a mass movement which meant that the evolution of the Marxist concept of ideology became subject to political factors. It should also be remembered that Marx's *The German Ideology*, where he dealt at great length with ideology, was not published until the mid-1920s. During this period there were three major developments in the Marxist treatment of ideology. First, in the Marxism of the Second International, the simplification of Marx's ideas into a general doctrine of economic determinism tended to bring the equation of ideology and false consciousness to the fore. Second – and in strong contrast with Lenin – the concept of ideology was stripped of its negative connotations and the idea of a socialist or Marxist ideology emerged. Third, with the failure of the revolutionary movement to develop adequately in the West, there was a growing impression that ideology might be a more powerful and independent force than had hitherto been imagined and consequently more attention and respect was paid to it among Western Marxists such as Gramsci and Althusser.

The systematization and vulgarization (in the best sense of the word) of Marx's theories was achieved above all by Engels. He alluded to ideology much more than did Marx (apart from *The German Ideology*), but in the context of general discussions of philosophy and history rather than as a foil for specific analyses. It is in his attempts to clarify the materialist conception of history that Engels most frequently mentions ideology. In a famous series of letters written in the late 1890s, he separated out economic, political and ideological relations and stated that, although the first two could affect the third, it was always the economic that determined them in the last instance:

> Men make their history themselves, only they do so in a given environment, which conditions it, and on the basis of actual relations already existing, among which the economic relations, however much they may be influenced by the other – the political and ideological relations – are still ultimately the decisive ones, forming the keynote which runs through them and alone leads to understanding.[1]

Taking over the base-superstructure metaphor from the Marx of 1859, Engels constructed a hierarchy of ideologies, citing religion and philosophy – in contrast to politics and law – 'as realms of ideology which soar still higher in the air',[2] Engels sometimes excluded politics and law from the ideological altogether and gave the impression that he considered ideologies to be more ideological the more removed they were from the material economic basis and the nearer they approached the top of the superstructure.

This connection of ideology with the ethereal was inspired by the influence on Engels of late nineteenth century rationalism and materialism and the straightforward methodological contrast with idealism. History, according to Engels, proceeded 'in the manner of a natural process and is subject to the same laws of motion'[3] and materialism began with recognizing this. Engels's main philosophical opponent, Dühring, was ideological in that he accepted an *a priori* method which 'consists in ascertaining the properties of an object by logical deduction from the concept of the object, instead of from the object itself'.[4] Dühring's ideas were 'pure ideology' which was 'deduction of reality not from itself but from a concept'.[5] On this view, ideology was an exclusive preoccupation with thoughts as opposed to reality:

> Every ideology, once it has arisen, develops in connection with the given concept material, and develops this material further; otherwise it would not be an ideology, that is, occupation with thoughts as with independent entities, developing independently and subject only to their own laws.[6]

Or again, in the passage already referred to, when Engels identified ideology with false consciousness, he described ideas as a process of thought in which the thinker derives its form as well as its content from pure thought, either his own or that of his predecessors. He works with mere thought material, which he accepts without examination as the product of thought, and does not investigate further for a more remote source independent of thought; indeed this is a matter of course to him, because, as all action is *mediated* by thought, it appears to him to be ultimately *based* upon thought.[7]

This view was founded on a kind of metaphysical materialism to which ideology was seen as the opposite. The falsity of ideology was not so much due to its origin or function as to its ontological status, its propensity to deal with things that simply were not there.

But there is also in Engels a strong connection between ideology and ignorance that reflects the influence of scientific rationalism. The false consciousness of the ideological thinker was so because 'the real motive forces impelling him remain unknown to him; otherwise it simply would not be an ideological process. Hence he imagines false or seeming motive forces.'[8] Engels's example here was taken from religion from what he called 'the erroneous, primitive conceptions of men about their own nature and external nature surrounding them'.[9] Engels's remarks on ideology obviously encountered the same difficulties as those of Marx. These were compounded in Engels by two further additions: first, the development of a rather jejune version of the materialist conception of history as an interaction of various factors in which ideology was neatly pigeonholed on the top of the superstructure, and second, the introduction of a materialist metaphysic in the shape of dialectical materialism which encouraged the narrow view of ideology as quite simply false. The effect of these two emphases was retrogressive when compared to Marx as they both neglect both the power and the subtlety of ideology.

Engels clearly retained a negative concept of ideology since he connected it with thought that was detached from reality and with ignorance. But he did sometimes talk generally of 'ideological superstructures'[10] as Marx did in 1859, and sometimes gave the impression that ideology was merely socially-determined thought. But the first person to declare roundly that Marxism was itself an ideology was Edward Bernstein whose attempts to revise Marx's ideas gained prominence around 1900. Bernstein based this conviction on the very revisionist idea that Marxism was based on a moral ideal and on the curious argument that Marxism must be an ideology because it consisted of ideas – and ideas were by definition ideological. Thus socialist conceptions of state and society were riddled with ideology. No political programme, including a socialist one, could do without 'a good dose of ideology'.[11]

If it was Bernstein's philosophically rather muddled revisions of Marxism that led him to describe it as ideological, the very opposite was the case with Lenin. For with him it was the sharpening of the class struggle that led him to ascribe an ideological position to every class – including the proletariat. Ideology thus lost its negative connotation: ideas were not deficient for their being ideological but solely from the class interest that they might serve. In the most famous passage expressing this idea, in his pamphlet *What is to be done?*, Lenin said:

> the *only* choice is – either bourgeois or socialist ideology. There is no middle course (for mankind has not created a 'third' ideology, and, moreover, in a society torn by class antagonisms there can never be a non-class or an above class-ideology). Hence, to belittle the socialist ideology *in any way, to turn aside from it in the slightest degree* means to strengthen bourgeois ideology.[12]

For Lenin these two very distinct forms of ideology were not the same as the consciousness of the classes concerned. Later in *What is to be done?* he stated that 'that history of all countries shows that the working class, exclusively by its own effort, is able to develop only trade-union consciousness'.[13] Therefore, socialist ideology had to be brought into the working class movement from the outside by a body of professional revolutionaries who had a superior grasp of political reality. The reason for this was that the workers, if left to themselves, would succumb to bourgeois ideology: 'The spontaneous development of the working-class movement leads to its subordination to bourgeois ideology . . . for the spontaneous working-class movement is trade-unionism, and trade-unionism means the ideological enslavement of the workers by the bourgeoisie.[14] An alternative ideology could only be generated by a socialist intelligentsia because bourgeois ideology was the ruling ideology: it has been around for so long that it appeared to be the natural way of looking at society and only the intervention of a vanguard party could point the workers in the right direction. Marxism was, moreover, a scientific ideology in that it corresponded to an objective reality. The success of the Bolsheviks in 1917 meant that Lenin's simplistic version of what ideology was became Marxist orthodoxy for generations and, in particular, his 'neutral' conception of ideology robbed it of any critical analytical power.

Lenin's view of ideology may have been simplistic but in the works of his Hungarian fellow-Communist Georg Lukacs it took on a much subtler form. First, it is clear that Lukacs's concept of ideology is as extensive as that of Lenin. It is true that, in certain passages, Lukacs seemed to equate ideology with false consciousness – as when he said that 'in the class struggles of the past the most varied ideologies, religions, moral and other forms of false consciousness were decisive'.[15] But this equation did not apply to all ideology, only to certain stages of it. What determined the validity of a view was not whether it was ideological or not, but the structural position of the class holding it: 'the bourgeoisie was quite unable to perfect its fundamental science, its own science of classes. . . . The barrier which converts the class consciousness of the bourgeoisie into "false" consciousness is objective: it is the class situation itself'.[16] And the superior class position of the proletariat did not make its views any less ideological – it just made them more scientific. Lukacs even talked of the degree of class consciousness of the proletariat being an indication of its ideological maturity. Historical materialism was, for him, an ideology, but not just an ideology: it was 'the ideological expression of the proletariat in its effort to liberate itself'.[17] Thus the validity of proletarian ideology lay in the future: it would be proved right in practice.

Where Lukacs did differ from Lenin was in his treatment of the difference between bourgeois and proletarian ideology. Previous to the arrival of the proletariat on the world stage, understanding the world had been blocked by the phenomenon for which Lukacs popularized the term 'reification'. Here Lukacs went explicitly to Marx's analysis of the fetishism of commodities in *Capital*, in which the social relations between persons became transformed – both subjectively and objectively – into relations between commodities. The world of things ruled human beings through objective laws that appeared to be independent of them; human beings thus became objects, passive spectators of a process that structured their lives for them. Starting from the economic division of labour, Lukacs traced the progress of this reification in the state and in modern bureaucracy – here borrowing from Max Weber's concept of 'rationality' inherent in industrial society.

According to Lukacs, the notion of reification was linked to that of totality. One of the results of reification was 'the destruction of every image of the whole'.[18] The specialization of labour and the general atomization of society meant that people and the world surrounding them were viewed as discrete, separate entities with no intrinsic connections. The bourgeoisie had necessarily to view things like this, for it was essential to their way of life to concentrate on some of the parts rather than the whole.

The central impetus of the reification process up until the present had been the all-pervasiveness of objectivity: in a reified world there were no subjects, no real choice. However, the oppressed, in order to free themselves, were forced to adopt the standpoint of the whole and question whether the parts were as objective and immovable as they seemed to be. Lukacs considered that the evolution of capital in society had not reached a point where the proletariat could destroy reification and become the subject and initiator of the historical process. Thus, while for Lenin the power of bourgeois ideology was due largely to its control of institutions for disseminating its views, for Lukacs the ideological subordination of the proletariat was more embedded in the very economic and social organization of capitalist society.

The difficulties of Lukacs's account of ideology are that it is excessively abstract and lacks almost any empirical reference. For the proletariat is not its own creator – it is created by the capitalist mode of production. And Lukacs had no theory of *how* the proletariat developed its own consciousness, except in the ultra-Left view that the Party alone was capable of representing the proletariat's 'ascribed' class consciousness. For the class consciousness of the proletariat that Lukacs talked so much about did not necessarily have any palpable existence. It was simply 'the thoughts and feelings appropriate to their objective situation'. 'This consciousness is, therefore'. Lukacs continued,

> neither the sum nor the average of what is thought or felt by the single individuals who make up the class. And yet the historically significant actions of the class as a whole are determined in the last resort by its consciousness and not by the thought of the individual – and these actions can be understood only be reference to this consciousness.[19]

Here Lukacs's idealist approach stands in stark contrast to the materialism of Engels. For whereas Engels attempted to give his concept of ideology a materialist basis by sometimes almost equating Marxism with natural science, Lukacs went in the opposite direction and posited a radical break between natural and social science and particularly gave an overwhelming role to ideology. From being a pale reflection of reality perched on the summit of the superstructure it became in Lukacs the driving force of history. But it was an account of ideology that was, in its way, just as removed from material reality as that of Engels.

With Antonio Gramsci the Marxist discussion of ideology reaches its high point. Gramsci took over the positive or neutral concept of ideology outlined by Lenin and Lukacs, but he devoted considerable space to discussing both the concept of ideology and also the details of its history and contemporary influence. There is another difference too: Lenin and Lukacs were writing at the time of the high tide of Marxist success; Gramsci's thinking about ideology was marked by the ebb of Marxism in Western Europe and the rise of Stalinism in Russia. There is, therefore, a less confident treatment, more of a resigned analysis, even a 'pessimism of the intellect', in Gramsci's famous phrase, however much this might be accompanied by optimism of the will. This tendency both to pay more attention to ideology and to treat it as more a matter of theoretical discussion than practical political activity is characteristic of Western Marxism as a whole.

Unlike Lenin and Lukacs, Gramsci did consider the negative concept of ideology, only to reject it. He did this on the grounds that the negative concept of ideology was too reductionist. He enumerated the steps leading to this error as follows:

(1) ideology is identified as distinct from the structure, and it is asserted that it is not ideology that changes the structures but vice versa;
(2) it is asserted that a given political solution is 'ideological'; i.e. that it is not sufficient to change the structure, although it thinks that it can do so; it is asserted that it is useless, stupid, etc.;
(3) one then passes to the assertion that every ideology is 'pure' appearance, useless, stupid, etc.[20]

The result of this process, evident in the work of Engels and Bukharin, was that 'the bad sense of the word has become widespread, with the result that the theoretical analysis of the concept of ideology has been modified and denatured'.[21] Gramsci therefore distinguished between organic ideologies and those which were arbitrary. An organic ideology was one which was necessary to a given historical structure – organic ideologies 'organise human masses, and create the terrain on which men move, acquire consciousness of their position, struggle, etc.'[22] Gramsci's paradigm for this broad sense of ideology was religion which he saw, like ideology, as producing 'a unity of faith between a conception of the world and a corresponding norm of conduct'.[23]

Although Gramsci pointed to the 'common sense' nature of ideology, he also laid stress on the role of intellectuals in almost *creating* ideology. Here Gramsci drew a distinction between 'traditional' and 'organic' intellectuals. Traditional intellectuals were intellectuals who, mistakenly, considered themselves to be autonomous of social classes and who appeared to embody a historical continuity above and beyond socio-political change. Examples would be writers, artists, philosophers and, especially, ecclesiastics. They were those intellectuals who survived the demise of the mode of production that gave them birth. The fact that they were linked to historically moribund classes, and yet pretended to a certain independence, involved the production of an ideology, usually of an idealist bent, to mask their real obsolescence. While the notion of a traditional intellectual was primarily a historical one, that of an organic intellectual was much more sociological. The extent to which an intellectual was organic was measured by the closeness of the connection of the organization of which he or she was a member to the class which that organization represented. Organic intellectuals articulated the collective consciousness or ideology of their class in the political, social and economic sphere.

Gramsci also drew a close connection between ideology and his concept of hegemony which he inherited from Lenin and Lukacs. Lukacs in particular had emphasized how the bourgeoisie obtained the consent of virtually the whole of society to its governance through so organizing the relations of production that its own dominance seemed natural. Gramsci took up this conception and integrated it with his emphasis on the role of intellectuals:

> The intellectuals of the historically progressive class, in the given conditions, exercise such a power of attraction that, in the last analysis, they end up by subjugating the intellectuals of the other social groups; they thereby create a system of solidarity between all

the intellectuals, with bonds of a psychological nature (vanity, etc.) and often of a cast character (technical-juridical, corporate, etc.).[24]

In other words, the world view of the ruling class was so thoroughly diffused by its intellectuals as to become the 'common sense' of the whole of society, the 'structure of feeling' in which it lived.[25] The bureaucratic and technological rationalism analysed by Weber was part of the capitalist ideological hegemony which functioned to repress any creative or innovatory initiatives of the working class. Gramsci considered this realization that for the most part the ruling class did not have to resort to force to maintain its dominance to be the core of his theory: 'it is even possible to affirm that present-day Marxism in its essential trait is precisely the historical-political concept of hegemony'.[26]

This conception of ideological hegemony was Gramsci's answer to the puzzle of how capitalism had been able to survive in the bourgeois democracies of the West. Moreover, while the bourgeoisie continued to exercise such a cultural hegemony, a proletarian revolution was impossible. To establish its own hegemony the working class must do more than struggle for its own narrow sectarian interests: it must be able to present itself as the representative of the interests of society as a whole. The establishment of a proletarian counter-hegemony was impossible without the active participation of the intellectuals of the working class. The Party was also an essential element here. Gramsci had a broader view of the Party than Lenin, since he conceived of it as deeply committed to an ideological and cultural struggle as well as to the seizure of state power. Gramsci was convinced that the Leninist strategy of neglecting the ideological hegemony of the bourgeoisie would not work in the advanced industrialized countries of the West. Thus he advocated a Party that was an educational institution offering a counter-culture whose aim was to gain an ascendancy in most aspects of civil society (as opposed to directly political institutions) before the direct attempt was made on state power. Unlike both Lenin and Lukacs, he was interested in ideology not just in its highly rationalized form as systematic political ideology, but also as religion, as 'common sense', and even as folklore. Thus his work forms a bridge between classical Marxism and the investigation of the connection between ideology and everyday life that will be discussed in Chapter 6. In particular, Gramsci broke down the strict dichotomy between spontaneous consciousness and socialist ideology so prominent in the Bolshevik tradition and helped to emphasize the complex pervasiveness of ideology in contemporary society.

Finally, mention must be made of the contribution of the French philosopher Louis Althusser to the Marxist concept of ideology. This contribution combines two main ideas. The first is a strongly determinist view of society which sees people simply as bearers of social roles rather than as in any way autonomous subjects. The second is a strict separation between ideology and science. In both these ideas. Althusser, as an anti-humanist and an anti-historicist, differed sharply from Lukacs.

Like Gramsci, Althusser is against any conception of ideology as false consciousness. This is partly because he is not interested primarily in the possible falsehood of ideology but rather with the function it performs; more importantly he does not see ideology as a product of people's minds but as having itself a quasi-material existence which defines what people think and is embodied in our society in what he calls 'ideological state apparatuses' such as churches, trade unions and schools. He expresses this idea as follows:

> In ideology men do indeed express, not the relation between themselves and their conditions of existence, but *the way* they live the relation between them and their conditions of existence. This presupposes both a real relation and an '*imaginary*', lived relation.[27]

Thus ideology is not merely an illusory representation of reality: it is the means through which people live their relation to reality. As an example, Althusser cites the fact that

> In the ideology of *freedom*, the bourgeoisie lives in a direct fashion its relation to its conditions of existence: that is to say, its real relation (the law of the liberal capitalist economy), *but incorporated* in an imaginary relation (all men are free, including free workers). Its ideology consists in this word-play about freedom, which betrays just as much the bourgeois will to mystify those it exploits (free!) in order to keep them in harness, by bondage to freedom, as the need of the bourgeoisie to *live* its class domination as the freedom of the exploited.[28]

Thus it is a characteristic feature of ideology that it persuades people of their freedom and autonomy: 'all ideology has the function (which defines it) of "constituting" concrete individuals as subjects'.[29] The word 'subject' is taken here both in the sense of an independent person and also in the other sense of 'a subjective being, who submits to a higher authority, and is therefore stripped of all freedom except that of freely accepting his submission'.[30] On this pessimistic view, ideology inescapably makes us into prisoners of ourselves.

Althusser also believes that ideology (of some sort) is a permanent feature of society. He is strongly influenced by Freud here and declares that 'ideology is eternal, exactly like the unconscious'.[31] Ideology is a social cement and thus in contemporary capitalist society it cements a system of class domination. Nevertheless,

> Human societies secrete ideology as the very element and atmosphere indispensable to their historical respiration and life. Only an ideological world outlook could have imagined societies without ideology and accepted the utopian idea of a world in which ideology (not just one of its historical forms) would disappear. . . . Historical materialism cannot conceive that even a communist society could ever do without ideology.[32]

For even a communist society will need cementing.

The second main feature of Althusser's conception of ideology is more easily described. It is the sharp contrast he makes between ideology and science. By criticizing ideology, science poses the problem in an entirely different manner and therefore arrives at a different sort of solution. Epistemology is radically separate from sociology: the truth of scientific theory is not dependent on history as the methods and validation of theory, like those of mathematics, are internal and peculiar to it. The main science Althusser has in mind is, Marxism, though he is willing to admit psychoanalysis also into this category. Unfortunately he does not tell us how to judge whether or not a theory *is* scientific – many having considered both Marxism and psychoanalysis to be prime examples of *un*scientific thought.

A lot of Althusser's writing is obscure and ambiguous. It does, however, have the advantage of linking ideology to an institutional context and to the practices of everyday life. But the strict opposition of ideology to science is a mere assertion on his part and is inspired more by Lenin's opposition of trade union consciousness to the science available through the Party than by any argument.

Most importantly, the excessive structural determinism of his theory leaves no room for autonomous action by people and in particular their reflexive understanding of the structure in which they are embedded and the possibility of their doing something about it.[33] With the work of Althusser and Gramsci, building on some of Marx's own ideas, the Marxist concept of ideology has begun to incorporate some of the non-Marxist approaches to which we now turn.

The Non-Marxist Tradition

The attention devoted to Marxist conceptions of ideology is justified in that, until comparatively recently, discussions of ideology were not prominent in non-Marxist social and political thought. Nevertheless, parallel to the Marxist thinkers discussed in the last chapter, there were important developments in the social sciences in general which influenced the understanding of ideology. For example, the two thinkers who (with Marx) were the founding fathers of sociology – Weber and Durkheim – produced discussions about the genesis and validity of ideas which contributed substantially to subsequent treatments of ideology – Weber as the inspirer of much later empirical investigation in the Anglo-Saxon world and Durkheim as the forerunner of structuralist analyses. The turn of the century also saw the beginnings of psychoanalysis which has had its own rather pessimistic contribution to make to the discussion. Finally, we shall return to the German historicist tradition in the person of Karl Mannheim who produced a comprehensive theory of ideology that is still a reference point for today's discussions.

Weber very rarely mentioned the word 'ideology'. As we saw in the previous chapter, his discussions of the 'iron cage' of increasing bureaucracy and rationalization had a profound effect even on such a very different thinker as Lukacs. But his long, and heavily qualified, search for objectivity in politics places him uncertainly in the democratic tradition moving from Destutt de Tracy to much current Anglo-Saxon political science. Weber was well aware that the undermining potential of the Marxist concept of ideology could be turned against the Marxists themselves – a point later to be elaborated in full by Mannheim. 'The materialist conception of history', he wrote, 'is not to be compared to a cab that one can enter or alight from at will, for once they enter it, even the revolutionaries themselves are not free to leave it.'[1] Indeed, Weber went as far as to reject the idea of an 'absolutely "objective" scientific analysis of "social phenomena" independent of special and "one-sided" viewpoints according to which – expressly or tacitly, consciously or unconsciously – they are selected, analysed and organised for expository purposes'.[2] Nevertheless, he believed that a value-free social science was at least a legitimate aim. Whatever the particular values and prejudices of thinkers, their conclusions should be valid in terms which were in principle accessible to everyone – even, as he unfortunately put it, to a Chinaman. It is this aspect of Weber's thought that has been one-sidely taken up and so stridently pursued by many American studies of ideology in the post-war decades.

If Weber sometimes sounds ambivalent about his approach of ideology, Durkheim is much more firmly anchored in the tradition of Bacon and the *ideologues*. In *The Rules of Sociological Method*, ideology was firmly opposed to science. The 'ideological method' consisted in 'the use of notions to govern the collation of facts rather than deriving notions from them'.[3] Science, on the other hand, consisted in the study of social facts which 'constitute a fixed object, a constant standard which is always to hand for the observer, and which leaves no room for subjective impressions or personal observations'.[4] Durkheim was not interested in the social origins of some preconceptions, but viewed them – like Bacon, to whom he makes explicit reference – as innate bents of the human mind. It is true that in the most famous of the works of his maturity, *The Elementary Forms of the Religious Life*, Durkheim located the source of religion in the social structure and perceived it as a factor of social integration. He saw the forms of religion and the form of society as being, in some sense, identical. Although Durkheim did not use the word 'ideology' to describe religion here, it seems applicable and, at first sight at least, incompatible with his earlier Baconian analysis of ideology. But presumably Durkheim would have said that he was considering religion as a social fact and his sociology was devoted to demolishing false ideas about religion by establishing its social function as society's collective representation of itself. In any case with his strong emphasis on objective structure and the rejection of the subjectivity of the German historical tradition, Durkheim laid the foundation for much of the later sociological discussion of ideology in the post-war world.

Neither Weber nor Durkheim could be described as having the confidence in reason that characterized Marx; but at least they were fairly optimistic about the possibility of improving society and thus qualified as progressive thinkers. But the end of the nineteenth century also witnessed currents of thought that profoundly mistrusted the power of reason and gave pride of place to the irrational in accounting for human beliefs and actions. This view tended to have strong conservative implications. Its most prominent representatives – whose influence is as strong today as ever – were Sigmund Freud and Vilfredo Pareto.

As is well known, Freud's main ideas were not immediately connected with the study of ideology. Psychoanalysis investigated the individual psyche. It was above all in the individual mind that Freud located the notions of repression – whereby the ego relegated unacceptable instinctual impulses to the realm of the unconscious – and of rationalization whereby the true causes of obsessional neuroses were concealed by an account of secondary motives. Nevertheless, the ideas of Freud do have social and political implications and indeed, when considering these implications, he worked on the assumption that 'we base everything on the psyche of the mass in which psychic processes occur as in the psychic life of the individual'.[5] Indeed it is striking how much Althusser, with his notion of ideology as largely unconscious of its own preconditions, takes from Freud. For Freud believed that the basic factor in politics was the erotic relationship of the group to the leader and that the function of ideology was to reinforce libidinal ties between rulers and ruled which would result in a positive attitude towards authority. In looking at artificial groups such as churches and armies, Freud claimed that groups capable of subsisting had to have 'many equals, who can identify themselves with one another, and a single person superior to them all'.[6] In consequence, Freud modified the widespread description of human beings as 'herd animals' and asserted that man was 'a horde animal, an individual creature in a horde led by a chief'.[7] This view was most clearly worked out in *Totem and Taboo* where Freud firmly placed the question of the origin and maintenance of political power in the context of the Oedipus complex and described the continued acceptance of political authority to feelings of guilt. Positing some kind of initial rebellion of sons against their father, Freud continued:

> The situation created by the removal of the father contained an element which in the course of time must have brought about an extraordinary increase of longing for the father. Thus the bitter feelings against the father which had incited to the deed could subside in the course of time, while the longing for him grew and an ideal could arise having as a content the fullness of power and the freedom from restriction of the conquered primal father as well as the willingness to subject themselves to him.[8]

Thus every revolution ended in restoration and all political arrangements were counter-revolutionary responses to the archetypal origin rebellion.

In Freud's later and more rationalistic work, *The Future of an Illusion*, the problem of ideology received a wider treatment. Here the attachment of the led to their leaders was viewed as to some extent the product of a defence mechanism whereby human beings protect themselves against an object which causes fear by identifying themselves with it and assuming some of its features. Like Durkheim, Freud was interested in examining primitive society and the origin of religion in order to understand ideology. At times he talks as though culture, and particularly religion, involved a repressive element necessary for the maintenance of any civilization. But at the same time, again like Durkheim, he put faith in the ability of scientific investigations to bring about a more rational society. Nevertheless, the impact of Freud's work has undoubtedly been conservative: his Hobbesian view of human nature, and his undermining of the concept of reason, have generally yielded pessimistic social and political conclusions which have been widely used in the United States to discredit radicalism.[9] But psychoanalysis can be turned to radical, as well as conservative, ends, as is shown by Freud's maverick disciple Wilhelm Reich.

It was the rise of Fascism that Reich was particularly concerned to explain with the help of psychoanalytical categories. Fascist ideology, according to Reich, arose from sadistic impulses that were given a political rationalization in times of crises. These sadistic impulses were the result of age-old sexual repression, particularly in the authoritarian family which was 'the factory in which the state's structure and ideology are moulded'.[10] He continued:

> When sexuality is prevented from attaining natural gratification, owing to the process of sexual repression, what happens is that it seeks various kinds of substitute gratifications. Thus, for instance, natural aggression is distorted into brutal sadism, which constitutes as essential part of the mass-psychological basis of those imperialistic wars that are instigated by a few.[11]

Unlike Freud, Reich's conclusion was libertarian and socialist; removal of repression, particularly in the sexual field, was the necessary precondition for all emancipation.

The psychological approach of Freud was given a more general form by Vilfredo Pareto. In Pareto's view, the part played in social phenomena by un-logical behaviour was overwhelming. He was more sceptical than Freud and held that any belief in reason, truth or progress was to be classed as non-logical. Basic to human activity were what Pareto called 'residues' – feelings which correspond to certain human instincts. In the social and political sphere, these 'residues' gave rise to 'derivations' which were would-be coherent sets of beliefs that directed people's actions. Pareto was not concerned to establish the falsity of these 'derivations', only the fact that they are not accepted on any rational grounds. But since Pareto also believed that all societies were inevitably governed by élites which replaced each other, he held that the role of derivations was to promote or undermine the established order in the interests of one or other élite. The content of the derivation was illusory in that it tended to promise the unattainable. Pareto's extremely prolix works exemplify the ultimate in conservative pessimism. They contain the positivist approach of Bacon and de Tracy shorn of its rationalist element. For Pareto's sceptical views allow no room for such ideas as truth, reason or progress which are, and always will be, illogical components of ideologies manipulated by élites in their own interests. It is a relief to turn from Pareto to Mannheim whose work represented the high point of the German historicist tradition aiming to assimilate the insights of both Marx and Weber.

If it was Marx and his followers who established the problem of ideology as an inescapable part of social-political discussion, it was Karl Mannheim who, in the words of the author of a magisterial work on the topic, 'produced the first and so far the last comprehensive elaboration of a theory of ideology'.[12] This theory was put forward in Mannheim's book *Ideology and Utopia* first published in 1929 in the midst of the political and social turmoil that was tearing apart the Weimar Republic. Mannheim's intention was to extend the insights of Marx and others so as to produce a comprehensive theory of ideology. This theory, or 'sociology of knowledge' as he came to call it, would uncover the historically limited and thus partial nature of all political viewpoints and so provide the groundwork for a more harmonious, integrative and progressive interpretation of the discordant politics of his time. It would provide a research programme to counter the corrosion of values produced by the spread of industrial capitalism.

As befitted a pupil of Lukacs, Mannheim was against any straightforward science of ideas based on unchanging concepts of reason and nature. He wrote:

> What we have to show, as against Enlightenment, is that the most general definitions and categories of Reason vary and undergo a process of alteration of meaning – along with every other concept – in the course of intellectual history. It is rather questionable in general whether 'form' can be sharply separated from 'content'. We always ask to what extent the particular content which, after all, is unqualifiedly historical, determines the particular formal structure. If however, one tries to evade the problems involved in historicity by assuming a timeless 'form as such', 'concept as such', 'value as such', and similar 'as such' structures, then it becomes impossible to say anything concrete in methodology at all.[13]

In his insistence that thought and expression were firmly embedded in history, Mannheim was much influenced by two late nineteenth century German theorists. Wilhelm Windelband had rejected the idea of a unity of the sciences and insisted that the natural and the human sciences had two radically different aims: the natural sciences searched for general and universal laws into which individual phenomena could be fitted; the historical sciences were concerned with the description of historical and cultural phenomena that were unique. Wilhelm Dilthey expressed this distinctiveness of the human sciences slightly differently; for him, they involved a reflective understanding of the meaning of cultural phenomena which placed a strong emphasis on the subjectivity of both the observer and the observed. This view – that all thought is historically conditioned – is sometimes known as 'historism'. This whole problem of how we can uncover the meanings of past events or writings (or even present ones springing from a different culture) is obviously both wide-ranging and crucial. The questions of how interpretation, understanding and explanation are possible between different epochs and cultures, whether they can be brought to some common denominator, whether the methods of the natural sciences (themselves viewed as problematic) can be applied to the human sciences, first formulated clearly in the late nineteenth century, have given rise to controversies that continue unabated today.

Although he was strongly influenced by the anti-positivist tendencies of Dilthey and others, Mannheim tried to avoid lapsing into relativism. Nevertheless, his treatment of ideology, leans heavily in the direction of his German 'historist' predecessors. This is very clear in his approach to Marxism which is his point of departure in developing his own self-reflective theory of ideology. Previous to Marx, there existed only a 'particular' conception of ideology. Mannheim traced the origin of this conception from Bacon and Machiavelli to the rational and calculating approach of the Enlightenment. This 'particular' conception 'will always strive in accordance with the psychology of interests to cast doubt upon the integrity of the adversary and to deprecate his motives' by pointing out the personal and psychological roots of intellectual bias. The particular conception of ideology merely rejected *what* was said and convicted its opponent of error – the very condition of which was a shared conceptual framework; with the 'total' conception of ideology, by contrast, it was the conceptual framework itself which was brought into question:

> When we attribute to one historical epoch one intellectual world and to ourselves another one, or if a certain historically determined social stratum thinks in categories other than our own, we refer not to the isolated cases of thought-content, but to fundamentally divergent thought-systems and to widely differing modes of experience and interpretation. We touch upon the theoretical or noological level whenever we consider not merely the content but also the form, and event the conceptual framework of a mode of thought as a function of the life-situation of a thinker.[14]

It was Marxist theory, Mannheim says quite justly, which 'first achieved a fusion of the particular and total conceptions of ideology'.[15] But Marxist positions could be formed against Marxism itself:

> As long as someone does not call his own position into question but regards it as absolute, while interpreting his opponents' ideas as a mere function of the social positions they occupy, the decisive step forward has not yet been taken. . . . In contrast to this special formulation, the general form of the total conception of ideology is being used by the analyst when he has the courage of subjecting not just the adversary's point of view but all points of view, including his own, to the ideological analysis.[16]

Mannheim's conclusion from the above was that with 'the emergence of the general form of the total conception of ideology, the simple theory of ideology develops into the sociology of knowledge. What was once the intellectual armament of a party is transferred into a *method of research* in social and intellectual history generally.'[17] This sociology of knowledge established a framework in which to investigate the relationship between changing structures of thought and changing historical situations. This raises two preliminary questions. First, what sort of knowledge does the sociology of knowledge investigate? It is not the knowledge of discrete facts of mathematical propositions, but rather 'the attempt to reconstruct the whole outlook of a social group, and neither the concrete individuals nor the abstract sum of them can legitimately be considered as bearers of this ideological thought-system as a whole.'[18] In other words, these 'ideological thought-systems' are rather like Weber's ideal types which are than imputed to social groups – though Mannheim did not always escape the danger of circularly defining the groups in terms of the imputed ideas. Second, what is the relationship of these thought systems to society? Mannheim did not define precisely the nature of this relationship which he referred to as the 'existential determination of knowledge'. He insisted that it was not a straightforward causal relationship, nor did he wish to reduce knowledge to its social origins.[19] The main point in investigating the connections between ideas and social structure was that this was at least a necessary condition for the very understanding of such ideas: those ignorant of social context would not know what they were talking about.

Mannheim was at pains not to be guilty of the 'genetic fallacy' – the deduction of the validity of an idea directly from its origins.

Indeed, he insisted that, in the first instance at least, his total theory of ideology was non-evaluative. This was in contradistinction to the 'special' theory of Marxism which, in his view, saw only its opponents' thought as ideological without subjecting itself to the same critique. Mannheim's aim was, initially, to conduct 'a purely empirical investigation through description and structural analysis of the ways in which social relationships, in fact, influence thought'.[20] This in turn could lead to the question of how far this interrelationship affected the validity of thought. But he pointed out that 'it is important to notice that these two types of enquiry are not necessarily connected and one can accept the empirical results without accepting the epistemological conclusions'.[21] Indeed, he went as far as to insist that 'the fact that our thinking is determined by our social position ... is often the path to political insight'.[22]

A major difficulty in grasping what Mannheim was saying is that he used the word 'ideology' in different senses according as to whether his interests were primarily historical or methodological. In the historical sections of *Ideology and Utopia*, for example, he described ideologies as 'the situationally transcendent ideas which never succeed *de facto* in the realization of their project contents'[23] and thus do not in the end disturb the existence of current social and political arrangements. These ideologies were incongruent with their period, either because they prevented human beings from adapting to the needs of the period, or because they cloaked other interests by reference to myths and ideals, or because they misdescribed social relations in terms of superseded historical categories.[24] They were, in other words, rather like the products of Gramsci's traditional intellectuals. Utopian ideas, by contrast, 'are not ideologies in the measure and in so far as they succeed through counteractivity in transforming the existing historical reality into one more in accord with their own conceptions'.[25] Since utopian ideas were 'only those orientations transcending reality which, when they pass over into conduct, tend to shatter, either partially or wholly, the order of things prevailing at the time',[26] the distinction between ideologies and utopias can only be clearly established after the event. But when he was dealing with broader questions of method, Mannheim adopted a wider definition of ideology. Indeed, when he talked of the sociology of knowledge, he preferred to substitute the term 'perspective' in order to avoid the pejorative moral connotation of 'ideology'.[27]

The central question raised by Mannheim's general total conception of ideology is whether it leads to a hopeless relativism. For he himself was careful to point out that his own conceptions were in no especially privileged position: 'The general form of the total conception of ideology is being used by the analyst when he has the courage to subject not just the adversary's point of view but all points of view, including his own, to the ideological analysis.'[28] But Mannheim refused the choice between an objectivity based on timeless principles unmediated by historical change and a relativism that would abandon any search for truth. Nor did he choose a middle path between them, for he rejected the presuppositions of both views, insisting that his own approach 'becomes relativism only when it is linked with the other static ideal of eternal, unperspectivist truths independent of the subjectivist experiences of the observer, and when it is judged by this alien ideal of absolute truth'.[29] While not wishing to deny that there was 'an irrevocable residue of evaluation inherent in the structures of all thought', Mannheim claimed a distinction between 'relationism' (as he described his own view) and relativism:

> relationism does not signify that there are no criteria of rightness and wrongness in a discussion. It does insist, however, that it lies in the nature of certain assertions that they cannot be formulated absolutely, but only in terms of the perspective of a given situation.[30]

This relationist approach did not treat all perspectives as equal, for

> as in the case of visual perspective, where certain positions have the advantage of revealing the decisive features of the object, so here pre-eminence is given to that perspective which gives evidence of the greatest comprehensiveness and the greatest fruitfulness in dealing with empirical materials.[31]

The result of such investigations would be some sort of synthesis, but one which was neither simply additive nor capable of laying claim to any absolute status. Mannheim may have been optimistic about the possibility of achieving even such a limited synthesis and also suitably vague as to the criteria of success, but the charge of relativism is clearly misplaced.

In the task of advancing social knowledge, Mannheim attached a privileged role to intellectuals. Any progressive perspective would have to 'retain and utilize much of the accumulated cultural acquisitions and social energies of the previous epoch'.[32] He continued: 'such an experimental outlook, increasingly sensitive to the dynamic nature of society and to its wholeness is not likely to be developed by a class occupying a middle position but only by a relatively classless stratum which is not too firmly situated in the social order'.[33] He insisted that the class and status ties of such a 'socially unattached intelligentsia' did not simply disappear. On the contrary, it was precisely the social position of intellectuals that gave them their several advantages. First, they had benefited from an educational system which replicated the conflicting tendencies of society at large: most other citizens were confined to a particular sector of society through being embedded in the social process of production. Second, they tended to be recruited from several classes and thus already possessed at least the raw material for a dynamic and flexible approach. Third, a large part of their activity was directed towards the study of other periods and places and thus had to possess the skills of 'interpretative understanding' necessary for moving towards a total perspective. In summary, Mannheim said that

> we owe the possibility of mutual interpretation and understanding of existent currents of thought to the presence of such a relatively unattached middle stratum which is open to the constant influx of individuals from the most diverse social classes and groups with all possible points of view. Only under such conditions can the incessantly fresh and broadening synthesis, to which we have referred, arise.[34]

Mannheim's views on the potential role of intellectuals are open to several objections. It has been maintained, for instance, that intellectuals are not as free-floating as he suggested in that they have been largely incorporated into institutions themselves patterned on the needs of society.[35] Although it is remarkable how many prominent intellectuals from Aristotle to Marx, and Mannheim himself, had cosmopolitan backgrounds,[36] this tendency does seem to be on the wane, due to the increasing organization and bureaucratization of society in the twentieth century. Again, Mannheim seems over-optimistic about the ease with which those tied to partial insights might be persuaded to adopt a larger

perspective. But there are certain common charges against Mannheim which are clearly misplaced.

He is not particularly élitist, reserving a suitably modest role for
intellectuals in the tentative promotion of a progressive synthesis:
Mannheim himself is more inclined to think that those who lay claim
to absolute and unchallengeable forms of knowledge (or even
unchallengeable methods of acquiring it) are most liable to emerge
as an élite. But the central objection to Mannheim's treatment of
the intellectual is that it is self-refuting. In a widely-used book,
Robert Merton wrote: 'Mannheim's conception of the general total
ideology . . . leads at once, it would seem, to radical relativism with
its familiar vicious circle in which the very propositions asserting
such relativism are *ipso facto* invalid.'[37] But this so-called 'Mannheim paradox' is by no means so clear-cut and comparisons of
Mannheim with Baron Munchausen trying to extricate himself from
the bog by pulling on his own pigtail are wide of the mark. For
Mannheim was not saying that intellectuals escape social determination – nor did he identify social determination with falsehood. On
the contrary, it was the very social position of the intellectuals which
enabled them to achieve a broader perspective. 'New forms of
knowledge', he claimed, 'in the last analysis, grow out of the
conditions of collective life and do not depend for their emergence
upon the prior demonstration by a theory of knowledge that they
are possible; they do not need to be first legitimized by an
epistemology.'[38] Whether intellectuals are in fact capable of the
task Mannheim assigns to them is an empirical not a logical
question.

An eminent professor has characterized Mannheim as 'an
inferior thinker, if ever there was one'.[39] It is true that his thought is
both vague and ambiguous in crucial areas – particularly when he
uses ideology both in the broad sense of thought subject to social
determination that renders it partial, and in the more restricted,
negative sense of self-interested illusions perpetuated by social
groups, and his over-broad sense of ideology tends to rob it of its
critical edge. But, although Mannheim's writings often do lack
precision, it is more accurate (as well as more generous) to see
Mannheim as the thinker who, as far as ideology is concerned,
'remains the first and most prominent scholar to have touched on
almost every aspect of the arguments mustered by contemporary
writers'.[40] The rather bleak passages at the end of *Ideology and*

Utopia foreshadow the debate on the 'end of ideology' in the United States and his 'total' theory of ideology plays the same role with regard to discussions of interpretation, meaning and communication that are to be found in such current theories as those of Habermas. These points will be elaborated in the next two chapters.

Ideology in the United States

In spite of Mannheim's attempts to demonstrate the all-pervasiveness of ideological thinking, the positivist tradition of a restrictive definition of ideology and a discussion of it that claimed not itself to be ideological has been alive and well since the Second World War and living mainly in America. The comparatively recent growth of interest in ideology here is impressive; the prestigious *Encyclopaedia of the Social Sciences* (1930–35) contains no reference to ideology, whereas its successor of 1968, the *International Encyclopaedia of the Social Sciences*, has two lengthy articles on the subject.[1] Much of this positivist discussion of ideology harks back to Napoleon's dismissal of it as irrational and dangerously opposed to the pursuit of material interests.[2] This view reflected the predominance of behaviouralism in post-war American political science and the stress on ordinary language and linguistic analysis in British philosophy. The horrors of Nazism were fresh in many minds. Disillusion with Soviet Russia was also a factor making for an equation of ideology with extremism and the confidence that a value-free social science could establish some sort of adequate pragmatic approach to social improvement. An example of this attitude is to be found in the 'end of ideology' debate. Although many of the contributors to this debate were excellent examples of Mannheim's description of contemporary social scientists as 'talking past each other', they do bring into focus the approach to ideology still strong in Anglo-Saxon political science.

In one sense, Mannheim himself can be seen as a precursor of the 'end of ideology' thesis – or more appropriately, in his own terms, an 'end of utopia' thesis. In the final pages of *Ideology and Utopia*, he posed the pessimistic question:

> Must not the gradual reduction of politics to economics towards which there is at least a discernible tendency, the conscious rejection of the past and of the notion of historical time, the conscious pushing aside of every 'cultural ideal', be interpreted as a disappearance of every form of Utopianism from the political arena as well?[3]

While admitting the possibility that life in a world devoid of any transcendent element either in utopian or in ideological form was 'perhaps the only form of actual existence that is possible in a world which is no longer in the making', he nevertheless suggests that

> whereas the decline of ideology represents a crisis only for certain strata, and the objectivity which comes from the unmasking of ideologies always takes the form of self-clarification for society as a whole, the complete disappearance of the utopian element from human thought and action would mean that human nature and human development would take on a totally new character. The disappearance of utopia brings about a static state of affairs in which man himself becomes no more than a thing.[4]

One of the first post-war writers to give the idea of the end of ideology prominence ended his polemic against Marxism, entitled *Opium of the Intellectuals* (1955), with a conclusion headed 'End of Ideology?'. In spite of the question mark, Raymond Aron's view was quite clear:

> by different routes, either spontaneously or with the help of the police, the two great societies of our time have come to suppress the conditions of ideological debate, have integrated the workers, and imposed a unanimous adherence to the principles of the regime. The debate remains a burning one in those countries of the second rank who are not entirely at home in the ideological camp to which they belong; too proud to accept their *de facto* dependence, too arrogant to admit the dissidence of the internal proletariat reflects a national failure rather than a decree of history, fascinated by the power which spreads terror, prisoners of the geography which tolerates criticism and abuse but which forbids escape.[5]

Seymour Martin Lipset also ended his influential book *Political Man* with a chapter entitled 'The End of Ideology' (no question mark this time) which came to the same firm conclusion: since the fundamental problems of the industrial revolution had been solved, 'the democratic class struggle will continue, but it will be a fight without ideologies'.[6] This theme was given its most consistent elaboration by Daniel Bell, who in his book *The End of Ideology* (again!) declared that 'ideology, which was once a road to action, has become a dead end'.[7] Bell directly compared ideology to religion: ideology was religion's successor, appealing to the same sort of faith, passion and irrationality. But, unlike Gramsci who also drew strong parallels between religion and ideology, Bell drew the definitional boundaries of both very tightly, and his approach depends heavily for its validity on an equivocation between the decline of ideology and the decline of the 'old ideologies' – principally Nazism and Soviet Communism.[8]

Although much of the debate over the end of ideology thesis is semantic, the plausibility of the thesis does involve some substantive assumptions. Although the conclusions of the above authors can be debated even on their own terms, the point here is the more general one that the attempt to restrict the concept of ideology and even to eliminate it from Western society (and thereby by implication from the writings of the proponents of the thesis) has definite – and questionable – premises. The two most obvious of these premises are, first, the linkage made at the time by several prominent political theorists of the immediate post-war era between ideology and totalitarianism; and second, the attempt by sociologists to contrast ideology with science.

As to the first, Michael Oakshott's very influential essay *Rationalism in Politics* exalted practical, traditional knowledge, which could not be formulated in propositions and was only to be acquired in practice, with technical knowledge that was preoccupied with clearly formulated statements and a self-enclosed certainty whose main principle was rationalism. And rationalist politics were responsible for the advance of ideology in that they were 'the politics of the felt need, the felt need not qualified by a genuine, concrete knowledge of the permanent interests and direction of movement of a society, but interpreted by "reason" and satisfied according to the technique of an ideology: they are the politics of the book'.[9] In Oakshott's disciple Greenleaf this practical, traditional knowledge was to be found in Conservatism which, being a disposition, could not be ideological. In Minogue's even more extremely partial view, 'ideologies can be specified in terms of a shared hostility to modernity: to liberalism in politics, individualism in practice, and the market in economics', and therefore 'ideology is a direct attack on the modern liberal democratic state'.[10]

Writing from a very different point of view, Bernard Crick made a very sharp distinction between politics and ideology and identified the latter with totalitarianism:

> Totalitarian rule marks the sharpest contrast imaginable with political rule, and ideological thinking is an explicit and direct challenge to political thinking. The totalitarian believes that everything is relevant to government and that the task of government is to reconstruct society utterly according to the goals of an ideology.[11]

But it was in America that this identification of ideology and totalitarianism had been most clearly worked out, particularly by Hannah Arendt in her *Origins of Totalitarianism*.[12]

Here she delineated those specifically 'totalitarian elements that are peculiar to all ideological thinking': first, ideologies were not so much interested in what was the case as in the whole process of coming to be and passing away, in other words in a total explanation of all historical happenings; second, ideologies insist on a 'truth' behind that which is perceptible by the ordinary senses, a reality that requires for its detection a sixth sense only available to the initiate of the ideology; and, third, 'ideological thinking orders facts into an absolutely logical procedure which starts from an axiomatically accepted premise, deducing everything else from it; that is, it proceeds with a consistency that exists nowhere in the realm of reality'.[13] In sum, therefore,

> An ideology is quite literally what its name indicates; it is the logic of an idea. Its subject matter is history, to which the 'idea' is applied; the result of this application is not a body of statements about something that *is*, but the unfolding of a process which is in constant change. The ideology treats the course of events as though it followed the same 'law' as the logical exposition of its 'idea'. Ideologies pretend to know the mysteries of the whole historical process – the secrets of the past, the intricacies of the present, the uncertainties of the future – because of the logic inherent in their respective ideas.[14]

Since totalitarian politics became associated, in the post-war decades, with the Soviet Union, which was held to be Marxism in practice, the end of the ideology thesis often amounted to a thesis about the end of Marxism – 'the last great ideology' in Aron's words – and its irrelevance to advanced industrial societies.

The second, and rather broader, assumption lying behind the thesis was that it was possible to contrast ideology with science. 'Science' here involves an appeal to empirical observation and a rigid separation of fact from values. In contrast to the historist tradition discussed in the previous chapter, the scientific method is one and the same in the natural and social sciences. Typical of this approach are the two articles on ideology in the *International Encyclopaedia of the Social Sciences*. In the first article, Edward Shils allows that advances in scientific knowledge have been influenced by ideological thinking. But the progress of science involves an erosion of ideology. For, he continues,

> science is not and never has been part of an ideological culture. Indeed, the spirit in which science works is alien to ideology ... In so far as the social sciences have been genuinely intellectual pursuits, which have their own rules of judgement and observation and are open to criticism and revision, they are antipathetic to ideology.[15]

And his colleague Harry Johnson goes as far as to construct a definition of ideology in which 'ideology consists *only* of those parts or aspects of a system of social ideas which are distorted or unduly selective from a scientific point of view.'[16] This is firmly in the positivist tradition going back to Bacon's discussion of idols and de Tracy's construction of his science of ideas. Its most sophisticated recent exponent is Karl Popper who, although he would reject the label positivist, holds to a unified methodology for both natural and social sciences and to an appeal to immediate empirical observation to falsify hypotheses. Popper has used this methodology to attack Plato, Hegel and Marx as political theorists whose ideas are based on the dangerously ideological methods described by Hannah Arendt.[17]

The very bases of the mainstream American approach to the question of ideology have, naturally, come under heavy attack. There are some (of whom more in the next chapter) who have questioned the whole Enlightenment tradition of putting trust in reason and science as a force making almost inherently for social progress. For many of the Frankfurt School of social theorists, for example, the divide between natural and social science has broken down. In the words of its most extreme exponent: 'the very concept of technical reason is perhaps ideological. Not only the application of technology but technology itself is domination (of nature and men) methodic, scientific, calculated, calculating control.'[18] Thus there was no point in opposing science to ideology since science was itself ideological. Without going as far as that, it has frequently been pointed out how difficult it is to construct empirical and would-be value-free analyses without imparting some kind of ideological bias. All too often analyses of ideology are offered which brand the thoughts and beliefs of others as ideology, while not recognizing that their own analysis might rest on a framework which is equally vulnerable. The best way of illustrating this will be to take two fairly typical and specific examples in some detail. The purpose of having a closer look at these works is not to prove them mistaken but only to suggest that they are more ideological than their self-description would allow for.

The first example, appropriately, is a substantial article on ideology which has affinities with the 'end of ideology' school. In this article Giovanni Sartori aims to outline a concept of ideology that will be capable of serving as an analytical tool. As such, he tries to specify the nature of ideology in political belief systems and he contrasts ideology with pragmatism. Ideological belief systems spring from a cultural matrix which is rationalist; pragmatic belief systems spring from cultural matrices whose basis is empiricism. Thus ideology is impermeable to information which does not derive from an authoritative source within the ideology. By contrast, the pragmatic mentality is open-minded and tends to evaluate information on its own merits. The ideological mentality, therefore, 'can be legitimately understood to mean not only a rigid and dogmatic approach to politics, but also a principled and doctrinaire perception of politics'.[19] In addition, an ideological system has a high emotive content. Ideologies also have three other properties: they are articulate in that their concepts are explicit and contain a large number of elements; they are 'strongly constraining' in that these elements are 'tightly related in a quasi-logical fashion';[20] and, lastly, the first two properties mean that the holding of ideologies is confined to a relatively small minority. It follows that ideologies are articulate, highly constraining and held by an élite, while the beliefs of the masses have fewer elements and are altogether less sophisticated. Sartori's conclusion is:

the hetero-constraining potentiality of belief systems increases the
more the system is ideological and diminishes the more the system is
pragmatic. In short, ideologies are the *hetero-constraining* belief
systems par excellence. And this is the same as saying that ideologies
are the crucial lever at the disposal of elites for obtaining political
mobilization and for maximizing the possibilities of mass manipulation. That is, it seems to me, the single major reason that ideology is
so important to us. We are concerned about ideologies because we
are concerned, in the final analysis, with the powers of man over
man, with how populations and nations can be mobilized and
manipulated all along the way that leads to political messianism and
fanaticism.[21]

What are we to make of this? From the brief summary it will be clear
that, although Sartori's analysis is offered as a contribution to
empirical political theory,[22] the whole framework is heavily value-
laden: a very strong value-position flows out of the analysis. This
can be seen in three broad areas. First, by narrowing the concept of
ideology – in order, allegedly, to give it some empirical purchase – it
implies that there are some views, and in particular views which
severely restrict the scope of the concept of ideology, which are not
themselves ideological. Second, and more specifically, Sartori
rejects the charge that his definition of ideology represents an
anti-ideological bias. He does indeed define the ideological mentality as the rigid and dogmatic product of a closed mind, but
maintains at the same time that 'ideological closeness is bad and
pragmatic openness is good only according to an intellectual
yardstick – and one could well say an intellectualistic prejudice'.[23]
But this is surely disingenuous: the terms of the definition are
strongly normative and do bias us inevitably against ideology. It is
not simply a matter of 'intellectual prejudice' as to whether one is
for or against rigidity, dogmatism and a closed mind. One could just
as well defend calling someone a bastard on the grounds that such a
description could be construed as laudatory – and if anyone chose to
consider it differently this was simply due to prejudice. Third,
ideology is here closely associated with totalitarianism – the views of
Arendt and Friedrich cited above are quoted in this context. Even
more explicitly, Marxism is referred to as the typical ideology, and
liberalism is said to be a 'poor competitor, ideologically speaking, of
socialism, communism, egalitarianism and the like'.[24] The upshot of
this is inescapably to recommend one set of political doctrines over

others. Fourth, Sartori allows ideologies only an emotive content thus implying that they have no cognitive content: they are merely expressions of approbation or disapprobation which are 'causes' or 'triggering mechanisms' for actions. This, again, is to devalue ideologies in line with the previous points. It could easily be argued, on the contrary, that the significance of ideology in mobilization is not that it 'causes one to do' but that it 'gives one cause for doing'. It provides grounds or warrants for the political activity engaged in. Reference to purposes and evaluations gives meaning to political actions, making them comprehensible to oneself and others. To explain the mobilizing aspects of ideology in terms of triggering mechanisms or the release of 'ideological passion', therefore, ignores a vast and important aspect of how political actors understand and orient their political activities, and how observers, attempting to understand these activities, might explain their significance.[25] But to adopt such an attitude would be to take the content of ideology much more seriously than Sartori is prepared to do. Finally, the view that 'mass publics are likely to display, in whatever country, a poorly explicated, inarticulate, disconnected – and therefore relatively unconstraining – belief system'[26] leads to the conclusion that 'mass beliefs appear to be dependent variables of elite belief policies'[27] and that 'mass publics are, in general, hetero-constrained, in the sense that poorly articulated believers need guidance not only for the horizontal inter-belief linkage, but also for the event-principle linkage.'[28] The implicit conclusion must be that most people are easily misled (as they have been typically in the Soviet Union) and that any society is better off without ideologies, all of which have dangerous inherent tendencies towards political messianism and fanaticism. In other words, any society – and in particular the industrial societies of the West – would be better off without any radicals. This may be true but it cannot be true simply in virtue of any theory which is empirical.

The second example of covert ideological bias is the way in which theories of American society as pluralist are often put forward as being more or less straightforward accounts of how things are – descriptive theories, therefore, with no evaluative content. Pluralism can be conceived of as a middle road between the theory of a power élite and classical democratic theory. The power élite theorists claim that America is controlled by a single élite which controls all major decisions; the classical democratic image is that of a society in which the majority of individuals make the most important decisions. In contrast to both of these views, a pluralist theory claims that political power is diffused in American society in that it is based on a number of factors such as wealth, status, official position, or voting power. Groups or individuals whose political influence depends on one factor have to compete for political power with groups or individuals having a different base. Contrary to the theory of the power élite, no one group has a monopoly of political power, and, contrary to classical democracy, political decisions are seldom, if ever, the result of the wish of the majority, but result from competition between different centres of power.

Pluralism is more similar, however, to the classical model, in that it substitutes the groups engendered by modern industrial society for the isolated individuals as the basic unit of social interaction. This system has been described by one of its most lucid exponents as 'polyarchy', a system in which minorities rule in the sense that the competition of political parties for elective support reflects the pressures of various organized minorities. The system is an open one in that any organized and legal group can expect to have its point of view seriously considered by those taking political decisions. In the end, politics comes down to bargaining. Nevertheless, in *A Preface to Democratic Theory* (1956) R. Dahl writes:

> if the majority rarely rules on matters of specific policy, the specific policies selected by a process of 'minorities rule' probably lie most of the time within the bounds of consensus set by the important values of the politically active members of the society, of whom the voters are a key group.[29]

Thus it is also possible to claim that the majority does rule, in that 'politicians subject to elections must operate within limits set both their own values as indoctrinated members of society, and by their expectations of what policies they can adopt and still be re-elected'.[30] What is ordinarily understood as politics – election campaigns, differing party programmes, etc. – represents merely superficial conflicts. The emphasis in pluralist theory is rather on the underlying consensus: 'prior to politics, beneath it, enveloping it, restricting it, conditioning it, is the underlying consensus on policy that usually exists in the society among a predominant portion of the politically active members.[31]

In what way, then, does the pluralist view, which sets itself out as being a descriptive view with which every close observer of the political scene could agree, contain an ideology in Mannheim's sense of a perspective with which those adopting a different perspective could legitimately disagree? In so far as the pluralist model emphasizes the formal decision-making process, it must neglect the non-decision-making process by which what might become public issues never emerge as such. Pluralism assumes that the important issues are those which take place in the public arena of formal procedure. But, as has been pointed out,

> the pluralists suppose that because power, as they conceptualise it, only shows up in cases of actual conflict, it follows that actual conflict is necessary to power, but this is to ignore the crucial point that the most effective and insidious use of power is to prevent such conflict existing in the first place.[32]

And of course there is the point that if there is a winnowing out of issues beforehand, then there is also a toning down and re-interpretation of them afterwards. In his well-known study of politics in New Haven, Dahl examined the decision-making process with regard to several important issues. But how do we decide what is 'important'? The issues were chosen because 'they promised to cut across a wide variety of interests and participants. These were redevelopment, public education, and nominations in the two major parties'.[33] But the outcome of the investigation threatens to become self-confirming since these are exactly the sort of issues that would tend to be solved by the sort of bargaining that pluralism claims is characteristic of politics as a whole. A further difficulty in confining observation to observable decision-making processes is that often people will adjust their views and demands according to what they predict will be their effect on those in positions of power – which again means that some important issues and points of view may be ruled out by anticipation. Moreover, the pluralist assumption that everyone is able to know and articulate their interest is questionable. For if we take the view that people either may not be aware of their own interests or may misconceive them, then the claim of the pluralist world to be representative of, and responsive to, the interests of people, would be severely shaken.[34]

More fundamentally, the model of surface conflict and underlying consensus invokes an image of American society in which those in power simply apply to practical problems the values which are held in common. In this view of power as the collective product of society (a view most influentially presented in the sociology of Talcott Parsons), relations of power are reciprocal and realized mainly through authority and bargaining, both of which are sustained by a general commitment to the 'rules of the game'. But power could equally well be viewed as a zero-sum: if someone has a given amount of power, then someone else has concomitantly less. And if power is a scare commodity, then coercion and manipulation are liable to be more important than authority and bargaining. Moreover, although it might be agreed that there was such a consensus supporting the present power structure, it could equally be argued that it is a power élite which shapes the consensus since it also benefits most from it.

In effect, what pluralists are doing is to change the connotations of the word 'democracy' and make the concept compatible with, if not actually constituted by, a more conservative view of society. For the narrowing down of what constitutes rule by the people undoubtedly devalues the idea of popular participation. Thus the pluralist theory 'is in reality deeply rooted in an ideology, an ideology which is grounded upon a profound distrust of the majority of ordinary men and women and a reliance upon the established élites to maintain the values of civility and the "rules of the game" of democracy'.[35] Pluralism can also be seen, more generously, as an instance of Durkheim's account of ideology: it is the 'civil religion' of a society with no feudal past, a society which can seem classless in that its members were, in de Toqueville's phrase, 'born free'.

Dahl's model, therefore, of surface competition between interest groups founded on an underlying social consensus involves a particular view or perspective on politics. These two crucial variables – surface competition and underlying consensus – are being presented as the necessary conditions for democracy. But democracy is a concept with unavoidably normative overtones, and what purports to be a generalization from the experience of American politics turns into a recommendation of the status quo. This does not mean that pluralism is necessarily false or mistaken only that it does not have the obvious authority that would attend a descriptive or factual statement.

Empirical investigations of ideology have produced considerable information about the beliefs people hold, particularly in areas connected with mass communications, social psychology and voting behaviour. The extensive nature of these findings has been in proportion to the size of the resources and personnel available to these fields. But this mass of information (useful as most of it undoubtedly is) has not been matched by progress with theories as to how to order it to make it meaningful. Too many social scientists have sought to bracket the philosophical problems inherent in their research. This has been all the easier in the United States where the role of ideology has been less evident, though more pervasive, than elsewhere. It has often been pointed out, not least by Habermas, that capitalism seems to operate all by itself and without the need for any ideological justification in that its commodities and markets generate their own compelling logic. As we have seen, however, to step out of the ideological circle is more difficult than many are prepared to admit. Contemporary attempts to face this problem head-on are the subject of the next chapter.

Science, Language and Ideology

The analyses of ideology considered in the preceding chapter depend on the opposition between ideology and some sort of science. For much of mainstream Anglo-Saxon social science is continuing the tradition of de Tracy's science of ideas, a tradition which broadly goes under the label of positivism. Although there are many different sorts of positivism, there is general agreement among positivists that the social sciences should model themselves on the natural sciences, whose mode of procedure is the only one thought capable of producing valid knowledge. This valid social science must be strongly empirical by appealing to an objective world of facts and its method is one of rejecting all conceptions that cannot, in principle, be verified (or at least falsified) by appealing to such facts.

However, this assimilation of the social to the natural world has come under attack from those who question whether natural science (let alone social science) is quite as objective and neutral as is widely believed. Such people would not wish to deny that the vast emphasis of recent decades on empirical social science has indeed provided us with a lot of potential information about society, but would claim that there remains a still vaster problem of interpretation. It is obvious that to equate social facts with natural facts is to invest social facts with the same air of immutability that attaches to nature and thus has distinctly conservative implications. But some critics of positivism wish to go further and suggest that not only is there no sharp distinction between science and ideology, but that much of natural science is itself ideological. This disquiet over the status of natural science is prompted by the failure of scientific advance to deliver the blessings that many in the last century expected: the emergence of the ecological and anti-nuclear movements are only the most evident examples of this disquiet.

The best-known advocate of this view was Herbert Marcuse, but he shared the suspicion of natural science and the technology that accompanies it with Max Horkheimer and Theodor Adorno, who together formed the most prominent members of the Frankfurt School. While strongly influenced, at least originally, by Marx, they thought of Marxism as having been substantially misled by the Enlightenment's confidence in scientific reason and the consequential view of the growth of the productive forces as inherently progressive. According to Horkheimer, with the prestige of science, the use of reason had become almost exclusively 'instrumental'. In the great philosophical systems of the past, however misguided, at least there was debate about the ends of human life. Nowadays, reason had been reduced to technical talk about means, discussion about ends being the realm of propaganda. Debate about the goals of society had been occluded by the industrialization of reason, by its becoming the handmaiden of technical domination. Scientific method was held up as a norm, but, according to Horkheimer:

> Science has no realistic grasp of that comprehensive relationship upon which its own existence and the direction of its work depend, namely, society. . . . For Science, too, is determined in the scope and direction of its work not by its own tendencies alone but, in the last analysis, by social life as well.[1]

This attack on the supposed neutrality of science and its rise as a model for rational thought reached its extreme in Marcuse's best-selling *One-Demensional Man* whose central thesis was that

> the closed operational universe of advanced industrial civilization with its terrifying harmony of freedom and oppression, productivity and destruction, growth and regression is pre-designed in this idea of Reason as a specific historical project. The technological and pre-technological stages share certain basic concepts of man and nature which express the continuity of the Western tradition. Within this continuum, different modes of thought clash with each other; they belong to different ways of apprehending, organizing, changing society and nature. The stabilizing tendencies conflict with the subversive elements of Reason, the power of positive with that of

negative thinking, until the achievements of advanced industrial civilization lead to the triumph of the one-dimensional reality over all contradictions.[2]

Thus the destructive nature of instrumental reason called for a society based on other principles – though Marcuse was, naturally, not in a position to describe how such a society would come about and still less how it would operate.

A similar questioning of the status of natural science (though without the pessimistic conclusions of the Frankfurt School) has come from two Anglo-Saxon philosophers of science. Thomas Kuhn in his influential book *The Structure of Scientific Revolutions* contested the traditional empirical and rational image of science as a steady accumulation of agreed facts which progressively uncovered the real nature of the world. On the contrary, according to Kuhn, science proceeded by imaginative leaps and bounds from one 'paradigm' to another. A paradigm was instituted by 'universally recognized scientific achievements that for a time provide model problems and solutions to a community of practitioners'.[3] In time, every paradigm proved insufficient to accommodate discrepancies and anomalies whereupon one or more new paradigms would be proposed. Although Kuhn never went as far as claiming that there were no objective grounds for deciding between competing paradigms, he did stress that it was not a simple matter of experimentation and appeal to evidence. A more extreme proponent of the a-rationality of scientific method is Paul Feyerabend, who claims that the idea that natural science contains knowledge independent of ideology, social prejudice, etc., is simply a 'fairy tale' – there being no essential difference between natural science and the claims of mysticism or religion.

Although the ideas of Feyerabend do touch the wilder shores of relativism, there has been widespread criticism over the last two decades of the idea both that natural science is unproblematically objective and that the methods of the natural sciences can be applied to the social sciences.[4] But during the same period a method for analysis in the social sciences has risen to prominence which claims, on quite different grounds, to be scientific and which has obvious implications for the study of ideology. This is the method of structuralism.

Structuralism has its origin in the study of linguistics. Almost a century ago the Swiss linguist Ferdinand Saussure distinguished between *language* and *speech*. Language is a formal system (or structure) of arbitrary signs which are related to one another and which underlie all speech. The laws of language, i.e. the laws of structural linguistics, are not the laws of every day human speech: they are rather the laws of unmotivated, conventional categories of which the speaker is unconscious and powerless to alter. It is this underlying and unchanging system or structure which can be studied with scientific precision in abstraction from the superficial speech patterns which individuals may choose to adopt. By extension all social and intellectual activity can best be understood by referring it to an underlying system of meaning. It is easy to see the parallel with psychoanalysis. For in a manner reminiscent of Freudian psychoanalysis, a distinction is drawn between manifest content and latent content: the manifest content is the ordinary speech or activities of individuals, the latent content is the hidden structure of this speech or activity. And just as in Freud the 'slip' is to be explained by reference to the unconscious and its repressed contents, so the actual discourse or activities of individuals can be viewed as a screen hiding the underlying ideological structure of their words or actions.

Structuralism has had a considerable impact in anthropology and particularly the study of myth, so let us briefly consider the major thinker in this field, Claude Levi-Strauss, as an example, before considering in more detail the possible relation of language and ideology. Levi-Strauss uses the opposition of basic infrastructure to the conscious use of language to examine the role of myth. For him, mythical thinking, and cultural phenomena in general, are a sort of language in which societies express themselves in diverse ways but always according to the systematic universal laws of the unconscious structure. This underlying structure is both necessary and eternal and is the starting point for any account of human society. As an illustration of the primary nature of structures, Levi-Strauss likens them to the rules of a card-game: every game of cards is different since the number of possible variations is, for all practical purposes, infinite. But each game is strictly governed by the underlying rules which never vary and prescribe exactly which combinations are, and which are not, possible.

The idea of structural determinism has, according to Levi-Strauss, wide applicability. In the modern age, mythology is to be sought in political ideology – he refers to the French Revolution – and even in science itself. For the world of contemporary natural science and the world of myth yield two 'distinct though equally positive sciences'. It is only now that these two separate paths to knowledge unite: 'that which arrives at the physical world by the detour of communication, and that which, as we have recently come to know, arrives at the world of communication by the detour of the physical. The entire process of human knowledge thus assumes the character of a closed system'.[5] The same inbuilt cultural universal, the same logical system, underlies both and provides the only means of explicating them.

The structuralist approach to the study of myth certainly reveals connections that have stimulated the imagination of anthropologists. When it comes to considering ideology, the ideas of Levi-Strauss seem too general, since by privileging form over content and logical classification over practical results, it becomes difficult to distinguish between fact and imagination, between science, religion and myth. Levi-Strauss claims to show 'not how men think in myths but how myths operate in men's minds without their being aware of the fact'.[6] This is to reduce the whole of the conscious individual in a manner which goes far beyond even the psychoanalysis of Freud. Moreover, by explicating all intellectual activity in terms of a common structure, it is to emphasize the consensual element in human affairs at the expense of the conflictual.

However, the same schema of underlying structure determining surface phenomena has been applied – with the same would-be scientific rigour – to the connection between language and ideology. Previously language had been rather taken for granted, like a window through which we look at the world outside. The recent prestige of linguistics, itself the product of a hi-tech information society, has led to attention being paid to language itself: instead of simply looking through the glass, we look at it, since the shape of the window or the arrangement of the panes may determine what we see through them. On this view, ideology may go well beyond the scope of language as ordinarily conceived. For the study of linguistics leads us to suppose that other forms of human activity can be construed as languages, i.e. as systems of signs which have a meaning.

In any system of signs, according to the structuralist view, there is, as we have seen, a distinction between *speech* and *language*.

Speech is the manifest level, the one that is immediately apparent; language is the latent level, the hidden structure. It is in language that ideology is to be found. The ideological message is contained in the underlying structure, which is so packaged in speech as to be more or less inaccessible to both speakers and hearers. One of the most lucid, influential and readable exponents of this view, Roland Barthes, expresses this as a distinction between what a statement *denotes* and what it *connotes*. A famous example of this is the humorous reporting of a so-called 'blue-blood' cruise in which many royal personages gathered on a yacht for a trip round the Mediterranean. The public was vastly amused, but, says Barthes:

> Such a feeling of amusement carries a heavy pathological burden; if one is amused by a contradiction, it is because one supposes its terms to be very far apart. In other words, kings have a superhuman essence, and when they temporarily borrow certain forms of democratic life, it can only be through an incarnation which goes against nature, made possible through condescension alone. To flaunt the fact that kings are capable of prosaic actions is to recognize that this status is no more natural to them than angelism to common mortals, it is to acknowledge that the king is still king by divine right.[7]

In other words, when kings play at being men, what is *denoted* is their human side, but this only serves to *connote* their superhuman attributes.

In recent years there have been many attempts to give an account of the relation of language to ideology in structuralist terms, which are generally described as 'discourse analysis' and intended to have a critical edge to them. Elaborating on such cryptic remarks of Marx as 'language *is* practical, real consciousness',[8] discourse analysis takes as its subject the language of everyday life, the language of newspapers, magazines, classrooms, families, and it analyses the patterns of sentences in extended pieces of prose or in conversational exchanges. It also attempts less successfully to show how these patterns reflect relations of power on the grounds, again, that language is a form of activity – just as many forms of activity can be interpreted as languages. This goes further than the evident ideological context which informs the description of guerrilla forces as either 'freedom fighters' or 'terrorists'. It aims to uncover ideological implications in the apparently innocent structure of sentences. Some of these analyses yield little more than lists of categories, others try, more fruitfully, to connect their analyses to social relations. A simple example of this might be the sentence, 'The warder marched the prisoners', which can be broken down into (A) The warder caused X and (B) The prisoners marched. According to analyses of this sort,

> The actor of A becomes the imputed actor for the new sentence. The assumption that underlies the process is that power can be regarded as direct agency. The effect of this linguistic process is to reassign the actor roles in the two conflated models. The real actor of the process is denied credit and responsibility for the action he performs, and this credit is assigned to the syntactic participant who is regarded as more powerful. It is a thing not lightly done. The ideological function is clear.[9]

This may seem simply to be reconveying in terms of linguistic analysis what we all know prison life to be like anyway. But other, less obvious examples would be the frequent use of agentless passives ('The government has been criticized'), which by deleting reference to any agent deflects the force of the criticism, or the use of abstract nouns ('criticism of the government has been increased') which have the same effect. This is to give a critical edge to Chomsky's notion of transformation grammar:

> Below the surface of an utterance, in this view, are successive layers of structure, variously transformed or classified. A hearer or reader can attempt to recover these until the underlying set of basic forms is reached. Full decoding, then, is a journey into these depths, following in reverse the hypothesized genesis of the utterance: a description of the underlying forms, and a precise history of what has happened to them.[10]

With these latter analyses we have moved beyond structuralism to a kind of sociolinguistics.

If the concept of ideology is to have any critical edge, then structuralist principles require severe modification. Those principles have encountered three main difficulties. The first, and most evident, is that the meaning of a piece of writing is not to be deciphered simply by looking – however hard – at the words and sentences. Analysis that is strictly confined to the text breaks it down into units and then constructs models which are both drastic oversimplifications and often arbitrary. In a modern version of old idealist doctrines, discourse analysis sometimes seems to imply that only signs exist and that the universe is an endless round of signifiers with nothing signified: we cannot look through the window but remain condemned to stare at the glass. But the meaning of any set of words depends heavily on the conditions under which it is produced and those under which it is received by its readers or hearers. Language is a form of action and, like most forms of action, its efficiency depends very heavily on the context. Prime examples of this are the so-called 'performative' utterances, whereby the speaker performs an action by uttering certain words – for example, by saying 'I promise' in a marriage ceremony the speaker performs the act of getting married. But the meaning and effectiveness of the words depends on a whole set of institutional arrangements and presuppositions: it is not possible for just anyone to open a motorway by snipping some red tape and saying 'I open', or to condemn someone to death by putting on a black cap and saying 'I sentence'.[11] A different way of making the same general point would be to say the statements are *about* something, they suggest something, and to understand them is to understand their relationship to what they are about, i.e. to the world outside the statement. Irony, for example, is very difficult to discover without knowledge of the circumstances of a statement. Thus the meaning of a statement is bound up with its function, with what it *does*, and reference to the world outside the statement is essential to this: text is dependent on context.

A different sort of difficulty is that emphasis on the autonomy of *language* over speech removes it from social and historical influences. There is no evidence for the existence of independent rules of syntax lying behind speech and governing what can, or at least what cannot, be said. For as soon as such rules are stated it is possible in theory at least – and sometimes in practice – to find examples of their modification by social and historical circumstances.

A further criticism of structural approaches in general is that they tend to emphasize the consensual rather than the conflictual aspects of society and thus tend to legitimate the social order rather than to criticize it. For a structure is something objective and defines bounds beyond which we cannot step. It points to an underlying consensus in which we are all implicated. This is a version of the idea that in every society there is a dominant ideology in the shape of a coherent set of principles meeting general acceptance and serving to legitimate existing relations of power. This view has been highly contested. In anthropology the opinion of Edmund Leach that 'myth and ritual is a language of signs in terms of which claims to rights and status are expressed, but it is a language of argument, not a chorus of harmony'[12] is obviously at variance with the views of Levi-Strauss. In medieval society it might be claimed that the dominant politico-religious ethos served more to reinforce the *esprit de corps* of the ruling groups than to legitimate them in the eyes of the mass of the people who were either ignorant of, or indifferent to, this ethos.[13] In contemporary Western society there are many who claim that what stability it has depends not so much on any underlying consensus among its members but more on its fragmentation. As with the view of medieval society mentioned above, the acceptance of the values and norms of 'liberal democracy' are strongest among those at the top of the social scale: those at the bottom have no coherent or cohesive means to express their disaffection.

This point about consensus and conflict leads on to another difficulty in the structuralist approach – the apparent disappearance of the subject in the sense of a reflective, responsible and creative agent, a process elaborated in the varieties of post-structuralist and post-modernist writers examined in the next chapter. In reacting against the excessive subjectivity of existentialism with its emphasis on the absolute freedom and responsibility of every person, structuralism has gone to the other extreme. It is one thing to realize how bounded that freedom is by the structures of language and of society, and it is quite another to dissolve the subject into those same social relations and linguistic forms. More specifically, any understanding, whether of action or words, seems to involve the process of interpretation which implies a creative subjectivity. The would-be objective and scientifically determinable nature of structures can never be so overwhelming as to squeeze out entirely the subjective element in human action.

In sum, there is no doubt that the emphasis on language with its distinction between denotation and connotation has provided new insights. And obviously there is great importance in the kind of sociolinguistics which demonstrates how political, social or sexual prejudice is reinforced by language. But the hope that these could be formulated within the confines of a general scientific theory of structuralist inspiration has proved unfounded. For the underlying structures seem on inspection to be no different from the older idea of philosophical world-views between which no science can act as arbiter.

In order to draw together the threads of what has been rather a disparate discussion, let us look briefly at Jurgen Habermas, probably the most influential contemporary thinker in this area. Habermas has attempted, by drawing on the latest discussions in sociology, linguistics and many other areas to construct an analysis of society in which the concept of ideology would preserve its critical edge. The best way of introducing the complex thought of Habermas is to see what he borrows from the accounts of ideology we have already discussed.

Clearly, Habermas is much indebted to Marx. He accepts much of Marx's materialist conception of history in which the historical material conditions under which human labour has occurred have set the developing parameters for knowledge. Marx, according to Habermas, sets his conception of history in the context of a dialectic between the tools and instruments that human beings have at their disposal at any given time – the forces of production – and the institutional arrangements with their cultural and symbolic accompaniments. However, Habermas thinks that there is a tendency in Marx to over-emphasize the former:

> the productive activity which regulates the material exchange of the human species with its natural environment, becomes the paradigm for the generation of all the categories, everything is resolved into the self-movement of production. Because of this, Marx's brilliant insight into the dialectical relationship between the forces of production and the relations of production could very quickly be misinterpreted in a mechanistic manner.[14]

This tendency to emphasize economic determinism and assimilate the social to the natural sciences was taken much further by Engels, Bukharin and others. Habermas, by contrast, while not wishing to deny the importance of material labour and the technical innovations through which its forms develop, wants also to stress the importance of cultural tradition and institutional arrangements – which together he often refers to as 'interaction'. Unlike Marx – and more particularly unlike many of Marx's orthodox successors – Habermas claims that there is no 'automatic developmental relation between labour and interaction'.[15]

This attention to non-economic factors and the need for a drastic reformulation of Marx is justified, according to Habermas, by the changes in advanced industrial society over the last 100 years. He thinks that whereas in Marx's time the prevailing ideology was based on the idea of equal exchange in the market, the advance of technology in the twentieth century has given rise to a technocratic consciousness which reduces the political to the technical. The increasing intervention of the state in social and economic affairs has meant an equally increasing number of administrators and experts to take decisions based on the needs of the technocratic system: this involves a change in the ideology appropriate to such a society which moves from a consideration of just exchange and equality to justifying decisions in terms of technical questions appropriate to science and industry. This process involves at the same time a depoliticization of society. While being in a sense less ideological than its predecessors in that it does not represent an idealization or illusion over against 'real' life, this technocratic consciousness is at the same time more ideological: for it is both more pervasive and harder to oppose than its predecessors in that it simply suppresses all possible alternatives in the name of economy and efficiency and only allows debate to take place about different means to a predetermined end. Thus, while not going all the way with Marcuse in his condemnation of industrial society, Habermas is strongly inspired by this line of thought.

The distinction between labour and interaction involved a much enlarged conception of the crisis of capitalist society. Whereas Marx considered crisis mainly in economic terms, Habermas outlined a whole typology of crises inherent in late capitalism: an economic crisis, a crisis of rationality, of legitimacy, and of motivation. In Habermas's view, an economic crisis in late capitalism was not inevitable. But the steps taken by the state to avert it entailed a crisis of rationality. For the conflict of interests inherent in late capitalism and the contradictory demands on state intervention tended to mean that state aid was dysfunctionally distributed. This in turn created a crisis of legitimacy, for state intervention meant opening up the question of control and choice. The only solutions were buying off the most powerful parties or the creation of a new legitimizing ideology. In addition, growing public intervention involved lessening the scope of the private sphere which had motivated bourgeois society and thereby a crisis in motivation which had hitherto depended on the idea of the market as a fair distributor of values. Summarizing his conclusions, Habermas declared:

> Economic crises are shifted into the political system through the reactive-avoidance activity of the government in such a way that supplies of legitimation can compensate for deficits in rationality and extensions of organisational rationality can compensate for those legitimation deficits that do appear. There arises a bundle of crisis tendencies that, from a genetic point of view, represents a hierarchy of crisis phenomena shifted upwards from below. But from the point of view of governmental crisis management, these crisis phenomena are distinguished by being mutually substitutable within certain limits. These limits are determined by, on the one hand, the fiscally available quantity of value – the shortage of which cannot be validly predicted within crisis theory – and on the other by supplies of motivation from the socio-cultural system. The substitutive relation between the scarce resources, value and meaning, is therefore decisive for the prediction of crisis.[16]

This expanded idea of crisis and the relativizing of the economic sphere involved a drastic reformulation of Marx's historical materialism. Clearly Habermas's ideas have strong affinities with those of the Frankfurt School. His whole revision of Marx is governed by the School's criticism of instrumental reason, the scientific or technical reason which had come to dominate society in the twentieth century. Besides a legitimate interest in the instrumental reason which served to control objectified processes, Habermas claimed that human beings had two other interests: a practical interest in communicating with each other in forms of social organization and an interest in being self-reflective and self-determining, i.e. an emancipatory interest in autonomy. Also, like many members of the Frankfurt School, Habermas is interested in Freudian psychoanalysis as a model of emancipation. He thinks there are strong parallels between the development of the individual according to Freud and the development of the human species. Just as an individual whose ego organization is weak will find a neurotic solution to certain forms of inner repression, so societies generate ideologies which are rationalizations of asymmetrical power relations which have been repressed, elided or distorted in language. And just as the Freudian analyst leads the patient to self-awareness, so critical theory can do the same for a society by exposing the roots of its legitimating ideology.

The novel element in Habermas's theory of ideology is his emphasis on language. Like most writers influenced by the Western Marxist tradition, Habermas wishes to stress the importance of the superstructure as opposed to the rather rigid economic determinism of classical Marxism. But for him the key to the superstructure lies in language, in that 'today the problem of language has replaced the traditional problem of consciousness.'[17] His concentration on language, however, is far from being disembodied. It is closely linked to a study of society in that he believes that language not only constitutes social phenomena but is itself constituted (and distorted) by them. The study of ideology is therefore the study of systematically distorted communication.

What is distinctive about Habermas's interest in language is how he proposes to establish a criterion by which to judge ideology. If this enterprise involves the explanation of systematically distorted communication then it must also involve the 'mastery of the idea of undistorted communication or reasonable discourse'.[18] And this idea, he claims, is implicit in any use of language. For the very act of speech involves the supposition of the possibility of an ideal speech situation in which the force of the better argument alone will decide the issue. For people speaking to each other aim at reaching some kind of understanding. Communicative interaction presupposes that those engaging in it could sustain four types of validity claim: first, that what they say is comprehensible; second, that it is true; third, that it is legitimate in the context; and last, that it is sincerely meant. The redemption of these claims is only possible if all members of society have an equal chance to participate in the discussion; and this involves the notion of the transformation of society in a direction that would enable such a communicative competence to characterize all members of society. For technological society can only be rational if its policies are subject to public control. But, for this to happen, discussion and opinion have to be free from manipulation and domination. The ultimate goal of social emancipation is, therefore, inherent in any and every speech act.

In contemporary society there exist profound barriers to this 'discursive will-formation'. For

The validity of [contemporary] world-views is secured in a communication structure which excludes discursive will-formation ... the barriers to communication which make a fiction precisely of the reciprocal imputation of accountability, support at the same time the belief in legitimacy that sustains the fiction and prevents its being found out. That is the paradoxical achievement of ideologies, whose individual prototype is the neurotic disturbance.[19]

This approach allows us to gauge the extent of ideology in any society by counterposing to the actual state of affairs the question:

how would the members of a social system, at a given stage of development of productive forces, have collectively and bindingly interpreted their needs (and which norms would they have accepted as justified) if they could and would have decided on the organization of social intercourse through discursive will-formation, with adequate knowledge of the limiting conditions and functional imperatives of their society?[20]

Thus Habermas wishes to conclude that his criticism of ideology is not arbitrary but is 'inherent in the very structure of social action and language' into which, in their turn, most values are inextricably woven:

Only in an emancipated society, whose members' autonomy and responsibility had been realized, would communication have developed into the non-authoritarian and universally practiced dialogue from which both our model of reciprocally constituted ego identity and our idea of true consensus are always implicitly derived. To this extent the truth of statements is based on anticipating the realization of the good life.[21]

It is not surprising that Habermas's wide-ranging ideas have raised several objections. The parallel Habermas is keen to draw between psychoanalysis and social liberation is suspect both because it involves an illegitimate move from the individual to the social and also because in psychoanalysis the process is one of willing co-operation, whereas this is unlikely to be the case in liberation from social domination. More centrally, the equation of ideology with distorted communication is not specific enough since not all distorted communication is ideological. The whole concentration of language and communicative competence seems to neglect material domination and class interest: access to unfettered communication may not be enough to secure an emancipated society if access to wealth and status are not similarly equalized. But, however formal and abstract much of his presentation may be, Habermas has succeeded in uniting the themes of science, language and ideology more interestingly than any other contemporary thinker.

Ideology and the 'End of History'

Both structuralism and the very different approach of Habermas have recently come under attack from the increasingly influential view of the world known as postmodernism. Postmodernism is almost as elusive a concept as ideology itself.[1] This is because – like the terms post-Christian, post-Marxist, post-structuralism – it defines itself negatively. Critical and mockingly destructive, it rejects even very broad and tentative attempts to find some foundation for our thought. It turns all our 'isms' into 'wasms' and resolutely turns its back on efforts to give some overall account of our nature and destiny: it wishes to be post-everything, elevates incoherence to its defining feature, and sees even reason itself as the mere tool of a Nietzschean will to power. All this sounds confusingly relativist. However, no thinkers, not even postmodernists, can be consistently relativists without disappearing completely up their own backsides. So the most useful approach will be to ask whether postmodernism is not itself an ideology which will, in turn, suggest that we look at the social and historical context in which it has arisen and flourishes.

Postmodernism is a reaction to, and an extension of, modernity. It is 'in every respect parasitic on modernity: it lives and feeds on its achievements and on its dilemmas'.[2] By 'modernity' here is meant the Enlightenment project of achieving increasing material and moral progress for humankind through the application of science and reason. This project, like the Christianity it was in many ways intended to supercede, involved an account of where we have come from, where we are going, how we can get there, and why we should bother to go. Building on the subversion of the whole of the

Western philosophical tradition to be found in writers such as Nietzsche and Heidegger, Postmodernist thinkers are typically sceptical of such universal schemes which they call 'meta-narratives': they prefer to concentrate on smaller-scale accounts or narratives and deny that such accounts can be united, and judged, in terms of some over-arching account and judgement.

Postmodernist thinkers concentrate on three claims. First, according to a leading exponent such as Jacques Derrida, we have no direct encounter with reality through reason, but only through our images of it.[3] We construct our accounts of reality in words. Just as a building consists in its bricks, so reality consists in the words, images and metaphors that we use to describe it. By deconstructing the picture that we have made of reality we lay bare its (lack of) foundations. Thus 'today, culture impacts back on reality in ways that make any independent and, as it were, non- or extra cultural form of it problematical (in a kind of Heisenberg principle of mass culture which intervenes between your eye and the thing itself), so that finally the theorists unite their voices in the new doxa that the 'referent' no longer exists'.[4] There is a well-known story of an ancient sage who was asked about the foundation of the world. He replied that the world rested on an elephant. When asked what the elephant rested on, he replied that it rested on a turtle and when asked what the turtle rested on, he replied: 'it's turtles all the way down.' In postmodernist thought we are in danger of losing nature and reality completely and descending in a spiral of endless metaphor. Second, the self is held to be no longer the confident and sovereign being of much modernist thought. The self is no longer the potential lord of all it surveys and capable of shaping history in accordance with human aims. The self has been deconstructed or decentred, typically in the work of Foucault whose studies on attitudes to madness, the history of prisons and of sexuality claimed to show how human individuality is itself historically constructed and produced by all-pervasive impersonal relations of power. For Foucault, 'man is an invention the recent date of which is easily demonstrated by the archaeology of our thought, an invention which is also perhaps near its end. If there were to occur in the present times an intellectual revolution similar to that of the Enlightenment then it would be odds on that man would be effaced just like a picture drawn in the sand by the incoming tide'.[5] Third, postmodernism celebrates the existence of difference, variety and diversity for their own sakes. The effort to homogenize, to impose a false unity is characteristic of ideological thinking. Since there is no foundation or reality to which thought can be subjected and since even the self is divided in that the rational superego of Freud has given way to the amorphous and slippery Other of Lacan, there is no standpoint from which to impose a unity on the spontaneous diversity of existence.

The disappearance of a stable reality and of a stable conception of the self have obvious parallels with recent economic developments such as the anti-planning views that surfaced during the Reagan and Thatcher years. The dominance of the 'free' market led to an economic anarchy in which, in Marx's famous phrase, 'all that is solid melts into air'.[6] The impression of the lack of solidity in social and economic life was reinforced by the acceleration in the turnover time of capital fostered by the growth of information technology. This can be seen as the cultural logic of the late capitalism in which the 'information society' not only produces new theories of language but in which 'aesthetic production today has become integrated into commodity production generally: the frantic economic urgency of producing fresh waves of ever more novel-seeming goods (from clothing to aeroplanes), at ever greater rates of turnover, now assigns an increasingly essential structural function and position to aesthetic innovation and experimentation'.[7] In a society where packaging and imaging are crucial in the sale of politics as much as of beer, where time and space are increasingly compressed by information super-highways, where news reports are referred to as 'stories' and murderously armed nation states as 'players', it is not surprising that reality becomes virtual and people begin to lose any firm conception of their individualities.[8]

Some have seen postmodernism theories as subversive of old authoritarian ideologies and thus pointing to the emergence of an ultra-pluralist society in which different collective social practices could flourish. In this context the concept of civil society has made a striking return to political thought: the unifying state has failed as a moral project and civil society with its variety of institutions, clubs, professional associations and pressure groups is seen as the area where diversity can be fostered.[9] Others have suggested that the belief that all thought is ideological and merely the articulate expression of conflicting interests and desires is itself an ideology all of its own.[10] It confuses objectivity with disinterestedness – but we can have a very direct interest in finding out the truth. Postmodernism, by contrast, tends to give up on concepts such as truth which it dissolves into an interplay of rhetoric and power. By claiming that, since no one is disinterested, there is no such thing as objectivity but only an endless clash of perspectives, postmodernism seems, as Habermas has argued, to induce a scepticism and passivity which effectively favours a conservatism bolstering the *status quo*.[11] Moreover, some postmodernist writers, such as Baudrillard and Lyotard, tend to homogenize interests, to equate all desires and thus deprive themselves of saying which interests, desires and conflicts are more important than others: the interests of stamp-collectors and politicians are much the same.

Some have seen postmodernism as a recycling of the 'end of ideology' thesis discussed in Chapter 5. Postmodernism is certainly keen on ends in general. Indeed, as Jameson has remarked, postmodernism is constituted by 'an inverted millenarianism in which premonitions of the future, catastrophic or redemptive, have been replaced by senses of the end of this or that (the end of ideology, art, or social class; the 'crisis' of Leninism, social democracy, or the welfare state, etc., etc.)',[12] The end of ideology has recently been endorsed by Richard Rorty, the most prominent exponent of postmodernism in the United States. Rorty's playful and ironic liberalism springs from a postmodernism which expresses the continental European tradition of Nietzsche and Heidegger through an Anglo-Saxon analytical pragmatism. In his view, liberal democracy cannot have, and does not need, any philosophical justification. He believes that 'contemporary liberal society already contains the institutions for its own improvement – an improvement which can mitigate the dangers Foucault sees. Indeed, my hunch is that Western social and political thought may have had the last *conceptual* revolution it needs'.[13] In Rorty's view, echoing what he takes to be the later views of John Rawls, just liberal democracy 'will be a society which encourages the "end of ideology", that takes reflective equilibrium as the only method needed in discussing social policy. When such a society deliberates, when it collects the principles and the intuitions to be brought into equilibrium, it will tend to discard those drawn from philosophical accounts of the self, of rationality'.[14] Rorty's appeal here to 'our' common intuitions and traditional practices is reminiscent of Oakeshott's conservative ideological stance.[15]

The most successful proponent of the end of ideology and indeed of history itself, is Francis Fukayama. His article 'The End of History?' published in the summer of 1989[16] aroused immediate and enormous controversy and was followed by a book entitled *The End of History and the Last Man* which elaborated on many of its themes.[17] In his article Fukayama argued that 'the unabashed victory of economic and political liberalism' over all competitors meant 'not just the end of the cold war, or the passing of a particular period of history, but the end of history as such: that is, the end-point of mankind's ideological evolution and the universalisation of Western liberal democracy as the final form of human government'.[18] Fukayama was not claiming that there would be no more events, but only that the final conceptual and political framework in which these events would take place had already been achieved. In the past, war had been a great catalyst of change: but to date there had been no example of liberal democratic states going to war with one another since, with the decline of ideology, the particular interests hitherto pursued by armed conflict could now be absorbed into the competitions of liberal capitalism. Nor did Fukayama see the persistence of poverty in Western societies as casting doubt on his thesis: poverty was due, not to market forces, but to cultural disadvantage which would eventually be eliminated in the face of the consumer abundance produced by modern capitalism. Moreover, Fukayama did not claim that the end of history yielded a perfect society – only that there was no prospect of a better alternative to liberal capitalism. Nationalism might flourish outside the most historically advanced countries of the world, but the large economic powers would conduct their rivalry in the future only by wars of trade. The revival of religious fundamentalism, too, was peripheral: it was only of real significance in Islam and even here limited to a relatively small area of the world. As for socialism, the only plausible variant left after the collapse of communism was the politics of social democracy which posed no threat to Fukayama's thesis since it fully accepted the primacy of market relations.

Fukayama's thesis was that there was an underlying evolutionary direction to history and that it arrived at an end state in which human nature's inbuilt struggle for individual recognition would at last be satisfied – and that the framework for this satisfaction was provided for in a liberal democratic and capitalist society. The form of this account is reminiscent of Marx's theory of history but the philosophical mentor of Fukayama is Marx's teacher Hegel. The philosophical background to which Fukayama appeals is Hegel's *Phenomenology* in the idiosyncratic interpretation given to it in Paris in the 1930s by the Russian emigré, Alexandre Kojève.[19] Central to Hegel's whole philosophy, according to Kojève, was the dialectic between master and slave: history continued in the past because the separation and struggle between masters who went to war and slaves who toiled precluded any mutual respect and recognition of individual work and dignity. With the spread of the principles of the French Revolution, however, universal equality was achieved. Each person received universal recognition 'as a Citizen enjoying all political rights and as a "juridical person" of the civil law' and 'desire thus being entirely satisfied, struggle and labour cease: history is over, there is nothing more *to do*'.[20] This absence of effort was not all to the good, however, and at the end of his article Fukayama painted a rather gloomy picture of the capitalist eternity he foresaw in which 'the end of history will be a very sad time. The struggle for recognition, the willingness to risk one's life for a purely abstract goal, the worldwide ideological struggle that called forth daring, courage, imagination and ideal-ism, will be replaced by economic calculation, the endless solving of technical problems, environmental concerns, and satisfaction of sophisticated consumer demands. In the post-historical period there will be neither art nor philosophy, just the perpetual caretaking of the museum of the human spirit'.[21] The owl of Minerva did indeed paint grey on grey.

Thus Fukayama's position is a bit more ambivalent than his reputation as a bourgeois triumphalist might suggest. These am-biguities were strengthened in the three years that elapsed between his original article and its elaboration in book form. Here Fu-kayama provides an overall theory of history which stresses the role of science, unleased by capitalism, in the satisfying of human wants. He buttresses Hegel's account of the quest for existential recog-nition with a description of the spirited or wilful element in human nature drawn from Plato's *Republic*. This rather abstract and generalized philosophizing is supplemented by an extended and fluent account of the recent progress of democracy across the globe. The general message is still that 'if we are now at a point where we cannot imagine a world substantially different from our own, in which there is no apparent or obvious way in which the future will represent a fundamental improvement over our current order, then we must also take into consideration the possibility that History itself might be at an end'.[22] In the last section of his book, Fukayama turns to the second half of his title and imagines two criticisms from Left and Right to the effect that the very limited nature of human prospects that he describes does not allow for the most fundamental aspirations of human nature. From the Left comes the demand to extend human rights to promote a radical egalitarianism. Here Fukayama joins the recent backlash against 'political correctness' led by his teacher Alan Bloom.[23] It is, however, the challenge from the Right that Fukayama takes more seriously: that some will inevitably regard as shallow a society based solely on prosperity and efficiency and strive, not to be equal to others, but to be pre-eminent over them, thus subverting the very principles of liberal democracy. Fukayama is fairly optimistic about the capability of liberal democracy to cope with these criticisms, though the conclusion to his book does envisage the possibility of history's wagon train setting out on a new and more distant journey.[24] It is important to realize that on some crucial points Fukayama is deeply ambiguous. His strong historical metanarrative seems out of keeping with fashionable postmodernism but at the same time he endorses the directionless pluralism of contemporary society.[25] Further, as might be expected from anyone who tries to marry Plato to Hegel and their latter-day, if partial, disciples Strauss and Kojève, Fukayama sometimes retracts his confident assertion of the end of history. His readings of Plato and Hegel are, of course, extremely selective: for Plato, as his most articulate modern interpreter Simone Weil has shown, human achievement is due much more to self-transcendence than to self-aggrandizement. And central to Hegel's view of history is not struggle for recognition but progress in the consciousness of freedom.

Unsurprisingly, Fukayama's writing has generated a lot of controversy. Apart from the journalistic hype with which his first article was greeted, his ideas concentrate in an accessible form the enthusiasms and worries of the end of the twentieth century. Nevertheless his account does reveal serious gaps and weaknesses. It is surprising to find a complete neglect of Freud in a book which deals so extensively with the desires and motivations of the human mind. More importantly, Fukayama fails to engage seriously with either feminism – his individualistic description of the struggle for recognition is very male-orientated – or with ecological concerns – the global mass industrialization he envisages is likely to destroy the world's eco-system. In spite of the increasing gap between rich and poor nations, Fukayama is cavalierly confident about the stability and ever-widening appeal of liberal democracy. This confidence is based on the way in which he sees liberal democracy as bound up with capitalism. But this link is profoundly insecure since capitalism and democracy are very uneasy bedfellows. Capitalism is inevitably based on *some* form of exploitation and domination. As soon as democracy aspires to be more than a Schumpeterian competition among élites for the people's vote, it involves claims for equal economic entitlement and pressures which threaten the very inequalities on which capitalism depends. In other words 'capitalism as a system valorising motives of individual gain and self-realisation, and democratic citizenship as a source of social choice rooted in moral norms, point in different directions. There seems no reason to expect the hegemony of the first over the second to be a feature of all time'.[26] Indeed, Fukayama himself acknowledges this when he suggests that Western capitalism undermines any foundation of social solidarity and that if Asians appreciate the effect of corrosive individualism in Western societies, then 'a systematic illiberal and non-democratic alternative combining technocratic economic rationalism with paternalistic authoritarianism may gain ground in the Far East' and 'an overt rupture with democracy could occur in which the form itself would be rejected as a Western imposition, as irrelevant to the successful functioning of Asian societies as Western business management techniques are to their economies'.[27] Liberal democracy, with its self-destructive tendencies, would be just as doomed as Soviet communism and the end of history would be an East Asian Confucian capitalism with Lee Kuan Yew's Singapore as its model. Alternatively, if we take seriously the centrality accorded by Fukayama to Hegel's idea of the struggle for recognition, we might come to the conclusion that liberalism was seriously deficient. The criticism would be that 'the promise of universal, reciprocal recognition remains essentially unfulfilled in liberal societies: economic inequality brought about by capitalism *ipso facto* implies unequal recognition'.[28] The struggle, in other words, goes on until a radical egalitarianism, the only society which would ensure the full recognition of all, is achieved.[29] Either way, Fukayama's thesis of the end of history depends on that of Kojève and Kojève's claim that we are at the end of history 'stands or falls on the strength of the assertion that the recognition provided by contemporary liberal democratic states adequately satisfies the human desire for recognition'.[30] But if there is any validity in the above considerations, then the end of history, at least in Fukayama's sense, may yet by a very long way off.

8

Conclusion: An End to Ideology or Ideology Without End?

As we have seen in the foregoing chapters, the discussion of ideology over the last two centuries has divided into two different approaches. In the first, the dominant contrast is between ideology and science. In the French rationalist tradition of de Tracy the application of reason to society would rid society of the irrational prejudices that had been so noxious in the past: the science of ideas (ideo-logy) would demystify society just as natural science had demystified nature. With a little help from Marx (and Napoleon), ideology then became associated with those ideas that were contrasted with science – as in the work of Durkheim or Althusser. The same science/ideology dichotomy is present in the strongly empiricist English-speaking tradition. The difference between the two lies in their opposing conceptions of what constitutes the science that excludes ideology: in the work of Althusser, for example, it is Marxism itself (and possibly psychoanalysis) which is that science. For Popper, on the other hand, both are the supreme examples of pseudo-Archimedian sciences. In the second tradition, often called historicist and associated with German writing, the search for a foothold has been strongly relativized. The problems of studying society were seen as radically different from those of studying nature. Ideology was connected with sectional interests, with social perspectives from which it was impossible completely to escape. Various more or less Olympian viewpoints were proposed in the shape of Hegel's Absolute Spirit, or Mannheim's free-floating intellectuals, or Habermas's ideal speech situation – but all as aspirations rather than realities.

One of the strengths of the Marxist tradition, which gave the concept of ideology the prominence that it now enjoys, lies in its catholic attitude to these two approaches. Both the science/ideology dichotomy and the connection of ideology with the social determination of ideas can be found in Marx himself. Both Engels and Althusser subscribe to the former, but they differ fundamentally in the importance they assign to ideology. It is clear, however, that the most fruitful Marxist contributions are those in the Germanic tradition. The relegation of ideology to the superstructure, whether in the scientific version of Engels or in the purely political one of Lenin, were dead ends. Marxism has indeed produced much banal talk about ideology: but it has also undoubted successes. Consider the sketchy though enormously insightful discussion by Gramsci in his *Prison Notebooks* of the incorporation of intellectuals by the medieval Church and the parallels he draws with the socialist movement; or the detailed analysis of the connections between Jansenist thought in the work of Pascal and Racine and the changing class structure of French society by Lukacs' pupil Lucien Goldmann. Both these studies retain the critical sense of ideology but without appealing either to a dubious concept of science or to a reductionist view of social processes.

It is in the empiricist tradition that the science/ideology dichotomy appears at its most vulnerable. A recent and well-informed commentary can still declare that those propounding an 'end of ideology' thesis in the United States are merely 'speaking in terms of, and reference to, empirical phenomena far removed from the methodological self-doubts – certainly justified – of the social sciences'.[1] This idea that the facts can speak for themselves has its origin in rather a different fact, namely that, in the words of the American historian Richard Hofstadter, 'It has been our fate as a nation not to have ideologies but to be one'.[2] The view of empiricists is that facts and values are separate at least in the sense that they can be separated in expressions where they are conjoined. But to say that facts (particularly social ones) are simply there, whereas values are the subject of free choice, is itself an evaluative view. Moreover, much recent work on ideology has linked it to the study of language and the symbols of everyday practical life where it is much less vulnerable to dismissal by reason or science than when it is simply treated as a systematic body of 'ideas'.

But if the science/ideology dichotomy will not do, nor will its opposite – the pale view of the omnipresence of ideology which has the additional, dangerous implication of reducing all social and political arguments to the status of mere propaganda. This can come in the form of an indiscriminating 'vulgar' Marxism to which virtually any aspect of contemporary society is a symptom of 'bourgeois' ideology. This approach neglects the vast amount of empirical evidence against the existence of any pervasive dominant ideology. The ideas of the ruling class do not permeate the whole of society: rather their role is assured by the fragmented nature of opposition to them. Nor is the ecumenical concept of ideology espoused by Martin Seliger in his *Ideology and Politics* more fruitful. For Seliger's definition of ideology, whereby it is any and every action-oriented set of beliefs organized into a coherent system, robs the concept of any critical edge. It also, in spite of vaunting its inclusive nature, restricts the definition to political belief-systems and thereby neglects the link between ideology and everyday life. Although the latter objection certainly does not apply to Clifford Geertz's view of 'ideology as a cultural system,'[3] his work, also, is overly benevolent to the concept of ideology. Since ideologies are, according to Geertz, 'most distinctively, maps of problematic social reality and matrices for the creation of collective conscience',[4] they are not, as ideologies, open to criticism.

The problem here is to avoid a circular vacuity. Daniel Bell, nostalgic for cold war certainties, has lamented that 'the concept of ideology has unravelled completely'.[5] He is right in that the demands of gender and race have been added to those of class to reveal the 'performative contradiction' of contemporary western societies: their principles of universal freedom and equality are constantly at odds with their own practices.[6] The arbitrary incoherence of much liberal thought has been powerfully exposed, from a different point of view, in the recent work of Alasdair MacIntyre.[7] But we do not need to accept the conservative conclusions that some have drawn nor give up completely on ideas of progress. Genuine emancipation can never be based on domination. The science/ideology dichotomy and the vulgar Marxist view share at least one redeeming feature in that they both attempt, however unsuccessfully, to link ideology to domination. For successful accounts of ideology must combine two attributes. The first, emphasized by Mannheim, is a hermeneutic subtlety which sees both that it is necessary to understand ideology before criticizing it and also adopts a self-reflexive attitude towards its own premises. The second, stressed in most strands of the Marxist tradition, is to preserve the concept's critical potential by linking it with analyses of control and domination, thereby extricating it from the labyrinth of relativism associated with the hermeneutic circle. Ideology may be 'an irretrievably fallen word'[8] – but then we live in a fallen society and, until we mend it, we will continue to be implicated in ideology. It follows that, although in principle there could be an end to ideology, it is certainly nowhere in sight – not even on the horizon. This is because ideology is best viewed not as a separate system of signs and symbols that could be contrasted with – and eventually replaced by – another, e.g. science of some sort. Ideology is rather an aspect of every system of signs and symbols in so far as they are implicated in an asymmetrical distribution of power and resources. And of which system is this not the case?

Notes

Chapter 1

1 On this idea, see the original article: W.B. Gallie, 'Essentially Contested Concepts' *Proceedings of the Aristotelian Society*, 1955–6, vol. 56, particularly pp. 171ff. On attempts to define ideology, see: R. Geuss, *The Idea of a Critical Theory*, Cambridge University Press, Cambridge, 1981, Pt I; M. Hamilton, 'The Elements of a Concept of Ideology', *Political Studies*, 1987, vol. 35, pp. 18ff; and T. Eagleton, *Ideology*, Verso, London, 1991, Ch. 1.

2 On ideology as no mere reflection but an active agent moulding the desires of those in its thrall, see: J. Elster, 'Belief, Bias and Ideology', in M. Hollis and S. Lukes, eds, *Rationality and Relativism*, Blackwell, Oxford, 1982.

3 J. Habermas, *Towards a Rational Society*, Heinemann, London, 1970, p. 99. For a similar view of the modernity of ideology see, for example, K. Mannheim, *Studies on the Left*, Routledge, London, 1952, p. 55 and M. Oakeshott, *Rationalism in Politics and Other Essays*, Methuen, London, 1962, p. 21.

4 See further on this the excellent article: B. Halpern, ' "Myth" and "Ideology" in Modern Usage'. *History and Theory*, vol. 1, 1961, especially pp. 135ff.

5 See Ch. 7.

6 Baron d'Holbach. *The System of Nature* (translated by H.D. Robinson), Burt Franklin, New York, 1970, pp. viiiff.

7 K. Marx, *Selected Writings*, ed. D. McLellan, Oxford University Press, Oxford, 1977, p. 156.

8 Quoted in H. Barth, *Wahrheit und Ideologie*, Eugen Reutsch Verlag, Zurich and Stuttgart, 1961, p. 27.

9 The location of the 'Age' is a matter of dispute. Compare H.D. Aiken's *The Age of Ideology*, Mentor, New York, 1956, subtitled *The Nineteenth Century Philosophers* with K.D. Bracher's *The Age of Ideologies*, Weidenfeld, London, 1984, subtitled *A History of Political Thought in the Twentieth Century*.

10 See D. Coole, *Women in Political Theory*, Wheatsheaf, Brighton, 1988; S. Okin, *Gender, Justice and the Family*, Basic Books, New York, 1988; V. Bryson, *Feminist Political Thought*, Macmillan, Basingstoke, 1992.

11 See A. Dobson and P. Lucardie, *The Politics of Nature: Explorations in Green Political Theory*, Routledge, New York, 1993.

12 See particularly the trilogy by A. MacIntyre, *After Virtue*, 2nd edn, Duckworth, London, 1985; *Whose Justice? Which Rationality?*, University of Notre Dame Press, Notre Dame, 1988; *Three Rival Versions of Moral Enquiry*, University of Notre Dame Press, Notre Dame, 1990; and also the magisterial survey of the intellectual background to the moral dilemmas of the contemporary individual in C. Taylor, *Sources of the Self*, Cambridge University Press, Cambridge, 1985; and the useful collection of articles debating the issue in J. Horton and S. Mendus, *After MacIntyre*, Polity, Cambridge, 1994.

13 For an extreme example see the later work of J. Baudrillard in *Selected Writings*, ed. M. Poster, Polity, Cambridge, 1988.

Chapter 2

1 K. Marx, *Selected Writings*, ed. D. McLellan, Oxford University Press, Oxford, 1977, p. 64.

2 K. Marx, ibid. p. 164.

3 Ibid.

4 K. Marx, ibid. p. 169.

5 K. Marx, ibid., p. 176. For an argument that ruling ideas do not really rule subordinate groups in society but largely serve to give unity and direction to the ruling élite see: N. Abercrombie, S. Hill and Bill Turner, *The Dominant Ideology Thesis*, Allen and Unwin, London, 1980.

6 K. Marx, ibid., p. 164.

7 See J. Mepham, 'The Theory of Ideology in *Capital*', in *Issues in Marxist Philosophy*, eds J. Mepham and D.H. Ruben, Harvester, Brighton, 1979, pp. 143ff, and W. Mitchell, *Iconology: Image, Text, Ideology*, Chicago University Press, Chicago, 1986, Ch. 6.

8 K. Marx, op. cit., p. 436.

9 K. Marx, *Capital*, Lawrence and Wishart, London, 1972, vol. 3, p. 209.

10 For an elaboration of the contrast between 'lived' and 'intellectual' ideologies, see M. Billig, S. Condor, D. Edwards, M. Gane, D.

Middleton, A. Radley, *Ideological Dilemmas*, Sage, Beverly Hills, 1988 pp. 27ff.

11 K. Marx, *Selected Writings*, p. 455.

12 K. Marx, ibid., p. 164.

13 K. Marx, ibid., pp. 389f.

14 K. Marx, ibid., p. 172.

15 K. Marx, ibid., p. 389.

16 K. Marx, *Theories of Surplus Value*, Progress, Moscow, 1963, vol. 1, p. 285.

17 See especially, M. Seliger, *The Marxist Conception of Ideology*, Cambridge, 1977, pp. 28ff.

18 K. Marx, F. Engels, *Selected Correspondence*, Progress, Moscow, 1965, p. 459.

19 For an explicit rejection of the connection of ideology with false consciousness, see G. Therborn, *The Ideology of Power and the Power of Ideology*, Verso, London, 1980.

20 See further, W. Mitchell, *Iconology: Image, Text, Ideology*, University of Chicago Press, Chicago, 1986, Ch. 6; T. Eagleton, *Ideology*, Verso, London, 1991, pp. 70–80.

21 See L. Colletti, 'Marxism and the Dialectic', *New Left Review*, 1975, vol. 93.

22 B. Parekh, *Marx's Theory of Ideology*, Croom Helm, London, 1982, p. 219.

Chapter 3

1 K. Marx, F. Engels, *Selected Correspondence*, Foreign Languages Publishing House, Moscow, 1962. p. 467.

2 K. Marx, F. Engels, ibid., p. 423.

3 F. Engels, *Anti-Dühring*, Foreign Languages Publishing House, Moscow, 1971, p. 418.

4 F. Engels, ibid., p. 134.

5 F. Engels, ibid., p. 135.

6 F. Engels, *Ludwig Feuerbach*, Foreign Languages Publishing House, Moscow, 1968, p. 55.

7 K. Marx, F. Engels, *Selected Correspondence*, 1962, p. 459.

8 K. Marx, F. Engels, ibid., 1962, p. 455.

9 F. Engels, *Ludwig Feuerbach*, p. 55.

10 F. Engels, *Anti-Dühring*, Moscow, 1971, p. 135.

11 E. Bernstein, *Zur Geschichte und Theorie des Sozialismus*, Berlin, 1901, p. 282.

12 V. Lenin, *Selected Works*, Foreign Languages Publishing House, Moscow, 1963, vol. 1, pp. 156f.

13 V. Lenin, ibid., p. 149.

14 V. Lenin, ibid., p. 157.
15 G. Lukacs, *History and Class Consciousness*, Merlin Press, London, 1971, p. 224.
16 G. Lukacs, ibid., pp. 5ff.
17 G. Lukacs, ibid., pp. 258f.
18 G. Lukacs, ibid., p. 103.
19 G. Lukacs, ibid., p. 51. For a splendid example of Lukacs's method applied to literature and philosophy, see the study of the tragic world view of Pascal and Racine as expressive of the declining social power of their class in L. Goldman, *The Hidden God*, Routledge, London, 1955.
20 A. Gramsci, *Prison Notebooks*, ed. Q. Hoare and G. Nowell-Smith, Lawrence and Wishart, London, 1971.
21 A. Gramsci, ibid.
22 A. Gramsci, ibid., p. 377.
23 A. Gramsci, ibid., p. 326.
24 A. Gramsci, ibid., p. 60.
25 See R. Williams, *Marxism and Literature*, Oxford University Press, Oxford, 1977, Pt II Ch. 9 and also Ch. 6.
26 A. Gramsci, quoted in A. Davidson, *Antonio Gramsci*, Merlin, London, 1977, p. 260.
27 L. Althusser, *For Marx*, Allen Lane, London, 1969, p. 233.
28 L. Althusser, ibid., pp. 234f.
29 L. Althusser, *Lenin and Philosophy*, London, 1971, p. 160.
30 L. Althusser, ibid., p. 169.
31 L. Althusser, ibid., p. 152.
32 L. Althusser, *For Marx*, London, 1977, p. 232.
33 For an elaboration of this point, see W. Connolly, *Appearance and Reality in Politics*, Cambridge University Press, Cambridge, 1981, Ch. 2.

Chapter 4

1 Max Weber, 'Politics and Belief', *Gesammelte Politische Schriften*, Kaiser, Munich, 1921, p. 446.
2 Max Weber, *The Methodology of the Social Sciences*, Free Press, New York, 1946, p. 72.
3 E. Durkheim, *The Rules of Sociological Method*, ed. S. Lukes, Macmillan, London, 1982, p. 86.
4 E. Durkheim, ibid., p. 82.
5 S. Freud, *Totem and Taboo*, Penguin, Harmondsworth, 1939, p. 156.
6 S. Freud, *Group Psychology and the Analysis of the Ego*, Hogarth Press, London, 1967, p. 53.
7 S. Freud, ibid., p. 53.
8 S. Freud, *Totem and Taboo*, Harmondsworth, 1939, pp. 147f.

9 See, as a rather extreme example, L. Feuer, *Ideology and the Ideologists*, Blackwell, Oxford, 1975, particularly Ch. 4.
10 W. Reich, *The Mass Psychology of Fascism*, New York, 1970, p. 30.
11 W. Reich, ibid., p. 31.
12 M. Seliger, *Ideology and Politics*, Allen and Unwin, London, 1976, p. 13.
13 K. Mannheim, *Essays on the Sociology of Knowledge*, Routledge, London, 1957, pp. 90f.
14 K. Mannheim, *Ideology and Utopia*, Routledge and Kegan Paul, London, 1936, p. 51.
15 K. Mannheim, *Ideology and Utopia*, p. 66.
16 K. Mannheim, *Ideology and Utopia*, pp. 68f.
17 K. Mannheim. *Essays on the Sociology of Knowledge*, op. cit., p. 69.
18 K. Mannheim, ibid., p. 52.
19 cf. K. Mannheim, *Ideology and Utopia*, p. 239.
20 See particularly K. Mannheim, *Ideology and Utopia*, p. 239.
21 K. Mannheim, ibid., p. 239.
22 K. Mannheim, *Essays on the Sociology of Knowledge*, op. cit., p. 111.
23 K. Mannheim, ibid., p. 175.
24 cf. K. Mannheim, ibid., pp. 84ff.
25 K. Mannheim, ibid., p. 176.
26 K. Mannheim, *Ideology and Utopia*, p. 173.
27 K. Mannheim, *Essays on the Sociology of Knowledge*, op. cit., p. 239.
28 K. Mannheim, ibid., pp. 68f.
29 K. Mannheim, *Ideology and Utopia*, p. 270.
30 K. Mannheim, *Essays on the Sociology of Knowledge*, op. cit., p. 254.
31 K. Mannheim, ibid., p. 271.
32 K. Mannheim, ibid., p. 137.
33 K. Mannheim, *Ideology and Utopia*, p. 137.
34 K. Mannheim, *Essays on the Sociology of Knowledge*, op. cit., pp. 143f.
35 See A. Arblaster, 'Ideology and the Intellectuals', in R. Benewick, R. Berki, B. Parekh, *Knowledge and Belief in Politics*, Allen and Unwin, London, 1973, pp. 117ff.
36 cf. J. Gabel, 'Une pensée non-ideologique est-elle possible?' in *Sociologie de la Connaissance*, ed. J. Duvignaud, Sevil, Paris, 1979, pp. 17ff.
37 R. Merton, *Social Theory and Social Structure*, Free Press, Glencoe, New York, 1957, p. 503.
38 K. Mannheim, *Ideology and Utopia*, p. 259.
39 M. Cranston, 'Ideology and Mr. Lichtheim', *Encounter*, vol. 31, 1968.
40 J. LaPalombara, 'Decline of Ideology: A Dissent and an Interpretation', *American Political Science Review*, vol. 60, 1966, p. 13.

Chapter 5

1 See G. Sartori, 'Politics, Ideology and Belief Systems', *American Political Science Review* no. 3, 1969, p. 398.

2 Ibid., pp. 5f.
3 K. Mannheim, *Ideology and Utopia*, p. 230.
4 K. Mannheim, ibid., p. 236.
5 R. Aron, *Opium of the Intellectuals*, Norton, New York, 1962, p. 314.
6 S. Lipset, *Political Man*, Heinemann, London, 1960, p. 408.
7 D. Bell, *The End of Ideology*, Free Press, Glencoe, New York, 1960 p. 370.
8 In a recent defence of his avowedly normative definition, Bell still claims that 'ideology deals with social movements that seek to mobilize men for the realization of eschatological creeds in secular terms, and in this fusion of political formulas and passions, ideology provides a faith and a set of moral certitudes by which ends are used to justify immoral means'. See D. Bell 'The End of Ideology Revisited', Pt I, *Government and Opposition*, vol. 23, 1988.
9 M. Oakeshott, *Rationalism in Politics and Other Essays*, Methuen, London, 1962, p. 22. For a useful account of Oakeshott and his school, see H. Williams, *The Concept of Ideology*, Harvester, Brighton, 1989, Ch. 3.
10 K. Minogue, *Alien Powers: The Pure Theory of Ideology*, Weidenfeld and Nicholson, London, 1985, p. 4, and K. Minogue 'Ideology after the Collapse of Communism', in *The End of 'Isms'? Reflections on the Fate of Ideological Politics after Communism's Collapse*, ed. A. Shtromas, Blackwell, Oxford, 1994, p. 17. See also W. Greenleaf, *The British Political Tradition: the Ideological Heritage*, Methuen, London, 1983, vol. 2 and the criticism of this view in A. Vincent, 'British Conservatism and the Problem of Ideology', in *Political Studies*, vol. 42, June 1994.
11 B. Crick, *In Defence of Politics*, Penguin, Harmondsworth, 1964, p. 34.
12 See also the contributions to *Totalitarianism* ed. C.J. Friedrich, Harvard University Press, Cambridge, Mass. 1954.
13 H. Arendt, *The Origins of Totalitarianism*, Harcourt Brace, New York, 1973, p. 471.
14 H. Arendt, op. cit., p. 469.
15 E. Shils, 'The Concept and Function of Ideology', *International Encyclopaedia of the Social Sciences*, vol. VII, 1968, p. 74.
16 H. Johnson, 'Ideology and the Social System', op. cit. p. 77.
17 See K. Popper, *The Open Society and Its Enemies*, Routledge, London, 1952.
18 H. Marcuse, *Negations*, Penguin, Harmondsworth, 1972, pp. 223f.
19 G. Sartori, 'Politics Ideology and Belief Systems,' *American Political Science Review*, vol. 63, 1969, p. 403.
20 G. Sartori, ibid., p. 406.
21 G. Sartori, ibid., p. 411.
22 G. Sartori, ibid.
23 G. Sartori, ibid., p. 401.
24 G. Sartori, ibid., p. 402.

25 W. Mullins, 'On the Concept of Ideology in Political Science', *American Political Science Review*, vol. 66, 1972, pp. 509f.

26 G. Sartori, op. cit., p. 407.

27 G. Sartori, ibid.

28 G. Sartori, ibid., p. 410.

29 R. Dahl, *A Preface to Democratic Theory*, Chicago University Press, Chicago, 1956, p. 132.

30 R. Dahl, ibid., p. 132.

31 R. Dahl, ibid.

32 S. Lukes, *Power: A Radical Analysis*, Macmillan, London, 1974, p. 23.

33 R. Dahl, *Who Governs?* Yale University Press, New Haven, 1961. See, however, the evolution of Dahl's views in R. Dahl, *A Preface to Economic Democracy*, Yale University Press, New Haven, 1984, for a sharp re-thinking of property rights.

34 On the difficulties inherent in the concept of 'interests', see further W. Connolly, *The Terms of Political Discourse*, Martin Robertson, London, 1983, pp. 45ff.

35 P. Bachrach, *The Theory of Democratic Elitism*, University Press of America, Washington DC, 1980, pp. 83f.

Chapter 6

1 M. Horkheimer, *Critical Theory*, Herder and Herder, New York, 1972, p. 8.

2 H. Marcuse, *One-Dimensional Man*, Routledge and Kegan Paul, London, 1964, pp. 105f.

3 T. Kuhn, *The Structure of Scientific Revolutions*, Chicago, 1973, p. viii.

4 For a nuanced statement of this point of view with regard to ideology, see P. Ricoeur, *Hermeneutics and the Human Sciences*, ed. J. Thompson, Cambridge University Press, Cambridge, 1984, pp. 232ff.

5 C. Levi-Strauss, *The Savage Mind*, Chicago, Chicago University Press, 1966, p. 269.

6 C. Levi-Strauss, *The Raw and the Cooked*, Cape, London, 1970, p. 12.

7 R. Barthes, *Mythologies*, Paladin, London, 1973, p. 32. For an extended demonstration of how the media exposure of the British royal family affirms their regal image, see M. Billig, *Talking of the Royal Family*, Routledge, London, 1992.

8 K. Marx and F. Engels, *The German Ideology, Collected Works*, vol. 5, Lawrence and Wishart, London, p. 44.

9 G. Kress and R. Hodge, *Language as Ideology*, Routledge, London, 1979, p. 9. See also the later writings of Pierre Bourdieu which contain micro-sociological accounts of how the 'symbolic violence' of contemporary society regulates our actions in accordance with unconscious norms and excludes and silences those who cannot compete.

10 G. Kress and R. Hodge, ibid., p. 10.
11 The classic work on this is J.L. Austin, *How to do Things with Words*, ed. J.O. Urmson and M. Sbisa, Clarendon Press, Oxford, 1962, pp. 4ff. On the politics of discourse analysis, see S. Hall and M. Jaques, *New Times: The Changing Face of Politics in the 1990s*, Lawrence and Wishart, London, 1989.
12 E. Leach, *Political Systems of Highland Burma*, Bell, London, 1954, p. 278.
13 cf. N. Abercrombie, S. Hill, D. Turner, *The Dominant Ideology Thesis*, Allen and Unwin, London, 1980, pp. 59ff.
14 J. Habermas, *Theory and Practice*, Heinemann, London, 1971, p. 169.
15 J. Habermas, ibid.
16 J. Habermas, *Legitimation Crisis*, Heinemann, London, 1976, p. 93.
17 J. Habermas, *Logik der Sozialwissenschaften*, Frankfurt, 1970, quoted by T. McCarthy in 'Introduction' to *Legitimation Crisis*, London, 1976, p. xiii.
18 J. Habermas, 'Summation and Response', *Continuum* vol. 8, 1970, p. 129.
19 Quoted by T. McCarthy, 'A Theory of Communicative Competence', *Philosophy of Social Science*, vol. 3, 1973, p. 140.
20 J. Habermas, *Legitimation Crisis*, London, 1976, p. 113.
21 J. Habermas, *Knowledge and Human Interests*, Heinemann, London, 1978, p. 314.

Chapter 7

1 For a careful discussion see M. Rose, *The Post-modern and the Post-industrial*, Cambridge University Press, Cambridge, 1992, Ch. 1.
2 A. Heller and F. Feher, *The Postmodern Political Condition*, Polity, Cambridge, p. 11.
3 See P. Kamuf, *A Derrida Reader*, Columbia University Press, New York, 1991, Part 1; and R. Gaschè, *The Turn of the Mirror: Derrida and the Philosophy of Reflection*, Harvard University Press, Cambridge, Mass., Ch. 8.
4 F. Jameson, *Postmodernism, or, The Culture Logic of Late Capitalism*, Verso, London, 1991, p. 277.
5 This is the last sentence of M. Foucault's *The Order of Things*, Tavistock, London, 1970.
6 K. Marx and F. Engels, *The Communist Manifesto*, Oxford University Press, Oxford, p. 6.
7 F. Jameson, op. cit., p. 4.
8 See here particularly D. Harvey, *The Condition of Postmodernity*, Blackwell, Oxford, 1990, Pts III and IV.

9 See particularly V. Perez-Diaz, *The Return of Civil Society*, Harvard University Press, London, 1993, Ch. 2. Civil Society has been celebrated from the Right by such writers as Gray and Oakeshott and from the Left by Keane and most recently by J. Cohen and A. Arato in *Civil Society and Political Theory*, MIT Press, Cambridge, Mass., 1992, with its postmodern apogee being reached in E. Laclau and C. Mouffe, *Hegemony and Socialist Strategy*, Verso, London, 1985.

10 See T. Eagleton, *Ideology*, Verso, London, 1991, p. 165.

11 cf. J. Habermas, *The Philosophical Discourse of Modernity: Twelve Lectures*, MIT Press, Cambridge, Mass., 1977.

12 F. Jameson, op. cit., p. 1. See also, more explicitly, p. 263; T. Eagleton, op. cit., p. xii; and J. Derrida, 'A Lecture on Marx', *New Left Review*, vol. 205, 1994, pp. 49ff.

13 R. Rorty, *Contingency, Irony, and Solidarity*, Cambridge University Press, Cambridge, 1989, p. 63.

14 R. Rorty, 'The Priority of Democracy to Philosophy', in R. Vaughan, ed., *The Virginia Statute of Religious Freedom*, University of Wisconsin Press, Madison, 1988, p. 264.

15 Ibid., p. 53.

16 F. Fukayama, 'The End of History?', *The National Interest*, vol. 16, Summer, 1989.

17 F. Fukayama, *The End of History and the Last Man*, The Free Press, New York, 1992.

18 F. Fukayama, 'The End of History?', pp. 3f.

19 See A. Kojève, *Introduction to the Reading of Hegel*, Basic Books, New York, 1969.

20 A. Kojève, ibid., p. 237.

21 F. Fukayama, 'The End of History?', p. 18.

22 F. Fukayama, *The End of History and the Last Man*, p. 51.

23 See A. Bloom, *The Closing of the American Mind*, Simon and Schuster, New York, 1987.

24 cf. F. Fukayama, *The End of History and the Last Man*, p. 339.

25 See Kojève, op. cit., p. 238 on the disappearance of 'man' and the advent of an animal society driven solely by the mindless merry-go-round of pleasure and play.

26 M. Rustin, 'No Exit from Capitalism?', *New Left Review*, vol. 193, 1992, p. 107.

27 F. Fukayama, *The End of History and the Last Man*, p. 243.

28 Ibid., p. 289.

29 See further the excellent article by J. McCarney, 'Shaping Ends: Reflections on Fukayama', *New Left Review*, vol. 202, 1993.

30 J. McCarney, ibid., p. 207.

Chapter 8

1 W. Carlsnaes, *The Concept of Ideology and Political Analysis*, Green-wood Press, Westport, 1981, p. 238.
2 Quoted in S.P. Huntington, *American Politics: The Promise of Disharmony*, Belknap Press, New York, 1981, p. 25.
3 See Geertz's influential article 'Ideology as a Cultural System' in *Ideology and Discontent*, ed. D. Apter, Free Press, New York, 1964.
4 C. Geertz, ibid., p. 64.
5 D. Bell, 'The End of Ideology Revisited', Pt II, *Government and Opposition*, 1988, p. 321.
6 See the sharp exposition in D. Turner, *Marxism and Christianity*, Blackwell, Oxford, 1983, Ch. 3.
7 See J. Horton and S. Mendus, *After MacIntyre: Critical Perspectives on the Work of Alasdair MacIntyre*, Polity, Cambridge, 1994, particularly Chs 1, 13, and 14.
8 D. Bell, op cit., p. 331.

Further Reading

Chapter 1

On the origins of the concept of ideology, see Ch. 1 of Hans Barth's *Truth and Ideology*. There are shorter accounts in Seliger's *The Marxist Conception of Ideology*, Lichtheim's *The Concept of Ideology*, pp. 12ff, and Bendix's article, 'The Age of Ideology: Persistent and Changing', pp. 296ff. For the French *ideologues*, see particularly Cheryl Welch's *Liberty and Utility* and the two books on Destutt de Tracy by Kennedy and Head.

A virtually exhaustive account of the manifold senses of the concept is given in Arne Naess *et al.*, *Democracy, Ideology and Objectivity*, pp. 143ff. There is a shorter version in Robert Lane's 'The Meanings of Ideology'. See also Geuss's *Idea of a Critical Theory*, Ch. 1, Eagleton's *Ideology*, Ch. 1, and Hamilton's article 'The Elements of the Concept of Ideology'.

Attempts to distinguish ideology from the related concepts of myth and utopia can be found in the following articles: Lee McDonald, 'Myth, Politics and Political Science'; Ben Halpern, ' "Myth" and "Ideology" in Modern Usage'; and Willard Mullins, 'On the Concept of Ideology in Political Science'.

For Michael Oakeshott's strictures on ideology, see the title essay of his *Rationalism in Politics*. This approach is carried out in more detail in a collection by Oakeshott's disciples: David Manning, ed., *The Form of Ideology*. For the same scepticism about received thinking on ideology see Kenneth Minogue's recent lively polemic, *Alien Powers: The Pure Theory of Ideology*. For a good commentary on the Oakeshottian view of ideology, see Williams's *Concepts of Ideology*, Ch. 3.

Among more general works on ideology, Norman Birnbaum's 'The Sociological Study of Ideology 1940–1960', is immensely useful, though necessarily chronologically confined. Perhaps the best book is Jorge

Larrain's *The Concept of Ideology*, written from a mildly Marxist viewpoint. John Plamenatz's *Ideology* combines rather uneasily the historical and the analytic. Always stimulating is Alvin Gouldner's disorganized *Dialectics of Ideology and Technology*. Martin Seliger's *Ideology and Politics* pursues the theme of an inclusive conception of ideology through virtually all the recent literature. Two short treatments which deal knowledgeably and clearly with the more 'continental' aspects of recent discussion are Anthony Giddens, *Central Problems in Social Theory*, Ch. 5, and Stuart Hall's 'The Hinterland of Science: Ideology and the "Society of Knowledge"'. Boudon's *The Analysis of Ideology* usefully blends continental European and Anglo-Saxon approaches, while Eagleton's *Ideology*, witty, powerful, neo-Marxist, is highly recommended.

Chapter 2

A book-length treatment is available in Bhikhu Parekh's *Marx's Theory of Ideology*, which is a good exposition with sensible criticisms. See also Larrain's two books: Ch. 1 of *The Concept of Ideology* and Ch. 2 of *Marxism and Ideology*, which are sound and thoughtful, though over-protective of Marx. Seliger's critique in *The Marxist Conception of Ideology* suffers from an over-hasty identification of Marx's concept with that of 'false-consciousness'. The same is true of Ch. 2 of Carlsnaes's *The Concept of Ideology and Political Analysis*, which is the best example of a critique of Marx from a positivist/analytical viewpoint. But see also, in the same vein, Ch. 3 of Plamenatz's *Ideology*. A very sharp account of Marx which tries forlornly to harmonize his conception with that of Lenin is Ch. 1 of McCarney's *The Real World of Ideology*. Mepham's 'The Theory of Ideology in *Capital*' stresses the differences between *Capital* and *The German Ideology*. On the former see Geras's article 'Marx and the Critique of Political Economy' and on the latter Mitchell's *Iconology*, Ch. 6. For brief treatments sympathetic to Marx see Hans Barth, *Truth and Ideology*, Ch. 3; John McMurtry, *The Structure of Marx's World View*, Ch. 5 and Cohen's *Karl Marx's Theory of History*, Ch. 5. A fascinating attempt to reconstruct Marx's theory on the basis of methodological individualism is to be found in Jon Elster, *Making Sense of Marx*, Ch. 8. See also Jakubowski's *Ideology and Superstructure*, Williams's *Concepts of Ideology*, Ch. 1, Peffer's *Marxism, Morality and Social Justice*, Ch. 6 and Eagleton's *Ideology*, Ch. 2.

Chapter 3

General background to this chapter can be found in Jordan's *The Evolution of Dialetical Materialism* and McLellan's *Marxism After Marx*. See also the huge though patchy collection by Nelson and Grossburg, *Marxism and the Interpretation of Culture*.

For the view that there is more to Engels on this subject than had previously been thought, see Balibar's *Masses, Classes, Ideas*, Chs. 4 and 6. Lenin's most accessible work in which there is reference to ideology is *What is to be done?*, available in most collections. An excellent general treatment of Lenin is Harding's *Lenin's Political Thought*. His views on ideology are given sympathetic treatment in Ch. 2 of Larrain's *Marxism and Ideology* and even more so in Ch. 2 of McCarney's *The Real World of Ideology*; a fuller exposition and criticism is to be found in Ch. 3 of Carlsnaes's *The Concept of Ideology and Political Analysis*.

For Lukacs's more philosophically oriented version of Lenin, see his *History and Class Consciousness*, paticularly the three central essays on class consciousness, reification and historical materialism. There is commentary, again, in Ch. 2 of Larrain's *Marxism and Ideology*, and in Ch. 2 of McCarney's *The Real World of Ideology*; also in Roizin McDonagh's 'Ideology and False Consciousness: Lukacs', also in Eagleton, Ch. 4 and Perkins's *Marxism and the Proletariat*, Chs 5 and 6. For a more hostile treatment, see Martin Seliger, *The Marxist Conception of Ideology*, especially Ch. 4.

Gramsci's remarks on ideology are to be found scattered throughout his *Prison Notebooks*, especially in the sections entitled 'The State and Civil Society' and 'Problems of Philosophy and History'. There is thorough discussion in Chantal Mouffe, 'Hegemony and Ideology in Gramsci'. See also Stuart Hall *et al.*, 'Politics and Ideology: Gramsci', and Ch. 3 of Larrain's *Marxism and Ideology*. For a thoroughly post-modern reading, see Renate Holub's *Antonio Gramsci*.

Finally, Althusser's conception of ideology can be found most easily in his essay in 'Ideology and Ideological State Apparatuses', though *For Marx, Reading Capital*, and *Essays in Self-Criticism* should also be consulted. Two accessible commentaries are Gregor McLennan's 'Althusser's Theory of Ideology' and Paul Hirst's article of the same title. For a recent attempt to think about ideology in an Althusserian mode, see Therborn's *The Ideology of Power and The Power of Ideology*. See also the excellent books by Benton and Elliott, the two readers edited by Kaplan and Sprinkler and by Elliott, and the careful commentary in Ricoeur's *Lectures on Ideology and Utopia*, Chs 7, 8 and 9.

Chapter 4

The contributions of Durkheim and Weber are very briefly discussed in Bendix's article 'The Age of Ideology: Persistent and Changing'. Durkheim's explicit references to ideology are mostly in his *Rules of Sociological Method*, though a different approach seems to be implicit in his *Elementary*

Forms of the Religious Life. There is a clear account at the end of Ch. 3 of Larrain's *The Concept of Ideology.* See also Turner's collection *Emile Durkheim: Sociologist and Moralist,* Part I. Weber has no concept of ideology as such, but see his *The Protestant Ethic and the Spirit of Capitalism,* together with Gidden's introduction for his general approach, and the concise commentary provided by Frank Parkin's *Weber,* especially Ch. 2, also Ricoeur's *Lectures on Ideology and Utopia,* Chs 11 and 12, and Turner's *Max Weber: From History to Modernity.*

The main works of Freud of interest here are *Totem and Taboo, The Future of an Illusion,* and *Civilization and its Discontents.* See further Larrain's *The Concept of Ideology,* Ch. 3, the general comments by Roazen in *Freud: Social and Political Thought,* especially Ch. 4 and the collections by Neu, *The Cambridge Companion to Freud,* particularly the contributions by Paul and Deigh, and by Spurling, *Sigmund Freud: Critical Assessments,* Parts I and II. The relevant works of Reich and Pareto are in the bibliography.

Mannheim's classic work on the subject is *Ideology and Utopia.* See also the collection *From Karl Mannheim,* with a useful introduction by Kurt Wolff. David Kettler's *Mannheim* is a good short introduction. Post-war interest in Mannheim was given impetus by Merton's *Social Theory and Social Structure,* Ch. 13. Expositions and criticisms of Mannheim are to be found in Larrain's *The Concept of Ideology,* Ch. 4 and Carlsnaes's *The Concept of Ideology and Political Analysis,* Ch. 4. The subtlest and best discussion is in Simonds's *Karl Mannheim's Sociology of Knowledge.* See also Remmling, *The Sociology of Karl Mannheim,* Loaders's *The Intellectual Development of Karl Mannheim,* and Williams, *Concepts of Ideology,* Ch. 2.

Chapter 5

Two short and influential summaries of the mainstream conception of ideology in the United States are available in the articles by Edward Shils 'The Concept and Function of Ideology' and Harry Johnson, 'Ideology and the Social System'. Sartori's 'Politics, Ideology and Belief Systems' is an unabashed attempt to put such conceptions to work. For more would-be empirical discussions of ideology, see Robert Lane, *Political Ideology,* and the articles by Robert Putnam, 'Studying Elite Political Culture: The Case of Ideology' and by Philip Converse, 'The Nature of Belief Systems in Mass Publics'. A conceptually more subtle approach can be found in two contributions from Willard Mullins: 'On the Concept of Ideology in Political Science' and 'Sartori's Concept of Ideology: A Dissent and an Alternative'. A more basic critique of this whole approach is in William Connolly's book *Political Science and Ideology* and in Charles Taylor's article 'Neutrality in Political Science'.

The connection between a certain concept of ideology and 'totali-tarianism' is spelt out in Friedrich and Brzezinski, *Totalitarian Dictatorship and Autocracy*, the last two chapters of Hannah Arendt's *The Origins of Totalitarianism*, and Hansen's *Hannah Arendt*.

The two main exponents of an end of ideology thesis are Daniel Bell, *The End of Ideology*, and Seymour Lipset, in the last chapter of *Political Man*. Further contributions and criticism are available in Chaim Waxman's collection, *The End of Ideology Debate*. See also Bell's reprise in his two 1988 articles and the reading referred to under Ch. 7. For a view that the old enemy is renascent under the bizarre description of political correctness see Bloom, *The Closing of the American Mind*, and D'Souza *Illiberal Education*. For good surveys, see Hoeveler's *Watch on the Right*, Himmel-stein's *To the Right* and Faulkner's contribution to the Shtromas collection *The End of Isms?*

Chapter 6

For the attack on the modern applications of science through technology, see Horkheimer and Adorno, *Dialectic of the Enlightenment*, and Marcuse, *One-Dimensional Man*, particularly Ch. 6. A questioning of the objectivity of natural science itself is to be found in Thomas Kuhn's *The Structure of Scientific Revolutions* and, in a more extreme form, in Paul Feyerabend's *Against Method*.

Two classics of the structuralist approach to ideology are Roland Barthes, *Mythologies*, and (more difficult) Levi-Strauss, *The Savage Mind*. A good general introduction to structuralist thought is John Sturrock's *Structuralism and Since*. A more specific discussion is in Ch. 5 of Larrain's *The Concept of Ideology*. Accessible introductions to Levi-Strauss are Leach's *Levi-Strauss* and Badcock's *Levi-Strauss: Structuralism and Socio-logical Theory*. Marxist attempts to assimilate this line of thought can be found in the works of Louis Althusser and its effluents discussed in Ch. 3 above.

For more strictly linguistic discussions of ideology of structuralist inspiration, see Robert Fowler *et al. Language and Control*, Kress and Hodge, *Language and Ideology*, and Lee's *Competing Discourses*. An excellent discussion of this whole difficult area is John Thompson's *Studies in the Theory of Ideology*. See also the sharp and uncompromising account in Part I of Denys Turner's *Marxism and Christianity*.

For Habermas, see his various works listed in the bibliography below. Good commentaries are David Held, *Introduction to Critical Theory*, Chs 9–11; David Held and John Thompson, eds, *Habermas: Critical Debates*; and Alvin Gouldner, *The Dialectic of Ideology and Technology*, Chs 11 and 12. See also the careful discussion in Geuss, *The Idea of a Critical Theory* and White, *The Recent Work of Jürgen Habermas*.

Chapter 7

The classic here is Lyotard's *The Postmodern Condition* on which see Drolet's article on 'Lyotard's Post-Modern Politics'. See also the Derrida reader by Kamuf. For a favourable account from the Left, see Jameson's magisterial *Postmodernism*; for a hostile account, equally from the Left, see Harvey's coruscating *The Condition of Postmodernity*. The two most accessible introductions are Margaret Rose's *The Post-modern and the Post-industrial* and Stephen White's *Political Theory and Postmodernism*. There is also a good discussion in Heller and Feher's *The Postmodern Political Condition* and in Wagner's *A Sociology of Modernity*, Parts IV and V.

For Rorty, see his *Contingency, Irony and Solidarity*, and the discussions in Bernstein, Chs 8 and 9 and in Malachowski's collection *Reading Rorty*, Parts IV and V.

On Fukayama, see the articles by Halliday and Rustin. Also the excellent discussions in McCarney's 'Shaping Ends' and Anderson's *A Zone of Engagement*, Ch. 13.

Bibliography

Abercrombie, N., Hill, S. and Turner, B., *The Dominant Ideology Thesis*, Allen and Unwin, London, 1980.

Aiken, H., *The Age of Ideology*, Mentor, New York, 1956.

Althusser, L., *For Marx*, Allen Lane, London, 1969.

Althusser, L., 'Ideology and Ideological State Apparatuses', in *Lenin and Philosophy*, New Left Books, London, 1971.

Althusser, L., *Essays in Self-Criticism*, New Left Books, London, 1976.

Althusser, L., and Balibar, E. *Reading Capital*, New Left Books, London, 1970.

Anderson, P., *A Zone of Engagement*, Verso, London, 1992.

Ansell-Pearson, K., *Nietzsche contra Rousseau: A Study of Nietzsche's Moral and Political Thought*, Cambridge University Press, New York, 1991.

Arblaster, A., 'Ideology and the Intellectuals', in *Knowledge and Belief in Politics*, ed. R. Benewick, R. Berki, B. Parekh, Allen and Unwin, London, 1973.

Arendt, H., *The Origins of Totalitarianism*, Harcourt, Brace, Jovanovich, New York, 1973.

Aron, R., *The Opium of the Intellectuals*, Norton, New York, 1962.

Bachrach, P., *The Theory of Democratic Elitism: A Critique*, University Press of America, Lanham, 1980.

Badcock, J., *Levi-Strauss: Structuralism and Sociological Theory*, Hutchinson, London, 1975.

Balibar, E., *Masses, Classes, Ideas: Studies on Politics and Philosophy Before and After Marx*, Routledge, New York, 1994.

Barth, H., *Truth and Ideology*, University of California Press, Los Angeles, 1977.

Barthes, R., *Mythologies*, Paladin Books, London, 1973.

Bauman, Z., *Intimations of Postmodernity*, Routledge, New York, 1992.

Bell, D., *The End of Ideology – On the Exhaustion of Political Ideas in the Fifties*, Free Press of Glencoe, New York, 1960.

Bell, D., 'The End of Ideology Revisited', Parts I and II, *Government and Opposition*, vol. 23, 1988.

Bendix, R., 'The Age of Ideology: Persistent and Changing', in *Ideology and Discontent*, ed. D. Apter, Free Press, Glencoe, New York, 1964.

Benton, T., *The Rise and Fall of Structural Marxism: Althusser and His Influence*, Macmillan, London, 1984.

Bernstein, R., *The New Constellation: The Ethical Political Horizons of Modernity/Postmodernity*, Polity, Cambridge, 1991.

Billig, M., Condor, S., Edwards, D., Gane, M., Middleton, D., Radley, A., *Ideological Dilemmas: A Social Psychology of Everyday Thinking*, Sage, Beverly Hills, 1988.

Birnbaum, N., 'The Sociological Study of Ideology 1940–1960, A Trend Report and Bibliography', *Current Sociology*, vol. 9, 1960.

Bloom, A., *The Closing of the American Mind*, Simon and Schuster, New York, 1987.

Boudon, R., *The Analysis of Ideology*, Polity, Cambridge, 1989.

Bourdieu, P., *Outline of a Theory of Practice*, Cambridge University Press, Cambridge, 1977.

Bracher, K., *The Age of Ideologies: A History of Political Thought in the Twentieth Century*, Weidenfeld, London, 1984.

Carlsnaes, W., *The Concept of Ideology and Political Analysis*, Greenwood Press, Westport, 1981.

Cohen, G., *Karl Marx's Theory of History: A Defence*, Clarendon Press, Oxford, 1978.

Cohen, J. and Arato, A., *Civil Society and Political Theory*, MIT Press, Cambridge, 1992.

Colletti, L., 'Marxism and the Dialectic', *New Left Review*, vol. 93, 1975.

Connolly, W., *Political Science and Ideology*, Atherton Press, New York, 1967.

Connolly, W., *Appearance and Reality in Politics*, Cambridge University Press, Cambridge, 1981.

Converse, P., 'The Nature of Belief Systems in Mass Publics', in *Ideology and Discontent*, ed. D. Apter, Free Press, Glencoe, New York, 1964.

Crick, B., *In Defence of Politics*, Penguin, Harmondsworth, 1964.

Dahl, R., *A Preface to Democratic Theory*, Chicago University Press, Chicago, 1956.

Dahl, R., *Who Governs?*, Yale University Press, New Haven, 1961.

Derrida, J., *Spectres of Marx: The State of the Debt, the Work of Mourning, and the New International*, Routledge, New York, 1995.

Dobson, A. and Lucardie, P., *The Politics of Nature: Explorations in Green Political Theory*, Routledge, New York, 1993.

Drolet, M., 'The Wild and the Sublime: Lyotard's Post-Modern Politics', *Political Studies*, vol. 42, 1994.

D'Souza, D., *Illiberal Education: The Politics of Sex, Race and Gender on Campus*, The Free Press, New York, 1991.

Duncan, G., 'Understanding Ideology', *Political Studies*, vol. 35, 1987.

Durkheim, E., *Elementary Forms of the Religious Life*, 2nd edn, Allen and Unwin, London, 1976.

Durkheim, E., *Rules of Sociological Method*, and Selected Texts on Society and its Method, ed., S. Lukes, Macmillan, London, 1982.

Eagleton, T., *Ideology: An Introduction*, Verso, London, 1991.

Eatwell, R., and Wright, A. *Contemporary Political Ideologies*, Pinter, London, 1993.

Elliott, G., *Althusser: The Detour of Theory*, Verso, London, 1987.

Elliott, G., ed., *Althusser: A Critical Reader*, Blackwell, Oxford, 1994.

Elster, J., 'Beliefs, Bias and Ideology' in *Rationality and Relativism*, eds M. Hollis and S. Lukes, Blackwell, Oxford, 1982.

Elster, J., *Making Sense of Marx*, Cambridge University Press, Cambridge, 1985.

Engels, F., *Anti-Duhring*, Foreign Languages Publishing House, Moscow, 1971.

Feuer, L., *Ideology and the Ideologists*, Blackwell, Oxford, 1975.

Feyerabend, P., *Against Method*, New Left Books, London, 1975.

Fish, S., *There's No Such Thing as Free Speech, and It's a Good Thing, Too*, Oxford University Press, New York, 1994.

Fowler, R., *Language and Control*, Routledge and Kegan Paul, London, 1979.

Freud, S., *The Future of an Illusion*, Hogarth Press, London, 1928.

Freud, S., *Totem and Taboo*, Penguin, Harmondsworth, 1938.

Freud, S., *Civilization and its Discontents*, Norton, New York, 1951.

Freud, S., *Group-Psychology and the Analysis of the Ego*, Hogarth Press, London, 1967.

Friedrich, C., and Brzezinski, Z., *Totalitarian Dictatorship and Autocracy*, 2nd edn, Harvard University Press, Cambridge, 1965.

Fukayama, F., *The End of History and the Last Man*, The Free Press, New York, 1992.

Gallie, W., 'Essentially Contested Concepts', *Proceedings of the Aristotelian Society*, vol. 56. 1955–6.

Geras, N., 'Marx and the Critique of Political Economy' in *Ideology in the Social Sciences*, ed. R. Blackburn, Fontana, London, 1972.

Geuss, R., *The Idea of a Critical Theory*, Cambridge University Press, Cambridge, 1981.

Giddens, A., *Central Problems in Social Theory*, Macmillan, London, 1979.

Goldstein, J., ed., *Foucault and the Writing of History*, Blackwell, Oxford, 1994.

Gouldner, A., *Dialectic of Ideology and Technology*, Macmillan, London, 1976.

Gramsci, A., *Selections from the Prison Notebooks*, eds Q. Hoare and G. Nowell-Smith, Lawrence and Wishart, London, 1971.

Gutting, G., *Michel Foucault's Archaeology of Scientific Reason*, Cambridge University Press, Cambridge, 1989.

Habermas, J., *Towards a Rational Society*, Heinemann, London, 1970.

Habermas, J., *Theory and Practice*, Heinemann, London, 1971.

Habermas, J., *Legitimation Crisis*, Heinemann, London, 1976.

Habermas, J., *The Theory of Communicative Action*, vol. I: *Reason and the Rationalization of Society*, Heinemann, London, 1984; vol. 2: *Lifeworld and System: A Critique of Functionalist Reason*, Polity, Cambridge, 1987.

Hall, S., 'The Hinterland of Science: Ideology and the "Sociology of Knowledge"', in *On Ideology*, Centre for Contemporary Cultural Studies, Hutchinson, London, 1977.

Hall, S., 'Politics and Ideology: Gramsci', in *On Ideology*, Centre for Contemporary Cultural Studies, Hutchinson, London, 1977.

Halliday, F., 'An Encounter with Fukayama', *New Left Review*, vol. 193, 1992.

Halpern, B., '"Myth" and "Ideology" in Modern Usage', *History and Theory*, vol. 1, 1961.

Hamilton, B., 'The Elements of the Concept of Ideology', *Political Studies*, vol. 35, 1987.

Hanninin, S. and Paldan, L., eds, *Rethinking Ideology: A Marxist Debate*, International General, New York, 1983.

Hansen, P., *Hannah Arendt: Politics, History and Citizenship*, Polity, Cambridge, 1993.

Harding, N., *Lenin's Political Thought*, 2 vols, Macmillan, London, 1977, 1981.

Harvey, D., *The Condition of Postmodernity*, Blackwell, Oxford, 1990.

Head, R., *Ideology and Social Science: Destutt de Tracy and French Liberalism*, Nihoff, Dordrecht, 1982.

Held, D., *Introduction to Critical Theory*, Hutchinson, London, 1980.

Held, D. and Thompson, J., eds, *Habermas: Critical Debates*, Macmillan, London, 1982.

Heller, A. and Feher, F., *The Postmodern Political Condition*, Polity, Cambridge, 1988.

Heywood, A., *Political Ideologies: An Introduction*, Macmillan, Basingstoke, 1992.

Himmelstein, J., *To the Right: The Transformation of American Conservatism*, University of California Press, Berkeley, 1990.

Hirst, P., 'Althusser's Theory of Ideology', *Economy and Society*, vol. 5, 1976.

Hoeveler, J., *Watch on the Right: Conservative Intellectuals in the Reagan Era*, University of Wisconsin Press, Madison, 1991.

Holub, R., *Antonio Gramsci: Beyond Marxism and Postmodernism*, Routledge, New York, 1992.

Horkheimer, M. and Adorno, T., *Dialectic of the Enlightenment*, Herder and Herder, New York, 1972.

Howard, D., *The Politics of Critique*, University of Minnesota Press, Minneapolis, 1989.

Jakubowski, F., *Ideology and Superstructure in Historical Materialism*, Allison and Busby, London, 1976.

Jameson, F., *Postmodernism, or, The Cultural Logic of Late Capitalism*, Verso, London, 1991.

Johnson, H., 'Ideology and the Social System', *International Encyclopaedia of the Social Sciences*, vol. 7, 1968.

Jordan, Z., *The Evolution of Dialectical Materialism*, Macmillan, London, 1967.

Kamuf, P., ed., *A Derrida Reader: Between the Blinds*, Harvester Wheatsheaf, Hemel Hempstead, 1991.

Kaplan, E. and Sprinker, M., eds, *The Althusserian Legacy*, Verso, London, 1993.

Kennedy, E., *Destutt de Tracy and the Origins of 'Ideology'*, American Philosophical Society, Philadelphia, 1978.

Kettler, D., *Mannheim*, Tavistock, London, 1985.

Kolakowski, L., *Modernity on Endless Trial*, University of Chicago Press, Chicago, 1990.

Kress, F. and Hodge, R., *Language as Ideology*, Routledge and Kegan Paul, London, 1979.

Kuhn, T., *The Structure of Scientific Revolutions*, 2nd edn, Chicago University Press, Chicago, 1973.

Lane, R., *Political Ideology*, Free Press of Glencoe, New York, 1962.

Lane, R., 'The Meanings of Ideology', in *Power, Participation and Ideology*, eds C. Larson and P. Wasburn, David McKay, New York, 1969.

LaPalombara, J., 'Decline of Ideology: A Dissent and an Interpretation', *American Political Science Review*, vol. 60, 1966.

Larrain, J., *The Concept of Ideology*, Hutchinson, London, 1979.

Larrain, J., *Marxism and Ideology*, Hutchinson, London, 1983.

Larrain, J., *Ideology and Cultural Identity: Modernity and the Third World Presence*, Polity, Cambridge, 1994.

Leach, E., *Levi-Strauss*, Fontana, London, 1970.

Lee, D., *Competing Discourses: Perspective and Ideology in Language*, Longman, New York, 1992.

Lefebvre, H., *The Sociology of Marx*, Allen Lane, London, 1973.

Lenin, V., *Selected Works*, 3 vols, Foreign Languages Publishing House, Moscow, 1960.

Levi-Strauss, C., *The Savage Mind*, Chicago University Press, Chicago, 1966.

Levi-Strauss, C., *The Raw and the Cooked*, Cape, London, 1970.

Lichtheim, G., *The Concept of Ideology*, Random House, New York, 1967.

Lichtman, R., *Essays in Critical Social Theory: Toward a Marxist Critique of Liberal Ideology*, Peter Lang, San Francisco, 1994.

Lipset, S., *Political Man*, Heinemann, London, 1960.

Loader, C., *The Intellectual Development of Karl Mannheim: Culture, Politics and Planning*, Cambridge University Press, Cambridge, 1985.

Lukacs, G., *History and Class Consciousness*, Merlin Press, London, 1971.

Lukes, S., *Power: A Radical Analysis*, Macmillan, London, 1974.

Lyotard, J.F., *The Postmodern Condition: A Report on Knowledge*, University of Minnesota Press, Minneapolis, 1984.

McCarney, J., *The Real World of Ideology*, Harvester, Brighton, 1980.

McCarney, J., 'Shaping Ends: Reflections on Fukayama', *New Left Review*, vol. 202, 1993.

McDonald, L., 'Myth, Politics and Political Science', *Western Political Quarterly*, vol. 22, 1969.

McDonagh, R., 'Ideology and False Consciousness: Lukacs', in *On Ideology*, Centre for Contemporary Cultural Studies, Hutchinson, London, 1977.

McLellan, D., *Marxism after Marx*, Macmillan, London, 1980.

McLennan, G., 'Althusser's Theory of Ideology' in *On Ideology*, Centre for Contemporary Cultural Studies, Hutchinson, London, 1977.

McMurtry, J., *The Structure of Marx's World-View*, Princeton University Press, Princeton, 1978.

Malachowski, A., ed., *Reading Rorty*, Blackwell, Oxford, 1990.

Mannheim, K., *Ideology and Utopia*, Routledge and Kegan Paul, London, 1936.

Mannheim, K., *From Karl Mannheim*, ed. K. Wolff, Oxford University Press, New York, 1971.

Manning, D., ed., *The Form of Ideology*, Allen and Unwin, London, 1980.

Marcuse, H., *One-Dimensional Man*, Routledge and Kegan Paul, London, 1964.

Marx, K., *Selected Writings*, ed. D. McLellan, Oxford University Press, Oxford, 1977.

Marx, K., *Capital: An Abridged Version*, Oxford University Press, Oxford, 1995.

Mepham, J., 'The Theory of Ideology in *Capital*', in *Issues in Marxist Philosophy*, eds J. Mepham and D.H. Ruben, Harvester, Hassocks, 1979.

Merquior, J., *From Prague to Paris: A Critique of Structuralist and Post-Structuralist Thought*, Verso, London, 1986.

Merton, R., *Social Theory and Social Structure*, Free Press, Glencoe, New York, 1957.

Meszaros, I., *The Power of Ideology*, Harvester Wheatsheaf, Hemel Hempstead, 1989.

Mills, C., '"Ideology" in Marx and Engels', *Philosophical Forum*, vol. 16, 1985.

Minogue, K., *Alien Powers: The Pure Theory of Ideology*, Weidenfeld and Nicolson, London, 1985.

Mitchell, W., *Iconology: Image, Text, Ideology*, University of Chicago Press, Chicago, 1986.

Mouffe, C., 'Hegemony and Ideology in Gramsci', in *Gramsci and Marxist Theory*, ed. C. Mouffe, Routledge and Kegan Paul, London, 1979.

Mullins, W., 'On the Concept of Ideology in Political Science', *American Political Science Review*, vol. 66, 1972.

Mullins, W., 'Sartori's Concept of Ideology: A Dissent and an Alternative', in *Public Opinion and Political Attitudes: A Reader*, ed. A. Wilcox, Wiley, New York, 1974.

Naess, A. *et al.*, *Democracy, Ideology and Objectivity*, Blackwell, Oxford, 1956.

Nelson, C. and Grossberg, L., *Marxism and the Interpretation of Culture*, Macmillan, London, 1988.

Neu, J., ed., *The Cambridge Companion to Freud*, Cambridge University Press, Cambridge, 1991.

Oakeshott, M., *Rationalism in Politics and Other Essays*, Methuen, London, 1962.

Outhwaite, W., *Habermas: An Introduction*, Polity, Cambridge, 1994.

Parekh, B., *Marx's Theory of Ideology*, Croom Helm, London, 1982.

Pareto, V., *Sociological Writings*, ed. S. Finer, Pall Mall Press, London, 1966.

Parkin, F., *Weber*, Ellis Horwood, Chichester, 1982.

Peffer, R., *Marxism, Morality and Social Justice*, Princeton University Press, Princeton, 1990.

Perez-Diaz, V., *The Return of Civil Society*, London, 1993.

Perkins, S., *Marxism and the Proletariat: A Lukacsian Perspective*, Pluto, London, 1993.

Plamenatz, J., *Ideology*, Macmillan, London, 1970.

Putnam, R., 'Studying Elite Political Culture: The Case of Ideology', *American Political Science Review*, vol. 65, 1971.

Reich, W., *The Mass Psychology of Fascism*, Penguin, Harmondsworth, 1975.

Remmling, G., *The Sociology of Karl Mannheim*, Routledge and Kegan Paul, London, 1975.

Resch, R., *Althusser and the Renewal of Marxist Social Theory*, University of California Press, Berkeley, 1992.

Ricoeur, P., *Hermeneutics and the Human Sciences*, Cambridge University Press, Cambridge, 1981.

Ricoeur, P., *Lectures on Ideology and Utopia*, Columbia University Press, New York, 1986.

Roazen, P., *Freud: Social and Political Thought*, Hogarth Press, London, 1968.

Rorty, R., *Contingency, Irony and Solidarity*, Cambridge University Press, Cambridge, 1989.

Rose, M., *The Post-modern and the Post-industrial: A Critical Analysis*, Cambridge University Press, Cambridge, 1991.

Rossi-Landi, F., *Marxism and Ideology*, Clarendon Press, Oxford, 1990.

Rustin, M., 'No exit from Capitalism?', *New Left Review*, vol. 193, 1992.

Sartori, G., 'Politics, Ideology and Belief Systems', *American Political Science Review*, vol. 63, 1969.

Scott, P., *Religion, Ideology and Theology*, Cambridge University Press, Cambridge, 1994.

Seliger, M., *Ideology and Politics*, Allen and Unwin, London, 1976.

Seliger, M., *The Marxist Conception of Ideology*, Allen and Unwin, London, 1977.

Shaw, W., 'Ruling Ideas', in *Analyzing Marxism*, eds R. Ware and K. Nielsen, University of Calgary Press, Calgary, 1989.

Shils, E., 'The Concept and Function of Ideology', *International Encyclopaedia of the Social Sciences*, vol. 7, 1968.

Shtromas, A., *The End of 'Isms'?: Reflections on the Fate of Ideological Politics after Communism's Collapse*, Blackwell, Oxford, 1993.

Simonds, A., *Karl Mannheim's Sociology of Knowledge*, Clarendon Press, Oxford, 1978.

Simons, H. and Billig, M., eds., *After Postmodernism: Reconstructing Ideology Critique*, Sage, London, 1994.

Spurling, L., ed., *Sigmund Freud: Critical Assessments*, Routledge, New York, vol. 3, 1989.

Sturrock, J., ed., *Structuralism and Since*, Oxford University Press, Oxford, 1979.

Taylor, C., 'Neutrality in Political Science', in *Philosophy, Politics and Society*, eds P. Laslett and W. Runciman, Blackwell, Oxford, 1967.

Taylor, C., *Sources of the Self: The Making of the Modern Identity*, Cambridge University Press, Cambridge, 1985.

Therborn, G., *The Ideology of Power and The Power of Ideology*, Verso, London, 1980.

Thompson, J., *Studies in the Theory of Ideology*, Polity Press, Cambridge, 1984.

Turner, B., *Max Weber: From History to Modernity*, Routledge, New York, 1992.

Turner, D., *Marxism and Christianity*, Blackwell, Oxford, 1983.

Turner, S., ed., *Emile Durkheim: Sociologist and Moralist*, Routledge, New York, 1993.

Vincent, A., *Modern Political Ideologies*, Blackwell, Oxford, 1992.

Vincent, A., 'British Conservatism and the Problem of Ideology', *Political Studies*, vol. 42, 1994.

Wagner, P., *A Sociology of Modernity: Liberty and Discipline*, Routledge, New York, 1994.

Waxman, C., *The End of Ideology Debate*, Funk and Wagnall, New York, 1968.

Weber, M., *The Protestant Ethic and the Spirit of Capitalism*, ed. A. Giddens, Allen and Unwin, London, 1976.

Welch, C., *Liberty and Utility: The French Ideologues and the Transformation of Liberalism*, Columbia University Press, New York, 1984.

White, S., *The Recent Work of Jürgen Habermas: Reason, Justice and Modernity*, Cambridge University Press, Cambridge, 1988.

White, S., *Political Theory and Postmodernism*, Cambridge University Press, Cambridge, 1991.

Williams, H., *Concepts of Ideology*, Wheatsheaf, Brighton, 1988.

Williams, R., *Marxism and Literature*, Oxford University Press, Oxford, 1977.

Zizek, S., *The Sublime Object of Ideology*, Verso, London, 1989.

Index

27/10/22

Please return/renew this item by the
last date shown to avoid a charge.
Books may also be renewed by phone
and Internet. May not be renewed if
required by another reader.

BARNET
LONDON BOROUGH

K124

Also by L.J. Smith

Vampire Diaries

THE SALVATION

—

UNMASKED

Created by the #1 *New York Times* Bestselling Author

L. J. SMITH

Written by Aubrey Clark

Hodder Children's Books

A division of Hachette Children's Books

A NOTE ABOUT THE
HASHTAGS IN THIS BOOK

Elena's diary may be private, but this book doesn't have to be.

Everyone's talking about the biggest shockers, twists, and swoon-worthy moments.

Look for the hashtags throughout this book and share your own reactions on Twitter. To connect with other readers right now, tag your tweets with **#TVD13**

CHAPTER

1

'I'm going to plant the herb garden right there,' Bonnie told Zander, gazing out across their new yard. Green grass spread out in front of her, running right to the edge of a winding country road. There was a little space, half in sun and half in shade, that would be perfect for growing herbs for her spells and charms. Beyond the road rose white-topped mountains – *real* 'mountains, much higher than the rolling hills of Virginia'.

Behind her, Zander wrapped his arms around her waist and tucked his chin against her shoulder. Bonnie leaned back comfortably against his warm bulk. Taking a deep, satisfied breath of the crisp Colorado air, she told him, 'It's absolutely gorgeous here.'

They'd only been here for a few days, and each morning when Bonnie opened her eyes she was startled by her own happiness. She'd moved here because she couldn't bear to lose Zander, but she had never considered that she might actually like it.

Even on the plane flying here, she'd had an anxious feeling in the pit of her stomach. Bonnie had never lived so far away from her family before, never spent more than a few months some place where she couldn't drive to her mom or one of her sisters if she needed them. And she'd always had her *other* sisters, the ones she'd chosen, Elena and Meredith, by her side.

Bonnie had felt like a traitor leaving Elena and Meredith. They'd assured her that they understood and reminded her she was only a phone call away. But that didn't relieve Bonnie's guilt. Stefan, Elena's true love, had *died*. Meredith had been turned into a vampire. Surely it was *wrong* for Bonnie to abandon them, especially now.

But being here felt *right*. The Colorado sky stretched bright and blue overhead, so clear and deep that Bonnie almost thought she could hold her arms above her head and fly straight up into its limitless space.

There was something about that endless sky, something about the open country and nature all around her that made Bonnie feel like she was bursting with Power.

'I'm getting stronger every day,' she said, twining her fingers with Zander's and pulling his arms tighter around her.

'*Mmhmm*,' Zander agreed, kissing her neck softly. 'This place is really alive. Jared told me he ran for miles last night in the mountains as a wolf, and there was nothing to avoid, no cars or towns in his way. Pretty cool.'

He tugged her around by the hand, and Bonnie followed him into the house. *Our house. How awesome is that?* she thought. She'd liked their old apartments, she guessed, but this little white ranch house had no neighbours to complain about noise, no landlord laying down rules. It was *theirs*.

'We can do anything we want here,' she told Zander.

He grinned down at her with his slow, devastating smile. 'And what is it that you want to do, Miss Bonnie?'

Bonnie's face widened in a mischievous grin. 'Oh, I've got a few ideas,' she said lightly, and went up on her tiptoes to kiss him, her eyes fluttering closed.

The same familiar zing that Zander's kisses always gave her was there, but with something extra: they were *married* now. Till death do us part. He was hers.

She opened her eyes and looked up into Zander's warm, ocean-blue ones. A thrill of happiness shot through her. Channelling a shred of Zander's energy into herself, Bonnie concentrated for a moment. Joy shot through her as she felt the essence of her sweet, cheerful husband. In the fireplace, violet and green sparks flew, filling the space with light and colour.

'Beautiful,' Zander said. 'Like tiny fireworks.'

Bonnie was about to say something cheesy but honest, something like, *That's how I feel with you all the time – fireworks*. But before she could, her phone rang.

Meredith. Her friend no doubt wanted to know how the honeymoon had been and what Colorado was like. Bonnie answered, still smiling, 'Hey! What's up?'

There was a pause. Then Meredith's voice, thin and ragged. 'Bonnie?'

'Meredith?' Bonnie stiffened. Her friend sounded *broken*.

'It's Elena,' Meredith said, almost too quietly for Bonnie to hear. 'Can you come home?'

Sitting on the edge of Elena's bed, Damon closed his eyes, just for a moment. He was so tired, a bone-deep exhaustion worse than any he could remember feeling before. He'd sat by Elena's bedside for hours, her hand in his, silently willing her to keep breathing, and her heart to keep pounding.

Willing Elena to wake up.

And she'd kept breathing, somehow, although each slow, rattling breath seemed like it would be her last. All the way across the Atlantic from Paris, back to her home here in Virginia, she'd kept breathing. He could hear her heart beating, but weakly and irregularly.

But still, she was unconscious. It didn't matter how hard Damon willed her to wake up. It didn't matter if he pleaded with Elena herself, or if he pulled out

4

all the half-forgotten prayers of his childhood and begged a god who he was sure had turned away from him long ago.

Nothing Damon did mattered.

Gently, he brushed back a long strand of Elena's hair from her cheek. The once bright gold was duller now, tangled and matted, and her cheeks were sallow. She looked so close to death that Damon's heart clenched.

Lifting his hand away from Elena's face, Damon pressed his fist briefly against his chest. There was a dull empty ache there, where he was used to feeling Elena's emotions running bright and strong through the bond between them. He hadn't felt anything from their bond since Elena had fallen unconscious.

'Come as fast as you can,' he heard Meredith say in the living room. On the other end of the phone line, he could hear Bonnie's distressed voice promising to drop everything, to catch the first plane out. When Meredith finally hung up, there was a moment of pure silence before she gave a tearful sniff.

She was pinning her hopes on the little redbird's magic, he knew. Damon couldn't help a traitorous little spark of hope himself – Bonnie was so Powerful now – but, deep inside, he knew that even Bonnie wouldn't be able to help. The Guardians had made up their minds, and Elena was doomed.

Damon stood and paced across the bedroom to stare out of the open window. Outside, the sun was setting.

The bedroom's walls pressed in around him. He was achingly conscious of Elena, lying silent and still behind him.

Enough. He could sit by her bedside as long as he liked, but he wasn't helping her. Damon was *useless*. He had to get out of here, away from Elena's shallow breaths and the faint, dreadful scent of death that was slowly filling the room.

Damon concentrated and felt his body compact, his bones twisting and hollowing. Shining black feathers sprang from his new form. After a few moments, a sleek black crow spread his wings wide and flew through the window and out into the night.

Angling his wings to catch the evening breeze, Damon turned towards the river. Above him, dark-grey clouds gathered, mirroring his emotions.

Without consciously directing his flight, he soon found himself above Stefan's grave on the riverbank. Landing and transforming gracefully back to his natural form, Damon looked around. It had only been a few weeks since they'd buried Stefan, but grass had already grown over the earth where his younger brother lay. As Damon gazed at it, the ache in his chest intensified.

He bent and laid one hand against the ground over Stefan's grave. The earth was dry and crumbled under his fingers. 'I'm sorry, little brother,' he said. 'I failed you. I've failed Elena.'

Straightening, he wondered what he was doing.

Dead was dead. Stefan couldn't forgive him now, as much as it pained Damon to want him to.

They'd spent so much time hating each other. Damon could admit now that it was his fault. He'd resented his younger brother for a host of reasons, beginning with the fact that their father had loved Stefan best. His hatred had intensified after that dreadful day that they'd killed each other, and through centuries of watching from a distance as Stefan suffered through his vampirism and refrained from killing humans, Damon had grown more and more bitter. Even as a monster, Stefan had been more virtuous than Damon had been as a man, and Damon had loathed him for it.

But by the time Jack had come along, Damon hadn't hated Stefan any more. Jack. Damon's jaw tightened with hatred, and overhead, thunder rumbled in response.

Jack Daltry had pretended to be a human hunting a vicious, ancient vampire. It had all been a lie: Jack was a scientist who had created a new faster, stronger vampire race, who was on a mission to destroy older vampires. Including Stefan, Katherine and Damon himself.

Damon hadn't even been on the same continent when Stefan was killed. He'd come home in time for Stefan's funeral, in time to helplessly witness Elena's devastation. Damon rubbed at his chest with one hand, wincing at the memory of how Elena's pain had resonated through the magical bond between them, drawing him home. That pain was how he had known Stefan was dead. Nothing else could have hurt Elena so much.

Damon and Elena's bond was at the root of what had happened to Elena now. The Guardians had linked them to keep Damon under control. They'd rightly decided that if Damon and Elena were connected, it would prevent Damon from following his worst impulses. They'd spelled it out for him: if he fed on the unwilling, Elena would suffer. If he killed a human, Elena would die.

Fat raindrops were beginning to autumn, the light-brown earth of the riverbank turning a splotchy brown. Shoving his hands into his pockets, Damon spoke again, staring down at his brother's grave. 'I didn't know,' he said quietly.

All they had wanted, what had consumed him and Elena both, was vengeance. And they had succeeded. They had tracked Jack down and Damon had killed him, had avenged Stefan's death.

After Jack died, Elena had finally felt at peace about Stefan. She'd turned to Damon, and for the first time they could love each other, without feeling that they were betraying Stefan. Damon knew he didn't deserve her. Whatever soul he'd once had, it had been corrupted long ago. But Elena had wanted him anyway.

They'd had two glorious weeks travelling together,

enraptured with each other. Then Elena had collapsed, writhing in pain, and Mylea, the cold-faced Guardian who had bound them, arrived.

Damon had assumed it was safe to kill Jack Daltry because Jack was a vampire. It was humans who were forbidden; monsters were fair game to Damon. He'd been a fool. Jack had made *himself* a vampire, used science to replicate the strength and ferocity of the vampire while getting rid of a vampire's traditional vulnerabilities to wood, fire, sunlight.

He had changed himself through mortal means. He had never died; his human life had never ended. Jack wasn't a real vampire, just an imitation. There wasn't a drop of magic in him. As far as the Guardians were concerned, Damon had broken their bargain. And now was paying the price.

Dying.

Damon had brought her back to Dalcrest. Something in him had made him sure that she would want to be here, among the people she loved.

They'd battled unkillable monsters, saved the world together. Part of him – maybe foolishly – hoped that, together, they could all help him save her.

But, now that they were here and nothing had changed, he was terrified that they couldn't. Maybe Elena was beyond their reach. Damon shuddered at the thought, hunching his shoulders against the pounding rain.

'Stefan,' he whispered, looking at the rain-soaked dirt of his brother's grave, 'what can I do?' He had tried forcing his blood down her throat – she wouldn't have wanted it, but better a vampire than *gone* – but when he'd finally succeeded in making her swallow, it had done nothing.

Rage rose in him, and thunder cracked overhead. Damon turned his face up towards the sky, streams of water running through his hair, soaking his clothes. 'Mylea!' he shouted, his own voice sounding raw and broken beneath the steady pounding of the storm. 'I surrender! Punish me, I don't care. Anything. Just tell me what to do!' He paused and held his breath, listening and watching for some sign that the Guardians were prepared to bargain. He could feel tears running down his face, a little warmer than the raindrops. 'Please,' he whispered. 'Save her.'

There was no response, nothing but the sounds of the river and the rain. If the Guardian could hear him, she clearly didn't care.

CHAPTER

2

Meredith smoothed her hand across Elena's forehead. It was cold and clammy, and there were dark circles beneath Elena's eyes, startling against her pale skin. Meredith couldn't pull her eyes away from Elena's sleeping face, hoping against hope that something would happen, that she would suddenly crinkle her face in the half-annoyed way she always did in the mornings.

Stiffening, Meredith stared. Had there been a flicker of motion beneath Elena's closed eyelids?

'Elena?' Meredith said, keeping her voice soft and calm. 'Can you hear me?'

There was no response. Of course there wasn't. They'd been trying for days, first Damon in Paris and then, once he'd got Elena home, Meredith had tried to wake her every way she could think of.

In all that time, nothing had changed. Elena had lain as still and passive as a mannequin, with only a shallow, steady breathing to show that she still lived.

Damon had said that, before she fell into this coma, Elena had been in terrible pain. Meredith was glad she had missed that, glad that Elena wasn't suffering now. But this – this silent, pale creature – terrified Meredith. It couldn't be Elena. Not clever, quick Elena who had survived so much, who had been closer than a sister to Meredith since they were kids.

Meredith rose from her chair next to the big white bed, unable to bring herself to look at Elena any more. Instead, she moved around the bedroom, efficiently tidying: books off the nightstand and back on to the shelves, shoes neatly straightened on the closet floor. She kept her eyes fixed on what she was doing. She was not going to think about the still figure in the bed.

Meredith's teeth gave a hollow throb, and she rubbed absently at her gums with one finger. She would need to slip out to the woods soon to feed, but she couldn't leave Elena alone.

Alone. Their ranks were dwindling. Stefan was dead. Elena was *dying*. Alaric, Bonnie and Matt were all still on their way: Bonnie from her new home, Alaric from an academic conference, Matt from visiting his girlfriend, Jasmine's, parents. Who knew where Damon was? He had disappeared hours ago.

Meredith picked up a thin, silver-patterned scarf and folded it neatly. Elena had been wearing this the last time Meredith had seen her. 'I finally know,' she'd told Meredith, her face so full of joy it hurt to remember. 'Stefan wants me to live. He wants me to be happy. I can love Damon now . . . it's OK.'

Meredith blinked hard, pushing her tears away. Elena had been wrong. Everything was far from OK.

Clutching the scarf, Meredith jerked open a drawer. As she was about to stuff it inside, her hands faltered at the sight of the maroon book inside. Who would have guessed that poised, grown-up Elena Gilbert kept a high school yearbook in the nightstand next to her bed?

Gingerly, she pulled the book out of the drawer and flipped through its pages. Junior year. Their last real yearbook, the one before everything changed. There had been two yearbooks for senior year. The first, the one from the senior year Meredith remembered, had a memorial page for Elena Gilbert and Sue Carson. The other, for the changed world the Guardians had created, showed nothing but teams, classes and clubs. Neither felt true now. But there was only one version of their junior year.

Her own face, years younger, smiled up from a picture of Homecoming Court. Elena had been class Princess, of course. Junior dance committee. She, Elena and Bonnie had quit debate team after about a month, but they were in the picture, grinning like goons.

An action shot of Matt on the football field, his face set as he powered past a tackle. It all seemed so normal.

She turned to the back, and her own handwriting stood out at her.

> *Elena,*
>
> *What can I say? My best friend and sister, you're always there for me. But I'll remember the picnics up at Hot Springs, driving to the fraternity party at UVA, Matt and the guys crashing your birthday sleepover. All the times getting ready for a dance together – you, me, Bonnie and Caroline – was even better than the dance itself.*
>
> *Have a super-fabu time in Paris this summer, you lucky girl, and remember this! Only one more year till FREEDOM!!!*
>
> *XOXO*
>
> *Meredith*

Such an ordinary yearbook message, between two ordinary girls. Before Elena's parents had died. Before the Salvatore brothers had come to Fell's Church, and nothing had ever been ordinary again. Elena and Meredith hadn't got that freedom the message promised, the freedom to grow up and be normal, to determine their own destinies. Neither had Bonnie or Matt, nor had the people they'd fallen in love with as they got older.

Instead, they'd all been dragged under by the supernatural: vampires and werewolves, demons and Guardians. The responsibilities of saving everyone, of standing guard between everyday life and the darkness outside had pulled them all in, held them hostage.

Elena most of all, Meredith thought, and sneaked a look back at the bed. Elena's chest moved almost imperceptibly as she breathed, her rattling, slow breaths loud in the quiet room. Elena had never really had a chance, not once she'd fallen for Stefan Salvatore.

The bedroom door creaked open and Damon came in, silent and graceful. He looked to the bed first, a quick, worried glance, and then leaned against the doorjamb as if he was suddenly too tired to stand. His eyes, red-rimmed, met Meredith's, and she wondered if he'd been crying. Damon might rage or let himself be consumed with bitterness, but he never cried.

But maybe now, at the end of everything, he did.

Matt parked crookedly, one wheel up on the kerb, and bolted out of the car, slamming the door behind him. 'I knew this would happen someday,' he gritted out, teeth clenched, as he stormed down the sidewalk towards Elena's apartment building. 'I knew Stefan and Damon would get her killed.'

Jasmine followed more slowly, her golden-brown eyes serious. 'Don't say that,' she told him, laying a hand on his arm as they waited for the elevator. 'Elena's not dead. We can't give up on her.'

Matt bit his lip and stayed silent for the elevator ride up to Elena's apartment. The hall was quiet, and he hesitated a moment before knocking heavily on the apartment door.

'Take the worst possible thing you can imagine,' he muttered, his voice hoarse with rage, 'and that's it, that's the truth. Always.' Beside him, Jasmine sucked in a breath and raised a hand to touch him again, just as the door swung open.

Damon was in the doorway, his pale face pinched, his dark hair messy. He looked more human than Matt had ever seen him. Before anyone could speak, Matt balled up his fist and punched Damon in the face as hard as he could.

Damon's head rocked back slightly and he blinked in surprise, a red mark on his white cheek.

'Didn't think you had it in you,' he said with a thin, joyless smile. He touched his cheek lightly and then let his hand drop, the smile disappearing. 'I probably deserved that.'

'Yeah, I figured,' Matt said, shouldering past him into the apartment.

He stopped in the doorway of Elena's bedroom. His heart sank at the sight of her.

When he was little, there had been an amusement park up on Route 40 that'd had a fairy-tale theme to it. Matt's dad used to take him up there on Saturdays sometimes. He hadn't thought of it for years. But now it came rushing back. Silent and still, Elena reminded him of the Sleeping Beauty in the Hall of Fairies. The blonde princess, laid out like a sacrifice, not even a hint of movement. Pale and pretty and never changing.

Matt had always thought she'd looked dead.

Jasmine moved past him into the bedroom and felt Elena's throat for a pulse, then lifted one eyelid to look at her pupils. She bit her lip and looked back towards Matt. He could read the regret in her face.

'The doctors in Paris were baffled,' Damon said from behind him. 'They'd never seen anything like this. I tried the hospital there before booking a plane home, just in case. But it was useless.'

'Yeah, that makes sense,' Matt said. His mouth felt too dry, and his words sounded thick to his own ears. 'The Guardians wouldn't mess around with any kind of human illness. If they gave this to her, they're the only ones who can fix it. We just need to make them do it.'

Even as he said it, a cold rush of hopelessness spread through him. What did they have to offer the Guardians? What could possibly entice those clear-eyed, emotionless judges to give back Elena?

CHAPTER 3

'Well, how did you get the Guardians to come when Elena made the original bargain with them?' Meredith asked. 'Maybe we can convince them . . .' Her voice trailed off, as she clearly tried and failed to imagine the Guardians of the Celestial Court being moved by anything they had to say. They had only listened to Elena because she was valuable to them.

Damon gritted his teeth and tried to keep his temper. They were wasting time, he was sure of it. The Celestial Guardians had no interest in helping them.

'The little Guardian, Andrés, went into a trance and told them Elena was ready to kill me,' he said flatly. 'That brought Mylea fast enough. Unfortunately, we've got a shortage of Earthly Guardians around here now.'

'They saved you. Funny, isn't it, how everyone dies

except you, Damon?' Matt said, glaring at him with bloodshot eyes. 'Andrés. Stefan. And now—' His words broke off, and his mouth closed in a thin, miserable line.

A hot ball of hate burned in Damon's chest, and he momentarily imagined breaking Matt's neck. He could easily envision the shocked expression in the boy's blue eyes, the crisp snap of his spine. Then his shoulders slumped as he let the anger drain out of him. He deserved Matt's scorn. Everything Matt had said was true. The thing Damon was best at was survival, and now he'd outlived everyone – almost – who'd ever managed, despite everything, to love him. If Elena died, there would be no one.

He didn't want to think about it.

As footsteps approached the apartment door, he straightened, then rose from his seat. He thought he recognised the quick, light steps pattering down the hall, and the steady, heavier tread that followed. The door opened and Bonnie burst in.

'We got here as fast as we could,' she said rapidly. 'The airport was a zoo, and then the traffic coming down from Richmond was—' She broke off. 'Oh, *Meredith*.' She flung herself across the room and into the taller girl's arms.

They clung to each other for a minute, Bonnie's face buried in Meredith's shoulder, and then she raised her head and held it high, sticking out her chin bravely. 'So,

I'm gone for a couple of weeks and everything falls apart?' she said. Tears glimmered in her eyes, but her tone was casual, even joking.

Good girl. Damon knew the little redbird would stay brave, even though she was as scared as they all were.

Zander was leaning in the doorway, watching them all patiently. His longish white-blond hair fell over his forehead, and his eyes were solemn.

Letting go of Meredith, Bonnie took a deep breath. 'So, what can I do?'

'Well,' Meredith said, 'we think you're probably our best chance of getting in touch with Mylea or the other Celestial Guardians. If you can go into a trance and reach them, maybe we can convince them to save Elena.'

Bonnie grimaced. 'I've been trying,' she said. 'Ever since you called me. But . . . nothing. If they can hear me, they're not responding.'

'It's not going to work,' Damon said, unable to stop himself. Why would the Guardians listen to them? If they were letting this happen to Elena, the Guardians had written her and her Powers off. They'd never had the slightest interest in the rest of them, other than planning to kill Damon himself.

'You have a better idea?' Matt sneered.

'Try to contact Elena instead,' Damon said quickly, the idea coming to him as he spoke. 'You did it when Klaus had her, and we didn't have anything, not even a body then. Now we've still got Elena, she's just . . . We can't reach her.' His chest felt uncomfortably tight as he finished the sentence.

Whatever Bonnie heard in his voice, her face softened. 'I'll try,' she said, and made her way to where Elena laid.

The way Elena's hands were folded across her chest was too much like a corpse, and Damon grimaced.

'Oh, *Elena*,' Bonnie said, her brown eyes shining with tears. Standing at the bedside, she touched Elena's forehead gently, just for a moment.

The others trailed in after her. Jasmine and Matt stood on the other side of the bed, Matt only glancing at Elena briefly before fixing his gaze on the wall. Jasmine took his hand and squeezed it hard. Zander leaned against the wall, holding a bag of Bonnie's supplies, while Meredith hovered at the foot of the bed, her fingers twisting nervously. Damon stood in the doorway.

Bonnie took Elena's limp hands in hers and shut her eyes, her forehead crinkling in concentration. Then she opened her eyes again and shook her head, letting go of Elena. 'I'm going to need to focus,' she said. 'Can you guys wait outside?'

Damon stepped further into the room, crossing his arms across his chest. 'I'm staying.'

Bonnie sighed. 'Is it any use arguing with you about this?' she asked. When Damon stayed silent, she gave him a rueful half-smile. 'Then I won't bother. But everybody else out. I need quiet.'

Matt looked like he wanted to object, but he filed out with the others. As Zander left, he handed the bag he was holding to Bonnie, brushing his fingers against hers as he passed it over.

'OK,' Bonnie said, business-like, when the others were all gone and the door was closed behind them. 'If you want to stay, you have to help.' She handed him the bag. 'Pull out the purple and blue candles, and put them on the nightstand near her head. They're good for deep healing. I don't know if they'll help, but they can't hurt.'

Damon followed her directions. He kept his eyes fixed on the candles as he arranged and lit them.

Once the candles were in place, Bonnie took out a bronze bowl and set it on the padded bench at the foot of Elena's bed. Pulling out an assortment of little bags, she started adding pinches of dried herbs to the bowl. 'Anise for dreams,' she told Damon absently, and tipped in some limp dry flower petals. 'Chrysanthemum petals for healing and protection. Mugwort, that's for psychic powers and travelling. I just have to reach her.' She added a splash of oil from a small bottle, then pulled out a silver lighter and, with a flick of her finger, set fire to the small pile of herbs in the bowl. They smouldered slowly, a trickle of black smoke rising up towards the ceiling.

'Since when do you need anything to light a flame, redbird?' Damon asked, and Bonnie tilted her chin in acknowledgment of his point.

'I figure I should save my energy,' she said, and dug a thin silver dagger out of the bag. 'Cut me a piece of Elena's hair, please.'

Damon hesitated before moving back to the head of the bed. Elena's mouth was relaxed, a tiny bit open, and her thick golden lashes brushed her cheekbones. Thin, bluish capillaries ran across her eyelids, and her brow was smooth, untroubled. She looked like a doll or an empty image. As if there were no Elena left in there at all.

Her hair slid silkily across his fingers as he lifted a lock, and he could smell the citrus scent of her shampoo. Cutting through the hair, he winced as he accidentally pulled it tight, but Elena didn't react.

'OK,' Bonnie said, taking the lock of hair from him and dropping it into the bowl. The sickening smell of burning hair filled the room. 'Now, cut her arm.'

Damon's gaze shot up to meet hers. Bonnie looked at him squarely, her mouth set. 'We need her blood,' she said.

Of course. It always has to be blood. If anyone ought to know that, it was a vampire. Blood and hair, intimate and primal, would lead Bonnie to Elena if anything would. He lifted Elena's arm, and Bonnie slid the bowl beneath it as Damon used the silver knife to make a thin, shallow scratch on the underside of Elena's forearm. He half hoped for a twitch of pain as he cut, but again, Elena didn't react. A few drops of blood dripped into the bowl before Bonnie pulled it away. There was a soft, sizzling noise.

Damon could smell the richness of Elena's blood, and his canines ached and sharpened in response, but he barely noticed. Taking a tissue from the box by the bed, he pressed it against the spreading red line on Elena's arm for a few moments until the bleeding had stopped.

'Now what?' he began to say, but his voice died as he turned back to Bonnie. A sensation of Power rose and filled the room, making Damon's skin tingle. Bonnie had already slipped into a trance, her eyes wide and blank. Her pupils dilated as she stared down into the flames in the brass bowl.

Her hands rested lightly on the end of Elena's bed. Her breathing slowed and deepened. As Damon watched, Bonnie's eyes flickered, tracking something that only she could see.

Crossing the room, Damon let himself lounge against the windowsill, gazing out. Bonnie could be in a trance for a very long time. Outside the window it was still pitch-black, although it must be the early hours of the morning by now. He unloosed a questioning tendril of his own Power, searching into the darkness.

There wasn't much out there. The sharp, predatory

mind of an owl swooping silently through the sky. A wily fox slipped through the bushes near the apartment building. Further away, he could sense the quiet consciousness of the humans asleep through the town.

Behind him, Bonnie's mind was questing, gently but determined. He could feel the others too, each one's mind churning restlessly as they waited outside the bedroom.

But, even though she was right behind him, lying in that white-draped bed, he could feel nothing of Elena. Damon felt as if something inside him had been ripped apart. His Elena, just one last breath away from leaving him for ever.

And then he thought he saw one slender golden eyebrow twitch, just a millimetre.

'Bonnie,' he said, his throat constricting. But the little witch, deep in her trance, didn't hear him. He came closer to the bed again, close enough that he could feel the heat of the candles burning all around Elena.

Nothing. She could have been a statue. He sent his Power out desperately, but there was no glimmer of consciousness from her.

He must have imagined it.

Damon crouched down and brought his face closer to Elena's, watching her carefully. Time passed and he stayed still, his gaze intent on Elena's face. He was a predator; he could keep his mind clear and his eyes sharp for hours. But there was nothing.

He couldn't leave here, not while there was still that cruel drop of hope. But if Elena died, then it would be time to take off the ring that had let him walk in sunlight all these years. He could step into the sun and let go at last.

His jaw tightened. He wasn't going to give up yet. After all, Elena had survived so much before this.

Dawn was breaking, sending long swathes of pink and gold across the sky, by the time Bonnie finally stirred. She blinked at Damon, seemingly confused. There were dark shadows under her eyes, and her usually creamy skin looked pale and wan.

'Oh,' she said, her voice small. 'Oh, Damon.' She pressed one slim hand against her mouth, as if holding back her own words.

Damon straightened, feeling as if he were stepping in front of the firing line. Maybe, just maybe, he was wrong. The tiny spark of hope in his chest flickered and began to burn again. 'Well?' he asked.

Bonnie's eyes reddened, then overflowed, tears tracking down her cheeks. 'I don't know,' she said, shaking her head. 'I can't even begin to tell what's wrong. I couldn't reach her. It was like – like she's already gone.'

Damon jerked backward, and Bonnie reached out a trembling hand towards him. 'I think,' she sobbed, 'I think it might be time to start saying goodbye. Whatever the Celestial Guardians did to her, I don't think Elena's coming back.'

'*No.*' Damon heard his own voice, sharp as a whipcrack, and he strode forward, straight past Bonnie, and flung open the bedroom door. The others were out there, all of them, but he ignored their babble of questions as he shouldered past them. He had a brief impression of Meredith's face, anxious and strained, before he left the apartment.

He didn't know where he was going. But there had to be *something* Damon could do, *somewhere* he could go to help Elena. He'd lost everyone. Everyone he'd ever truly cared for was dead. He wasn't going to say goodbye to Elena – not now, not ever. He wasn't going to lose her.

CHAPTER 4

'I love you, Damon,' Elena whispered.

He couldn't hear her. None of them could hear her. Most of the time she couldn't hear them either, just enough to get the fleeting impression of tears and whispers and arguments. She couldn't understand more than a word or two, sometimes just enough to recognise a voice.

She thought she'd heard Damon. But she had to admit there was the possibility she'd imagined it, that she was imagining all the familiar distant voices, just to keep herself company.

She was dying. She must be. There had been that terrible pain, Mylea had appeared and then Elena had found herself in this place of emptiness.

Elena had hoped for a while that she might find

Stefan. She'd seen his ghost, she knew his consciousness still lingered somewhere, but the place she was in now didn't feel like any kind of spectral realm. She'd given up looking for Stefan when it became clear that there was no one here except Elena.

A soft grey light shone all around her, just enough to illuminate what seemed like a fog. It felt like a fog too. She was surrounded by a damp chill.

She'd walked for miles, but nothing changed. She might not have believed she was moving at all, except for the ache in her feet. When she stopped and stood still, the fog was just the same.

Elena clenched her fists and glared into the grey nothingness. She wasn't going to let this happen. She wasn't going to lie down and die, just because the Celestial Guardians wanted her to.

'Hey!' she shouted. 'Hey! I'm still here!' Her words sounded muffled to her own ears, as if she was wrapped in a thick layer of cotton wool. 'Let me out!' she shouted, trying to get louder, fiercer. Somebody had to be in charge here, and she would get their attention and make them let her go.

Elena's stomach jolted nervously. What if no one ever responded? She couldn't stay here forever. The moment she thought this, finally, something changed. The fog drew back and a sunlit road appeared.

Elena recognised the street. If she ignored the banks of grey nothingness on either side, it was the road that led to the house she had grown up in, back in Fell's Church. She recognised a long crack in the asphalt, the short grass growing at the edge of the road. But she hadn't lived there for years, not since that final year of high school. Stefan had bought it for her before he died, but she had been able to bring herself to visit only once.

Elena had a sudden, almost physical longing to walk down the path, to feel the sunlight on her shoulders, smell the summer scent of just-cut grass. As she watched, the sunshine intensified at the far end of the road, glowing so brightly Elena had to squint.

It was pulling her towards it, a steady, warm tug somewhere in the middle of her chest. There was peace down that road, she knew.

No. She stepped back, away from the road. They weren't going to trap her so easily.

'*Walk into the light?*' she shouted, suddenly furious. 'You've got to be kidding!'

The longing only increased. At the end of that road, she was sure, was almost everything she had ever wanted. Stefan, alive again, his leaf-green eyes shining with excitement at seeing her. Her parents, just as young and happy as they'd been when they died. Elena could almost see their welcoming faces, and it made her ache with love and loneliness.

Unwillingly, she raised a foot, ready to step forward, and then forced herself still.

'No,' she said, her voice cracking. She swallowed

hard and steadied it, then spoke again more firmly. '*No*. I refuse. I am Elena Gilbert, and I am a Guardian. I still have a part to play in the living world. Send me back.'

The road stretched further in front of her, sunlit and tempting. Grinding her teeth, Elena swung around and turned her back on it.

When she turned, she could see the same formless fog. But now there was a dark shape moving through it. *A person*, Elena realised. Her heart began to pound harder, and her mouth went dry. Was it someone coming in response to her call? For a panicky moment, she imagined a Grim Reaper, silent in black, come to collect her.

But no. As the figure came closer, Elena was able to make out that it was Mylea, the Celestial Guardian who had been overseeing Elena's life for years. When she finally halted in front of Elena, Mylea looked as serene and unruffled as ever, her golden hair pulled back into a bun, her ice-blue gaze level and cool.

'Elena, you made a bargain,' she said firmly. 'Damon killed a human, and so you have to die. You agreed to this, years ago.'

'That's not fair,' Elena said, scowling. She sounded like a child, she realised, and she made an effort to temper her voice so that she sounded more reasonable. 'Damon was working under the assumption that Jack Daltry was a vampire, and so he could be killed without

31

breaking our agreement. Jack *was* a vampire. He drank blood, and he had all the strengths of a vampire. He was a monster.'

Mylea sighed. 'As I've already explained to you, the fact that Jack Daltry chose to use his scientific gifts to mutilate himself did not make him less human.' Her face softened, just a fraction. 'He might have been a monster, but he was a human one.'

'But we didn't *know* that,' Elena told her, exasperated.

'You knew that he had never died, that he had never gone through the transformations every vampire suffers through. You knew that he and his creations did not have the flaws that weaken true vampires.' Mylea spread her hands. 'If anyone should have been able to recognise a true vampire, it would be you and Damon Salvatore.'

'Jack was dangerous,' Elena snapped. 'The Guardians ought to be *thanking* us. I'm supposed to protect people.'

Mylea shrugged, a graceful tilt of her shoulders. 'You were warned that he was not your concern.'

It was true; the Guardians had warned her. But in such a roundabout way that she'd had no idea of the possible consequences of hunting Jack. Fear ran through Elena, and she swallowed hard. This was real. She hadn't quite believed that the Guardians would kill her, but it was true. They would let her die.

'Please,' she said impulsively, reaching out for Mylea's arm. 'There must be something I can do. Isn't there any way to change this? I've served the Guardians for a long time.'

Mylea's expression remained as emotionless as ever, but Elena thought she saw a flash of sympathy deep in her eyes.

'There must be *something*,' Elena said desperately.

Mylea frowned, a tiny crease appearing between her slim eyebrows. 'There is one way you can change your future,' she admitted.

'Please,' Elena begged again. 'Anything.'

'If you can go back and change the course of things, prove that you and the Salvatore brothers can live without destroying one another or other people, you can have your life back.' Mylea tilted her head a little, watching Elena closely. Obviously she thought that she had made herself clear.

'What do you mean?' Elena asked, startled. *Destroying one another? They* loved *one another*.

Mylea shook her head. 'You and the Salvatore brothers have been in a dangerous cycle for years. *You* were the one who brought them back together after they'd been apart for centuries, Elena, and their rivalry over you led to everything that's gone wrong here since then. The destruction of Fell's Church was a direct effect of your relationship.'

Elena gasped, stricken.

Eyes narrowing, Mylea went on. 'The vampire Katherine's jealousy over both Salvatore brothers' obsession with you led to the beginnings of death and violence in Fell's Church. Her death as a result of her actions there led to the vampire Klaus's attacks on the town. Damon Salvatore's rage over your choosing his brother over him resulted in the kitsune demons gaining a foothold there and destroying Fell's Church at last.'

'But the Guardians brought Fell's Church back,' Elena objected.

'And yet the death continued,' Mylea told her. 'The students at Dalcrest College, Klaus's victims, the Guardian Andrés – all had their roots in the damaged love between the three of you. Everything has consequences, Elena.'

Elena pressed a hand to her forehead, feeling dizzy and sickened. It wasn't true, was it? She and Damon and Stefan were responsible for all the horror that had surrounded them. 'What do you mean "go back"?'

'I can send you back to when it all began,' Mylea said. Her eyes, a lighter blue than Elena's own, held Elena's gaze. 'William Tanner's death was the first time Damon Salvatore had killed in years, and it was the first link in the chain of violence. If you can prevent it from happening and keep Damon from giving in to the darkness within him, perhaps you can turn the course of events that will, in the present timeline, eventually kill you all.'

'Damon hadn't killed for years?' Elena said slowly.

She hadn't known that. Neither had Stefan, she was sure of it.

She'd thought her love had *saved* him. Had saved both Damon and Stefan. *The Guardians twist the truth*, she reminded herself, and swallowed hard, pushing away the tears that prickled at the back of her eyes. She wanted to argue with Mylea, but instead she asked, 'You can send me back in time?'

Mylea nodded briskly. 'You'll be back in your old body, in your old life,' she said. 'This is an opportunity to relive those days and change things.' Her eyes seemed to soften slightly, and she went on, 'Don't take this challenge lightly, Elena. What you change in the past will affect your future. Once you return, everything will be different. You might not be able to be with either of the Salvatore brothers.'

The grey mist seemed to swirl before Elena's eyes. She could lose Damon too? But their love was strong, she reminded herself. Even when she had been determined to only love Stefan, fate had pulled her and Damon together.

'I'll do it,' she said, trying to feel confident. She didn't know what she could do, not yet, but she would stop Damon from killing, somehow fix the hatred between the brothers before it could blossom into something that would affect more than the two of them. 'But how?'

Mylea's lips quirked up in an almost tender smile.

'Love is a very powerful force,' she said quietly, and raised one hand to press against Elena's forehead. Elena had a moment to feel the cool strength of that slender hand, and then everything faded to black.

CHAPTER

5

Dear Diary,

I can't believe it.

Here I am in my old home at 5.30 in the morning, just a few hours before my senior year of high school begins.

Again.

I remember this morning vividly, the last morning of my life before I met Stefan Salvatore. The Elena I was then – the one who should be here now – was so lost. I didn't feel like I belonged here, or like I belonged anywhere. I was searching for something that was just out of reach.

My bedroom looks just the way it always did, warm and cosy. My bay window gives me a view on to the quince tree outside. Down the hall are dear

Aunt Judith and my darling baby sister, Margaret, who's only four and tucked up tight in bed, not half grown and miles away.

Everything feels as if I might break it, it's so fragile. This moment has been gone for years.

Elena stopped writing and stared at her last line, shaking her head. Soon she'd see everyone, everything, unchanged. They'd been so naive – in a good way – focused on popularity and high school romances, and unaware of the darkness that hovered just outside their pleasant lives. She'd never appreciated what she had then. This time, she'd know to savour those moments of innocence.

But she wasn't just here to revisit her past.

Tapping her pen against the pages of the small book with the blue velvet cover, she thought for a moment, and then bent her head and began writing again.

Stefan is alive here. When I think about being with him, my hands start to shake and I can hardly breathe. Part of me died with him, and now I'm going to see him again. Whatever happens next, at least I'll have that.

If I'm going to save Damon, stop the destruction Mylea outlined, I can't be with Stefan this time. It hurts. It hurts a lot. But if I want Damon to listen to me, I have to be with him, not Stefan. I already

know how things turn out if I pursue Stefan now.
   I love them both. So much. I always have.
But I've learned my lesson about trying to have
them both. If I want them both in my life, things fall
apart. They always fall apart, no matter what we
do. I have to choose. And, if I can keep Damon from
killing Mr Tanner, maybe I can save us all.

With a click and a buzz, Elena's alarm clock went off. Closing her journal, she got up. Soon it would be time to go to school. Would she remember enough about who she had been then? She worried that somehow, everyone would see that she was the wrong Elena, in the wrong time.

A hot bath and some coffee, and I'll calm down, she thought. She had time.

After a leisurely bath, she took her time getting dressed. The clothes – all the gorgeous new outfits she'd got in Paris – looked outdated to her now, but she still sort of loved them. She remembered what she'd worn on this day, the first day of her senior year. A pale-rose top and white linen shorts. She pulled them on again. They made her look tempting, as sweet and refreshing as a raspberry sundae, she thought as she looked critically into the mirror, pulling back her hair with a deep-rose ribbon.

'Elena! You're going to be late for school!' Aunt Judith's voice drifted up from below. Glancing in the mirror one last time – her face was a trifle grim, as if she were headed into battle, but that couldn't be helped – Elena grabbed her backpack and headed for the stairs.

Downstairs, Aunt Judith was burning something on the stove and Margaret was eating cereal at the kitchen table. The sight of them stopped Elena in her tracks for a second. She'd forgotten how little Margaret was then. And Aunt Judith had still been wearing her flyaway hair long.

Elena pushed herself back into motion and kissed Aunt Judith quickly on the cheek. 'Good morning,' she said lightly. 'Sorry, I don't have time for breakfast.'

'But, Elena, you can't just go off without eating. You need your protein—'

It was all coming back to her. She felt like an actress, mouthing familiar lines she'd said a hundred times before. 'I'll get a doughnut before school,' she said, dropping a kiss on the top of Margaret's silky head and turning to go.

'But, Elena—'

'Don't worry, Aunt Judith,' Elena said cheerfully. 'It'll all be fine.' At the front door, she spun to take one last quick look at them. Margaret, still half asleep, licked her spoon. Aunt Judith, her eyes full of love, gave Elena a small, worried smile.

Elena's heart ached a little. Part of her wanted to go back, forget school and the future, and sit down at the table with them. So much had happened since this moment, and she'd never believed she would be back here like this again. But she couldn't stay. Margaret wiggled her fingers in a wave, and Elena, spurring herself into movement, winked at the little girl as she went through the door.

'Elena,' Aunt Judith said. 'I really think—'

She closed the door behind her, cutting off Aunt Judith's protests, and stepped out on to the front porch.

And stopped.

The world outside was silent, the street deserted. The tall, pretty Victorian houses seemed to loom above her. Overhead, the sky was milky and opaque, and the air felt oppressively heavy.

It was as if the whole street were holding its breath, waiting for something to happen.

Out of the corner of her eye, Elena saw something move. Something was watching her.

She turned and caught sight of a huge black crow, the biggest crow she had ever seen, sitting in the quince tree in her front yard. It was completely still, and its glittering black eyes were fixed on her with an intent, almost human gaze.

Elena bit back a laugh and turned away, letting her eyes slide over the crow as if she hadn't noticed it.

Damon. She had almost forgotten that this was the first time she'd seen him, that he'd watched her – frightened her – as a crow this first morning. There was a glad little bubble of joy rising in her chest, but she suppressed the urge to call out to him. It wasn't the time, not yet.

Instead, she took a deep breath, hopped off the porch and strode confidently down the street. Behind her, she heard a harsh croak and the flapping of wings, and she smiled to herself. Damon couldn't stand being ignored. She didn't turn back round.

It was only a few blocks to the high school, and Elena spent the walk reminiscing. There was the coffee shop she and Matt had gone to on their first date junior year; there was the little health food shop where Aunt Judith had insisted on buying her special organic cereal. There was the house of the terrible Kline twins, who Elena had babysat during her sophomore year of school.

In her real life, it hadn't been that long since Elena had been to Fell's Church, but things had changed since she was in high school. Stores had closed and opened, houses were remodelled. This was the way it had been when she'd lived here, the way it was supposed to be.

At the school, a crowd of her friends was gathered in the parking lot, chattering and showing off their new clothes. It was everyone who mattered, plus four or five girls who had hung around them in the hopes of gathering some scraps of popularity.

Elena winced. *Everyone who mattered*. The nasty thought had slotted right into her mind. The Elena who belonged here had thought that.

One by one, her best friends hugged her in welcome.

They looked so *young*, Elena thought, her heart aching. They all thought they were so sophisticated, but their seventeen- and eighteen-year-old faces still had childish curves, and their eyes were wide with thinly veiled excitement at the first day of their senior year.

Caroline, her green eyes narrow, laid one cool cheek against Elena's for a second and then stepped back. 'Welcome home, Elena,' she said drily. 'It must feel like the backwoods for you after Paris.'

Her expression was stiff and resentful, and Elena wondered at how she had managed to not notice then how much the other girl hated her.

Elena shrugged and laughed a little, feeling awkward. 'Paris was nice, but there's no place like home.'

For a moment, she tried to focus in on Caroline, to read her aura, but it was hopeless. Elena wasn't a Guardian here, and so she didn't have those powers any more. It was a strange, helpless feeling to lose them.

Then Bonnie flung her arms around Elena, her red curls tickling the taller girl's chin, and Elena relaxed.

'Do you like my hair? I think it makes me look taller.' Bonnie fluffed up her fringe and smiled.

'Gorgeous,' Elena said, laughing. 'But maybe not tall.'

Once Bonnie let go, Meredith moved forward for a warm hug. Raising one elegant eyebrow, she considered Elena. 'Well, your hair is two shades lighter from the sun . . . but where's your tan? I thought you were living it up on the French Riviera.'

Wait. Elena remembered this. She lifted her own pale hands and said, 'You know I never tan.'

'Just a minute, that reminds me!' Bonnie grabbed one of Elena's hands. 'Guess what I learned from my cousin this summer? Palm reading!'

There were a few groans, and someone laughed. Elena's breath rushed out of her. Of course; she had almost forgotten. This was the first time Bonnie had shown her Power. She'd seen the future in Elena's palm. Slowly, Elena flattened out her hand, opening it to Bonnie's gaze.

'Laugh while you can,' Bonnie said serenely, peering into Elena's palm. 'My cousin told me I'm psychic.'

There was something Elena had said then, the first time this happened, but she couldn't remember exactly what. It didn't matter anyway. What had mattered here was what Bonnie had seen in her hand: Stefan.

'OK,' Bonnie said, frowning as she traced the lines on Elena's palm with one finger. 'Now, this is your life line – or is it your heart line?' In the crowd around them, someone sniggered. 'Quiet. I'm reaching into the void. I see . . . I see . . .' Bonnie frowned. 'I don't get this. It says you have two loves, Elena.'

Elena's chest tightened. This wasn't right.

Bonnie touched one end of the line running across the centre of Elena's palm. The line forked there, splitting into two lines wrapping around the side of

Elena's hand. 'See? Your heart line divides into two.'

'Greedy,' Caroline said, not quite jokingly.

Elena blinked, bewildered. Bonnie should have started talking about Stefan. She was supposed to say he was dark and handsome, and he had been tall once. But instead Bonnie must be seeing something of what had happened in the time after this, the truths of Elena herself, the one who didn't belong here.

'I can see the two loves,' Bonnie went on. 'But there's something else here . . .' Her eyes widened and, with a quick, sudden movement, she dropped Elena's hand as if it had burned her.

'What's wrong?' Elena asked, suddenly frightened. She reached out to her, but Bonnie backed away, tucking her own hands behind her back.

'It's nothing,' she said. 'Palm reading's silly anyway.'

Elena was having trouble catching her breath. Bonnie's Power was incredibly strong, although in this time she didn't know how to use it. If there was something in Elena's future that frightened Bonnie this badly, then Elena should be frightened too. 'Bonnie?' Elena asked anxiously, reaching towards her again. '*Tell* me.'

There was something panicked in the smaller girl's face, and she shook her head. 'I don't want to talk about it any more. It's a dumb game.'

Unsure of what to do, Elena wavered. She couldn't *make* Bonnie tell her anything. But if what Bonnie saw in her palm had changed, maybe it was a clue to how her plan was going to work, how things would turn out differently. It might be important.

But maybe it was just showing all the awful things that had already happened to Elena after this moment – the future that hadn't yet appeared for Elena of the past. The future she was going to change.

Elena swallowed hard. That was it, it must be, she reassured herself. Bonnie was seeing things she didn't understand, frightening things. But it wasn't Elena's future, not now.

'We should head into class,' Meredith said, sounding slightly irritated as she glanced at her watch.

They were turning towards the school building when the roar of a finely tuned motor stopped them in their tracks. The group of girls swung round to look.

'Well, now,' Caroline said, her green eyes speculative. 'Quite a car.'

'Quite a Porsche,' Meredith corrected drily.

Elena didn't look; she kept her gaze firmly fixed on the brick façade of the school. But she could hear it, the purring of the sleek black Porsche's engine as its driver searched for a spot, and her heart pounded wildly in her chest.

A new student had arrived, one she'd been waiting for despite herself.

Stefan.

CHAPTER

6

Elena's heart clenched. She *had* to look. She couldn't help herself.

Talking to Stefan, touching Stefan, wasn't an option. But she was going to take this chance to at least see him, a chance she had thought would never come again.

The purr of the engine died, and she heard the car door open before she glanced up.

'Oh my God,' Caroline whispered.

'You can say that again,' breathed Bonnie.

Oh, *Stefan*.

He was alive. He was *here*. He looked just as he had that last night they'd been together. Elena wanted to run to him and wrap herself around his lean body, run her fingers through his wavy dark hair, kiss the sad curve of his mouth. Sunglasses shielded his face like a mask, but Elena knew Stefan well enough to see through the protection they provided. She could sense the misery that had driven him to enrol in school, had made him try to act like a teenage boy so that he could have some brief human contact.

Everything in her pulled towards him. But if she ran to him, everything would lead straight to where she had come from. Stefan dead, Elena dying, Damon broken.

Elena bit her lip so hard she tasted blood, and stayed where she was.

'Who is that masked man?' Meredith asked, and everyone giggled.

'Do you see that jacket?' one of the hangers-on asked. 'That's Italian, as in *Roma*.'

'How would you know? You've never been further than Rome, New York, in your life!' her friend answered.

Stefan was heading towards the school, a few rows of cars between him and the group of girls. The rhythm of his steps hitched and paused for just a moment. Elena felt a jolt. He had caught sight of her, she knew. There was a moment when he just stared from behind his sunglasses, his gaze burning into Elena. What was he seeing, she wondered? Her uncanny resemblance to Katherine, certainly, but Elena couldn't help hoping there was more to it than that. Even this early, could Stefan sense something more in her than the looks of his lost love?

After a moment, Stefan began to walk again, continuing smoothly on. Elena stared after him, feeling raw and exposed.

'Uh-oh,' another hanger-on said, a touch of envy in her voice. 'Elena's got that look again. The hunting look.'

'New Boy had better be careful.'

Elena pulled herself together and slapped on an expression of disdain. Tossing her head, she began to walk towards the school. 'Hardly,' she said. 'I've got big plans for this year. And they don't include some random boy, no matter how nice his car is.'

The other girls crowded behind her in a close-knit pack.

'What kind of plans?'

'Surely you can fit in Mr Cute-Dark-and-Mysterious.'

Without replying, Elena led them through the front door of the school. A long corridor stretched before them, and Stefan's lean figure was disappearing through the office doorway just ahead. Some of the other girls were already drifting towards the office window, eagerly craning their necks. 'Nice rear view,' someone said, giggling. Caroline was with them, but she wasn't looking through the window at Stefan. Instead, she was watching Elena speculatively.

Deliberately, Elena avoided her gaze. 'Do you have my schedule?' she asked Meredith.

'Sure,' Meredith said after a pause, handing it to her.

Elena remembered that her friend had picked it up for her when Elena had skipped orientation. 'We've got trig on the second floor in five minutes.'

A few of the girls who had been watching Stefan had turned away from the windows now, discouraged by Elena's lack of interest. *Good*, Elena thought. She couldn't have him, she knew, but somehow she didn't want anyone else going after him.

'Let's go,' she said to Meredith.

Meredith and Bonnie exchanged a look, and Meredith followed Elena upstairs. Just as they reached the classroom, Meredith laid a cool hand on Elena's arm, stopping her.

'Did something happen in France?' she asked quietly.

Elena frowned. 'What do you mean?'

'Nothing,' Meredith said slowly, her calm grey eyes scanning over Elena. 'You just seem different, that's all. Distracted.'

A semi-hysterical giggle rose up in Elena's chest – *Well, you see, Meredith, I've been sent back from the future to stop one of the vampires I'm in love with from killing someone, or I'll die* – and she choked it back and smiled at Meredith instead. 'I'm fine.'

All through trig, Elena shut out the teacher's droning voice, taking the textbook that was handed to her without glancing at it. She knew for a *fact* that she was never again going to use trigonometry. Tapping her fingers idly against her desk, she tried to plan instead.

She needed to meet Damon. But how? The first time they'd met, it had been partly because she looked like Katherine, but *mostly* because she was with Stefan, and the Damon she'd met then would be damned if he let his baby brother have her. But she couldn't wrap herself around Stefan and wait for Damon to come.

If Damon accepted that he was the one she wanted, if she could get him to love her now the way he would in the future, she could keep him from killing anyone. He wouldn't be so angry. He wouldn't be ready to strike out.

'Can anyone tell me what the sine function is?' the teacher asked, breaking in on Elena's thoughts. Mrs Halpern's eyes swept over the class, and Elena instinctively hunched a little, avoiding the teacher's gaze.

Meredith began to answer the question. She was so beautiful, Elena thought, with her olive skin and heavy black lashes. More than that, Meredith looked happy. And *human*.

She'd had troubles in her life at this point already, Elena knew. A vampire had attacked her grandfather, stolen her brother. But this confident high school Meredith was barely aware of the horrors in her family's past. She was already moving on.

Here, in this classroom, Elena could see exactly how miserable Meredith was in the future Elena had come from. Elena had known, of course, that Meredith hated being a vampire. But Elena hadn't seen this contentment in years.

Elena sighed and thoughtfully curled a long, silky strand of hair around her finger. Could she fix Meredith too, if she could keep Damon from killing Mr Tanner? The road that had led to Meredith's transformation was a long and twisting one, but it had started here. If Meredith was kept clear of the supernatural, if she never suspected the dangers beginning to descend on Fell's Church, maybe she would leave. Go to an Ivy League college as she'd planned, have a successful, human life.

The rest of the morning passed in a blur. Stefan was in none of her early classes, thank God, although she knew she'd see him in history that afternoon. She couldn't stop herself from looking for him in the halls. She didn't see him, but she had a constant, exultant awareness that he was here – and *alive*.

She tried to make plans, but she was constantly distracted. Everyone wanted Elena's attention: boys flirted with her; girls curried her favour with scraps of gossip. She had forgotten what it was like to be the queen of school. Matt *was* in one of her morning classes, and she met his smile with quiet panic. She didn't know what to do with Matt yet. Her friend was going to have to get his heart broken . . . again.

By lunchtime, she was sick of acting like she cared about the popularity, and she slipped down towards the cafeteria alone. Caroline was outside, posed casually against a wall in a model's slouch. The two boys she was talking to nudged each other as Elena came towards them.

Elena wanted to just walk on by. She remembered *this* too, and all the awful things Caroline had done later. She had plotted to destroy Elena, for no reason, out of jealousy and pure spite.

But Caroline's chin was tilted up, and her eyes staring deliberately past Elena, as if the other girl was beneath her notice. Every line of her body broadcast pure hostility. Her hatred would only increase. If Elena didn't deal with her now, it was bound to be worse later.

'Hi,' Elena said briefly to the boys. To Caroline she asked, 'Want to get lunch?'

Caroline barely glanced at Elena as she pushed her glossy auburn hair back. 'What, at the *royal table*?' she asked scathingly.

Elena suppressed an urge to roll her eyes and instead forced a smile. 'Please come,' she said gently. 'I want to hear about your summer. I missed you.' It was true, sort of. She'd known Caroline since kindergarten; they'd been good friends until this moment. Maybe she could change things here too. Maybe this was a chance to fix everything she regretted.

Elena kept going into the cafeteria, not giving Caroline a chance to snap back an answer. Caroline followed, but a few steps in her fingers fastened hard on Elena's arm. 'A lot of things changed while you were gone this summer, Elena,' she hissed warningly. 'And just maybe your time on the throne is running out.'

'You'd make a better queen than I do. Take it,' Elena said agreeably, scanning the crowd as Caroline stood dumfounded. 'Are you getting hot lunch?' It was a relief to see Meredith and Bonnie already sitting at their table. Caroline, temporarily silenced, followed as Elena got her lunch and went to join them.

'That new boy is in my biology class,' Bonnie announced. 'I sit right across from him. And his name is Stefan – Stefan Salvatore – and he's from Italy. He's boarding with old Mrs Flowers on the edge of town. He picked up your books when you dropped them, didn't he, Caroline? Did he say anything?'

'Not much,' said Caroline shortly. She was still watching Elena from the corner of her eyes, her forehead slightly creased.

'There he is,' Meredith said, looking across the lunchroom.

Elena's head shot up. There Stefan was, hesitating at the door of the cafeteria and then crossing it with long, smooth strides, heading for the hall that led towards the other side of the school. He wouldn't eat, of course. He had probably fed on the blood of a bird or small animal before school.

Stefan glanced towards their table, and Elena felt his

eyes slide over her as viscerally as if he'd touched her. And then he passed by, his jaw tight. Elena swallowed and looked away.

Caroline was still watching him. She had the slightest hint of a smirk on her lovely face.

Caroline wanted Stefan, Elena knew. A few days after this, they'd started hanging out during lunch, had gone to Homecoming together. And then Elena and Stefan had come together, and he'd forgotten Caroline completely. No wonder she'd hated Elena more and more.

On an impulse, Elena nudged her. 'You should talk to him,' she said.

It was the last thing she wanted, really. But Caroline's fury over Elena taking Stefan had led to so much horror. And if Stefan was out of the way, in Caroline's orbit, it would be easier for Elena to focus on Damon.

Besides, Stefan would never love Caroline. He'd be perfectly safe with her.

Caroline flicked a glance at Elena. 'Who says I want to talk to him?' she said coolly.

But a moment later, Caroline was staring at the door Stefan had gone through. Elena took a long drink of her water. She'd set something in motion.

It might be necessary, but that didn't mean she had to like it.

CHAPTER

7

'Aunt Judith wants me home right after school today,' Elena lied. 'I have to hear all about Margaret's first day of nursery school, I guess.' She was leaning against her locker, Matt looking down at her with his honest blue eyes. They ignored the people streaming past, all eager to get home now that the first day was over.

'I can give you a ride home at least,' Matt said, reaching for her hand.

'That's OK, I want to walk,' Elena said, gently disentangling her fingers from his. 'I've got some thinking to do. And you've got to get ready for practice, don't you?' She kissed him gently on the cheek, like a sister might instead of a girlfriend, and walked away.

Matt didn't object, but Elena could feel his puzzled gaze following her all the way down the hall towards the school doors.

Poor Matt, she thought, sighing. They'd been good friends for so long. Junior year, she'd hoped that he was the boy for her. The one who could be more to her than a trophy or an accessory. And he had been in so many ways – but she hadn't been in love with him, and she hadn't been able to see then how much he loved her.

It had taken Matt a long time to get over her the first time. Maybe that was something else she could fix while she was back here, Elena thought, resisting the urge to turn around and look at him again. If she handled their break-up better . . .

She pushed through the front doors of the school and set off. Crossing the parking lot, she tilted her face up towards the warmth of the late afternoon sun and hesitated for a moment.

Her biggest problem right now was how to approach Damon in the right way. If she was going to get him to fall in love with her before Halloween, she had better get started.

Tucking a stray hair back behind her ear, Elena turned down the sidewalk towards home and began to go over her first memories of him, ignoring the chatter of the other students leaving school all around her. He'd come to her in the school gym once, while she and her friends were planning the Haunted House, but that was after she knew Stefan. She didn't know if Damon would have come after her at school if not for Stefan. It wasn't really Damon's kind of place.

She'd met him at Alaric's house at the party Alaric had thrown looking for evidence of vampires. But Alaric wasn't here, wouldn't be here if she accomplished her mission, because he had come after Mr Tanner was murdered.

She'd sat through history class today, watched as Mr Tanner mocked Bonnie for her lack of knowledge of history, as Stefan coolly put him in his place. She was struck by how young Mr Tanner was – about the same age as Elena and her friends were in her real present. He was inexperienced and desperate to keep the attention and respect of a class of kids only a few years younger than he was. But despite all that, he'd known a lot about the Renaissance and spoken well about it. Maybe in a few years he'd be a good teacher. If he lived.

With renewed purpose, Elena walked faster, thinking hard. Damon had come to Bonnie's house. But that was when he was looking for Elena, after she'd already got his attention.

A caw came overhead. Elena stopped short and craned her head back to catch a glimpse of a fat black crow in the maple tree overhead. It wasn't Damon, she saw immediately. This bird was plumper, smaller. Probably just a bird, she told herself as it cawed again and then spread its wings and flew off, low, past the house behind her.

But the sight prompted the memory of a dark shape winging its way up from the oak trees at the edge of the cemetery, when she had gone there to visit her parents, before she had known Damon. He'd been keeping an eye on her, hadn't he?

Elena stopped dead. *The cemetery.*

The horrors of her senior year hadn't begun with Mr Tanner's death at Halloween. They'd begun *today* – when Stefan had fed from an old vagrant sheltering under Wickery Bridge. And it had happened because Stefan had watched Elena in the cemetery, then been caught by a wave of angry Power, leaving him dazed and ravenous.

Katherine's Power, which she had unleashed after witnessing Stefan's interest in Elena, driving Elena out of the churchyard.

The man hadn't died, but his injuries had been the first sign to the people of Fell's Church that danger lurked in their idyllic little town.

Hesitantly, Elena took a few steps towards home. If she didn't go to her parents' graves, the attack wouldn't happen. The old man would be fine, the town-wide panic wouldn't begin.

And yet . . . Elena stopped again and rocked back on her heels, thinking.

She hadn't been talking to Stefan, hadn't shown any interest in him this time. He wouldn't be following her, would he? And the graveyard would be a good place to try to find Damon. That was the most important thing.

A cloud passed over the sun and Elena felt a little colder, a little sadder. It had been a long time since she had visited her parents. Now that she lived a few hours away, she hardly ever made it back to Fell's Church. She could see them now, she thought longingly. The cemetery would be isolated and peaceful after her long day. She could be alone there, and Damon would be more likely to come to her when she was alone. Making up her mind, Elena hitched her backpack higher on her shoulders and headed towards the cemetery, her steps sounding loud and firm in her own ears.

It was a fairly long walk, almost to the edge of town. Coming close to Wickery Bridge, another rusty caw grabbed her attention. Wings spread wide, the huge crow glided to land on the bridge's parapet. Turning its head, it fixed one bright eye on Elena. It seemed to be waiting.

Elena smiled. *Challenge accepted, Damon.*

She had expected to be a little shaky crossing Wickery Bridge, the place where Katherine had pursued her, and Elena had driven off this bridge and drowned. She could still remember the horrible rending sound as the bonnet of Matt's car had smashed through the old bridge's side. She could almost feel how icy-cold the water had been as she struggled.

But with Damon here, she could be brave.

'Hello, bird,' she said casually. The crow stayed very

still, its shining dark gaze fixed on Elena. She glanced up at the blue sky, and back at the crow. Then, slowly and deliberately, holding the crow's gaze, Elena smiled, a smile full of secrets. And then she walked on, straight past him, her head high. The bird watched as she passed.

As she entered the cemetery Elena's gaze fell on the ruined church, and she felt a tremor of foreboding deep inside her. Katherine was down there in the dark passages of the crypts already, watching them all.

At the thought of Katherine, Elena's hands automatically clenched into fists, anxiety running through her. Katherine had been furious when Stefan and Elena had fallen in love, and had attacked them both, had gone after the whole town. It had been the beginning of everything terrible.

Elena's fingernails bit into her palms. How would Katherine feel when Elena went after Damon? Katherine considered both the Salvatores her property, Elena knew, but she had always thought the vampire girl was more possessive of Stefan. She'd even offered to let him live, if he left Damon and Elena to die. But Elena couldn't let herself forget that Katherine was a threat, whichever Salvatore brother Elena pursued.

Crossing past the old church, Elena lifted her chin defiantly. She'd have to solve the Katherine problem when she got to it.

Reaching the newer, well-kept part of the cemetery, Elena rested a hand on the big marble headstone with

GILBERT carved into the front.

'Hi, Mom. Hi, Dad,' she whispered. 'I'm sorry it's been such a long time.'

She missed them so much, not as sharply or painfully as when she'd been in high school the first time, but with a powerfully wistful longing. If her beautiful, artistic mother had lived, she could have guided Elena through those first rocky days of being an Earthly Guardian. If her funny, warm father had been there, she could have leaned on him through all the hard times. They would have liked Stefan, she thought, and they would have seen how Damon's stubborn, fiery nature complemented Elena's own.

She wished that she could have gone even further back, that the Guardians had sent her back to Fell's Church when she was twelve. She could have saved her parents. She could have kept them out of the car that terrible day that had ended their lives and changed hers and Margaret's for ever.

With a powerful rush of longing, Elena remembered her mother laughing as she chased her through the house when Elena had been very small, catching her and sweeping her up into her arms for a hug.

'I still miss you,' she whispered, brushing her hand across her parents' names.

A sudden wind caught her hair, whipping it across her face. Looking up, Elena saw the tops of the oak trees at the edge of the cemetery tossing violently. Dark clouds were massing above her and there was a sharp chill in the air. She shivered.

The sky grew darker still. This wasn't a natural storm, surely. It had been clear and sunny only a moment before.

Damon? He could change the weather when he wanted to. Or Katherine? She was far more powerful than Damon right now.

Elena shuddered. If it was Katherine, she might kill Elena without even thinking about it. She remembered how easily Katherine had torn Damon's chest apart with her long talon-like nails, as her fangs ripped through his throat. There had been so much blood.

Elena steeled herself. Running wouldn't make any difference; she knew that this time. She'd tried that, and Katherine had caught up with her eventually. Again, she remembered the cold of the water under Wickery Bridge and shivered.

'I'm not afraid,' she said stubbornly. 'Whatever's out there, I'm ready for you.'

The wind stopped. Everything grew still, the leaves hanging motionless from the trees. All around Elena was silence, without even the chirp of a bird or the sound of a car in the distance.

Something stirred in the shadows under the oak trees. Elena squinted, trying to see. A dark figure moved towards her. The dim sunlight caught pale skin and sleek, night-dark hair. Black boots, black jeans, black shirt, black leather jacket. An arrogant lift to his chin, as if he'd seen everything in the world and didn't think much of it. Damon.

Thunder crashed overhead and Elena, despite herself, jumped.

'Nervous?' Damon was smiling faintly, his dark eyes amused. He was so beautiful, she thought absently. That was always true, always had been true. Sculpted cheekbones and clean, fine features. But there was something unfamiliar in that smile. There was none of the affection, none of the tenderness she was used to.

Elena reached for the bond between them automatically, wanting to check on Damon's thoughts and emotions, and to reaffirm their constant connection. But there was nothing. The Guardian's bond didn't exist here.

Damon moved closer, his eyes fixed on her face. 'There's a storm coming,' he said, his voice low and intimate, as if he was telling her a secret. The thunder grumbled again. 'A bad day for a walk.'

Elena felt her own smile rise to meet his challenging one. 'I'm not afraid of a little rain,' she said.

'No, I imagine you're not afraid of much.' Damon lifted a hand to brush Elena's cheek, tracing a finger lightly down her throat. He was far too close, and something twisted uneasily inside Elena.

This was Damon. She had no reason to fear him. Damon *loved* her.

Only . . . not this Damon. Not yet. This Damon was a hunter, and he was looking at Elena as if she were prey. Despite herself, she stepped backward.

His eyes narrowed and his smile spread. Elena jutted her chin out stubbornly. She was not going to flinch away from Damon. She wouldn't give him the satisfaction.

'Someone could be watching you,' Damon went on, moving closer still. 'A young girl, alone in a graveyard, when night is beginning to fall.' His voice was soothing, hypnotic almost, and he moved towards her once more, so close that she could feel his breath on her skin.

Elena's chest ached. This wasn't her Damon, this Damon with the cruel set to his mouth and the malicious gleam in his eyes. He was dangerous, even to her.

But, after all, he *was* Damon, wasn't he? He didn't know her, not yet, but Elena knew *him*, inside and out. She felt a smile blossoming on her own face and her shoulders, which had lifted as if she was expecting a blow, dropped.

'It's all right,' she said. 'I know you'd never hurt me.'

Damon frowned and took a step back away from her. He hesitated for a split second, then opened his mouth to speak.

'Elena?' Startled, Elena turned to see Bonnie and Meredith approaching from the other end of the graveyard. 'Elena?' Bonnie called again.

A light breeze broke the stillness of the air, lifting

Elena's hair. The sun came out from behind the dark clouds, and a mockingbird sang an insistent trill from a nearby tree. A cool finger brushed across the nape of Elena's neck. She gasped and whipped back round, but Damon was gone. The green grass over the graves behind her was as smooth and empty as if he had never been there.

'Elena,' Bonnie said as they reached Elena, 'sometimes I *worry* about you. I really do.'

'Was somebody here?' Meredith said, confusion on her face. 'I thought . . .' Had Damon Influenced them to forget him? Elena wondered. Or had he simply moved so quickly they weren't sure what they had seen?

'It's just me,' Elena said slowly, her eyes still searching the graveyard. There were no dark figures among the trees. No black bird rose towards the sky. 'I didn't expect you guys to follow me.'

'You can tell us to go away,' Meredith suggested, glancing at the grey stone above Elena's parents' graves.

Elena shook her head. 'It's OK,' she said. 'I wanted to hang out with you guys anyway.' She sat down in the sun-warmed grass beside the headstone, pulling the others down next to her. The three girls sat quietly for a while, watching the soft white clouds blow across the sky.

Bonnie ran her fingers through Elena's ponytail, taking the ribbon out and twining it into little plaits. The gentle pulls on her hair felt good, and Elena relaxed, leaning back against her friend's leg.

'So,' Bonnie started, her hands not pausing in their plaiting, 'are you going to tell us why you've been acting so funny today?'

Elena opened her mouth, a denial springing to her lips, and caught Meredith's knowing gaze.

'I know I said you seemed distracted this morning,' Meredith told her, 'but it's more than that.'

'You've been getting the strangest look on your face when you look at people, even us,' Bonnie said thoughtfully, tucking a stray piece of hair into one of Elena's plaits. 'Like *we're* strangers.'

Elena turned at that, her hair slipping through Bonnie's fingers, and looked at her friend. Bonnie stared back at her, brown eyes wide and a little hurt.

'It's not like that.' Elena said. But it did feel, a little bit, like they were different people from the ones she knew. Bonnie and Meredith had been through so much with her – they'd even travelled to a different dimension together – but not yet, not *this* Bonnie and Meredith.

If Elena managed to change what happened now, if she could keep Damon from killing Mr Tanner and setting the future she already knew in motion, would her friendship with Bonnie and Meredith change too? She ached with sorrow at the idea.

'If something's wrong, we want to help,' Meredith said softly.

Warmth ran through Elena, soothing away that

sorrowful ache, and she reached for her friends' hands. 'I'm fine,' she said, gripping Bonnie's square, small hand and Meredith's long, cool one. 'Only . . . everything's changing, isn't it? It's our senior year, our last year together.'

'Nothing's going to change,' Bonnie said uncomfortably. 'Nothing important. Just school and stuff.'

'Elena's right,' Meredith said, turning her hand to thread her fingers through Elena's. 'Next year at this time, who knows where we'll all be?'

'You've both been such good friends to me,' Elena said in a rush. 'When my parents died . . . I couldn't have got through that bad time without you. I don't want to lose you guys, not ever.'

Bonnie sniffed and pulled away from Elena to wipe at her eyes. 'Don't make me cry,' she said, half laughing. 'My mascara will run, and then I'll look like a raccoon.'

'Let's swear an oath.' Elena said determinedly. 'An oath that we'll always be true friends.'

They'd sworn a blood oath in this graveyard the first time she'd lived this. Bonnie and Meredith had sworn that they would do anything Elena asked in relation to Stefan. And Elena had sworn not to rest until Stefan belonged to her. Not even if it killed her.

And, well, it had killed her in the end, hadn't it? It had killed both of them. An oath like that – sworn in blood in a graveyard – had true Power.

'Wait a minute,' Meredith said, as Elena had known she would. She let go of Elena's hand and unfastened a pin from her blouse, then jabbed it quickly into her thumb. 'Bonnie, give me your hand.'

'Why?' Bonnie asked, frowning suspiciously at the pin.

'Because I want to marry you,' Meredith said sarcastically, and Elena smiled a little. 'Why do you think?'

'But – but— Oh, all *right*. Ow!'

'Now you, Elena.' Meredith hesitated and then jabbed at Elena's finger, their eyes meeting for a moment. She held out her own thumb, a plump drop of blood swelling on its pad, and Bonnie and Elena pressed their thumbs against hers. Bonnie's eyes were still shining with tears and Meredith looked pale and earnest. Affection for them both swelled inside Elena. These were her *sisters*.

'I swear that I'll always be there for both of you,' Meredith said steadily. 'I'll be on your side and do everything I can for you, no matter what happens.'

'No matter what,' Bonnie said, closing her eyes. 'I swear.'

Elena, pressing her thumb hard against the other girls', ignoring the twinge of pain, said softly, 'I swear, I will always be there for you, no matter what.' She felt breathless and expectant. This was sacred.

A gust of cold wind blew through the cemetery,

lifting the girls' hair, and sending a flurry of dry leaves across the ground. Bonnie gasped and pulled back, and they all giggled. A flush of satisfaction filled Elena. Whatever happened, however the world changed now, at least she knew she'd have Bonnie and Meredith.

CHAPTER

8

Elena rested her head in her hands, staring down at the scratched surface of her desk as her classmates settled into their seats for trigonometry class. Ignoring their chatter, she went back over her meeting with Damon in the graveyard the day before. Was there something she should have done differently?

She knew she'd intrigued him. She had seen his pupils widen when he leaned in towards her, his eyes curious and hungry. She'd half expected him to appear at her window that night. But he hadn't.

Although . . . that morning she'd heard the caw of a crow and whipped round just too late to see the bird. All the way to school, she'd had the disquieting feeling that she was being watched.

Halloween was coming. The night Damon had killed

Mr Tanner. Shifting uneasily in her seat, Elena remembered how Mr Tanner's head had flopped lifelessly backward against the altar in the Halloween house of horrors. His throat had been caked with blood. Elena squeezed her eyes shut tight, trying to block out the memories.

Damon had been at the Haunted House that night, and seeing Elena and Stefan together filled him with jealousy and seething resentment. He had lashed out by feeding on Mr Tanner when Mr Tanner stuck a dagger into him. Damon had killed him out of surprised rage and pain.

According to Mylea, that was when Damon's fate had been sealed. If Elena didn't manage to change what happened, she would die. Stefan would die. And Elena couldn't imagine the Guardians would let Damon live, not without Elena to rein him in. They would all be doomed.

So far, she'd successfully avoided Stefan. In history class she tried to close her mind off, scowling with concentration as she chanted multiplication tables or dialogue from old movies in her mind – anything to drown out whatever part of her might call to Stefan. He didn't try to talk to her either. She'd had to pursue him last time; he hadn't wanted to be reminded of Katherine, hadn't wanted to connect with her.

But Elena could feel him watching her in the halls, as clearly as she could feel Damon watching her on the streets. The other day, she'd glanced at Stefan in class without meaning to and seen his green eyes fixed on her. His gaze had been soft and longing, *hungry*. She wanted to comfort him, but Elena already knew how that would end.

The speaker set high on the classroom wall crackled, jolting Elena out of her thoughts. She half listened to the morning announcements, snapping to attention as the vice principal's voice said, 'Senior Homecoming Court nominations have been tallied. This year's nominees for Homecoming Queen are Sue Carson, Caroline Forbes, Elena Gilbert, Bonnie McCullough and Meredith Sulez. Voting will take place in the cafeteria over the next week. Congratulations to all the nominees.'

Elena gripped the edge of her desk, a sudden panic running through her. No. No way.

Homecoming had been when it all began. A dizzying whirl of images rose up in Elena's mind's eye. Herself, determined that Stefan wouldn't turn her down. Leaving the dance in Tyler Smallwood's convertible, the taste of whisky sharp in her mouth, her hair blowing wildly in the wind as they sped down the highway. The lid of the tomb in the ruined church shifting under her hand. The ripping sound as Tyler tore her dress.

Stefan saving her, taking her in his arms. Her whole world changing.

She couldn't let it happen again.

'Congratulations, girls,' Mrs Halpern said to Meredith and Elena as the speaker clicked off. 'There's a meeting for all the Homecoming Court nominees with the faculty sponsors in the office third period.'

Elena raised her hand. 'Mrs Halpern,' she said. 'I don't want to be on the Homecoming Court. Is there something I have to do to drop out of the race?' She heard Meredith's gasp of surprise behind her.

There was a moment of utter silence as everyone contemplated the thought. Elena Gilbert, queen of the school, refusing to compete? She was sure to win, they all knew that.

'Uh, no,' Mrs Halpern said, her forehead crinkled in a puzzled frown. 'If you're sure, Elena, I can just let the sponsors know.' At Elena's nod, she made a note on her clipboard.

Ignoring the whispers around her, Elena waited out the rest of the period. When the bell rang, she pretended not to see Meredith striding towards her and slipped out the door alone. She would have to figure out some kind of explanation to give Bonnie and Meredith.

Outside, Matt was waiting, a smile stretching across his handsome, all-American face. 'Congratulations,' he said, pulling her close and kissing her easily, just a sweet press of his lips. 'You're a shoo-in for Queen. Tell me what colour dress you're wearing and I'll make sure to get the right kind of corsage.' Despite his words, there was a wary look in his eyes, as if he was bracing himself for a blow.

'Oh, Matt,' Elena said, feeling stricken. She'd been avoiding him, avoiding this moment, and of course he'd noticed.

Whatever happened, her relationship with Matt was over, and she couldn't keep him hanging on. She needed to let him go, kindly, before she went after Damon.

The smile slipped off Matt's face and he bowed his head. 'I'm guessing you've got something to tell me, huh?'

Elena pulled him aside into a little alcove past the lockers, ignoring the curious looks of students passing by. It wasn't nice – it wasn't fair – to spring this on him here, right in the middle of the school day, but she couldn't string Matt along any longer.

'I *do* love you,' she said in a fierce whisper, when they were as private as they could be. 'I do.'

Matt flinched a little and then gave Elena a smile that was almost a grimace. 'I guess that's why you're dumping me, huh? Because I'm just that lovable. I should have realised before.' His voice was hoarse and, spontaneously, Elena wrapped her arms around him, pushing her face against the rough fabric of his letterman's jacket.

Unbidden tears rose in her eyes. 'Oh, Matt,' she said, muffled against his shoulder. 'You're my friend. My true friend. Don't love me like this any more.'

Matt sighed and stroked the back of Elena's head, running his strong fingers through her hair. 'It's not that easy, Elena. I can't just stop how I feel. But I won't try to hold on to you, not if you don't want me to.'

When she lifted her head to look at him, there was devastation on his face, beneath the steady eyes and the crooked grin. How had she not seen this the first time? She barely remembered this conversation. It had just been a means to an end: getting Matt squared away so that she had an open field to go after Stefan.

A curl of self-disgust twisted inside Elena and she lowered her head again, wiping her eyes against Matt's shoulder. She'd gone through this part of her life with blinkers on. And poor Matt, once he'd got over her, his next girlfriend had become a vampire and finally killed herself. All the craziness here – Fell's Church, Dalcrest, all along the ley lines – had ruined so much of Matt's life.

When she pulled back from their hug, Matt was staring at her, his forehead creased with concern. 'Are you all right?' he asked.

Elena bit her lip to keep back a hysterical giggle. If she kept up with these mood swings, remembering the future that might not come, everyone was going to think she was having a nervous breakdown. 'Listen, Matt,' she said. 'We're good friends, we really are. I love you so much. But there's nothing for you here. As soon as we're out of school, you should go. Take a football scholarship. You're bound to get one.'

He had been offered one, hadn't he? A good one, at some big football school. And he'd turned it down. He'd come to Dalcrest to help them protect the innocent.

Elena thought of Jasmine, with her easy smile and soft eyes, her fiercely loyal heart. 'You'll meet the right person for you someday,' she told him, trying to make him believe. 'She'll be smart and kind, and it'll be so much better than we could have been together.'

The smile was gone from Matt's face. 'You're the only person I want to be with,' he said flatly. His eyes narrowed. 'Does this have anything to do with the new guy? He's always watching you.'

'Stefan?' Matt had always seen more than she'd given him credit for. Elena met his gaze squarely. 'I don't want to date Stefan Salvatore,' she said honestly, and after a moment, Matt nodded, his shoulders slumping.

'I guess there doesn't have to be someone else for you to break up with me,' he said. 'You always know what you want, Elena. And what you don't.'

'You're one of my best friends,' Elena told him. 'I just want the best for you.'

Matt shook his head, confused. 'You're different since you came back from France,' he said. Then the corners of his mouth tilted up in a small, sad smile. 'Maybe the trip was good for you, too.'

* * *

'But if you broke up with Matt, who are you going to go to Homecoming with?' Bonnie asked after school, as they turned down the walk to Bonnie's house. It was a warm afternoon and Bonnie had invited Meredith and Elena over to hang out.

'I don't know,' Elena said. 'Does it matter?'

Meredith and Bonnie stared at her with identical expressions of shock.

'Does it—' Bonnie echoed incredulously.

'Elena, is there something *wrong* with you?' Meredith interrupted. 'You're really not acting like yourself.'

Feeling defensive, Elena shrugged. 'I guess I just don't think Homecoming is all that important.'

'That's what she means when she says you're not acting like yourself,' Bonnie said tartly, opening the front door.

Yangtze, Bonnie's family's fat, elderly Pekingese, greeted them with shrill, yapping barks, trying to wiggle his chubby body out through the open door. Bonnie pushed him back, and he growled and snapped at Elena's ankle as she went by.

Katherine had killed Yangtze, Elena remembered. Bonnie's mother had cried off and on for days. The dog was so spoiled she was the only one who could stand him. But there had been no sign of Katherine in the cemetery the other evening, no wild surge of Power to send the girls running screaming across Wickery Bridge. Maybe if Elena and Stefan didn't fall in love, none of the terrible things from Elena's first time around – not even Yangtze's death – would happen.

Gingerly, Elena reached down and patted the dog's back, earning another snarl. But wait, she thought, pulling back her hand. If Yangtze didn't die, wouldn't the world be different, in ways Elena couldn't even predict? The dog was the smallest part of all this, but every piece of the world made a difference.

Something terrible might happen, Elena thought, suddenly cold with panic. What if Bonnie tripped over the dog's small, round body on the stairs and fell, cracked her spine and ended up in a wheelchair? What if the dog finally managed to push its way out, ran into the road and caused a fatal car accident? *Anything could happen*. At the realisation, all the breath went out of Elena's body in a sudden gasp, and she clapped her hand over her mouth.

'What is it?' Meredith asked warily, but Elena just shook her head, her mind spinning. Anything could happen. The Guardian had told her that, but she hadn't really thought about it. Elena was changing everyone's lives, and what if she accidentally changed them for the worse? At least in Elena's own reality, Bonnie, Meredith and Matt were more or less safe.

Not Stefan though. Stefan had died.

Not Elena, who was dying.

And not Damon. She was the last one he had left. For a long time, Stefan had been the only person in the world Damon gave a damn about. And then Elena had come, and their bond had tethered Damon to her, to humanity. And now, in her reality, Elena was dying and Damon was losing the last bit of that humanity he had left.

In the McCulloughs' living room, Bonnie's sister Mary was unpinning a nurse's cap from her wavy red hair. 'Hey, girls,' she said, dropping her cap on the table. She looked exhausted, dark circles under her eyes.

'Long shift?' Bonnie asked. Mary worked at the Fell's Church clinic, which was always busy.

Mary sighed and closed her eyes for a second. 'We got a pretty bad case in today,' she said. 'You girls go down to the cemetery sometimes, don't you? Down by the Wickery Bridge?'

'Well, sure,' Bonnie said slowly. This wasn't something they talked about. 'Elena's parents . . .'

'That's what I thought.' Mary took a deep breath. 'Listen to me, Bonnie. Don't ever, ever go out there again. Especially not alone or at night.'

'Why?' Bonnie asked, bewildered.

Elena's stomach clenched. It shouldn't have happened. Things had been different this time, down near Wickery Bridge.

'Last night somebody was attacked out there,' Mary said. 'They found him right under Wickery Bridge.'

Meredith and Bonnie stared at her in disbelief, and Elena with a dull, wondering dread. Bonnie clutched Elena's arm, her fingers pinching painfully tight. 'Somebody was attacked under the bridge? Who? What happened?'

'I don't know,' Mary said, shaking her head. 'This morning one of the cemetery workers spotted him lying there. He was some homeless person, I guess. He was probably sleeping under the bridge when he was attacked. But he was half dead when they found him, and he's still unconscious. He might die.'

Stefan. Elena felt weighed down by guilt. She had thought things had changed. Was Stefan following Elena in this reality too? Had he been overcome with the need for blood and attacked the homeless man anyway?

Or was it Damon who had attacked the man under the bridge? Damon had been at the cemetery.

Maybe fate wasn't changeable after all, Elena thought, chilled. Maybe the man had been destined to be terribly hurt that night at the bridge, no matter what.

If so, perhaps her mission was doomed to failure. Maybe she and Stefan and Damon would continue on the same path, no matter how she tried to alter things. It was possible, wasn't it, that all roads would end with Stefan falling, a false friend's stave in his heart, with Elena drifting to death in her big white bed? With Damon's heart breaking, all his steps towards redemption lost?

'His throat was nearly ripped out,' Mary said grimly.

'He lost an incredible amount of blood. They thought it might have been an animal at first, but now Dr Lowen says it was a person. And the police think whoever did it may be hiding in the cemetery.' She looked at each of them, her mouth tight.

'You don't have to scare us,' Bonnie said, her voice strained. 'We get the point, Mary.'

'All right. Good.' Mary rubbed the back of her neck and sighed. 'I've got to lie down for a while. I didn't mean to be crabby.' She left the living room, heading for the stairs.

'It could have been one of us.' Meredith said. She bit her lip. 'Especially you, Elena. You went there alone.'

'No,' Elena said absently. 'It would never have been one of us.' She barely noticed the way the other girls stared at her, shocked by the certainty in her voice.

Elena clenched her fists, her nails biting into the palms of her hands. It couldn't all be inevitable. There was a way to save Mr Tanner, a way to keep the town safe from all the havoc Katherine, Damon and Stefan had, in their own separate ways, brought down upon it.

She had to find Damon, and soon. Halloween was coming fast, and she would need time with him if he was going to fall in love with her, if she was going to show him there were things more pleasurable than destruction.

Elena needed a plan.

CHAPTER

9

A chilly breeze swept through Elena's hair and she wrapped her arms around herself for warmth. The sun hadn't set yet, but there was already a pale moon high in the sky, and dark shadows were spreading under the trees.

She'd really thought Damon would have come to her by now. Elena had made excuses to dodge Bonnie and Meredith after school, and headed out to the woods. She had to draw Damon to her again, needed to start building a connection between them. And here, isolated beneath the ancient oak trees, was just where he was likely to appear.

A bird crashed through the top of the tree above her, and Elena looked up with a burst of relief. But it was just a blue jay, not the sleek black crow she was waiting for.

Maybe she should give up on subtlety and just shout Damon's name until he answered her. No, that would only make him suspicious.

If he was nearby, there was one thing that ought to draw him out. Blood.

Elena uncrossed her arms and looked around carefully. A rough grey boulder lay half buried between two trees with twisted roots growing up around it. That might do. Steeling herself, Elena wandered towards it.

Her toe caught on a root and Elena tipped forward, eyeing the sharp-edged rock. About right. Pretending to lose her balance, she threw herself on to the ground hard.

Her teeth clacked together as she hit the ground more violently than she'd meant to. There was a jolting, blinding pain in her knee. Her palms were stinging, scraped by tree roots. Winded, Elena lay gasping for a moment, fighting back tears of pain. She glanced down at her leg and was relieved to see a trickle of red blood. She didn't want to have to try that again.

'Let me help you.' The voice, husky and a little unsure, was so familiar, so loved. But it was the wrong one.

Elena looked up to see Stefan Salvatore standing above her, his hand extended. His face was shadowed so that she couldn't quite see his expression. Tentatively, she laid her hand in his and let him pull her gently to her feet.

Upright again, she winced a little, and Stefan quickly turned her hands palm-up, carefully brushing away dirt and bits of dry leaves. 'Just a scrape,' he told her quietly.

'My leg,' she said, looking up into his face. Her voice cracked, and she had to swallow hard. He hadn't changed. Of course he never changed; he was a vampire. Elena's heart ached, and for one mad moment she wanted to forget everything and throw herself into his arms and hold him tightly, weep with joy that he was alive.

'Let me see,' Stefan said, letting go of her hands. He didn't look her in the eyes, but instead knelt in the dirt, pulling a white silk handkerchief from his pocket. Unfolding it, he tucked something small – Elena couldn't see what it was – back into his pocket. Gently, he blotted at her knee and then tied the handkerchief around it as a makeshift bandage. 'There, that should get you home.'

He rose, eyes still averted, and backed away. Impulsively, Elena stepped forward and took hold of his leather-jacketed arm. He was so close, so solid and *real*. A warm flush of love and relief ran over her. 'Thank you,' she said. 'Stefan—'

Almost faster than her eyes could follow, Stefan pulled away from her, and stepped back, deeper into the shadows of the trees. 'I—' he said and stopped, then began again. 'You're welcome. You should be careful though, out here alone. Did you hear about the attack?'

'Yes, I did,' Elena said, moving closer to him again, her eyes searching the shadows, trying to make out his face.

'They're saying whoever did it must have been a monster.' There was an ugly, harsh note in Stefan's voice. Without the sunglasses, he looked vulnerable and terribly tired.

'I don't believe it,' she said firmly.

For a moment, their eyes met. Elena could see a wild flicker of hope rise in Stefan's and then disappear, leaving nothing but grim hopelessness. 'Anyone who would do such a thing is a monster,' he said.

Elena was almost touching him now. She wanted to run her hands across the chiselled lines of his face, remind herself how smooth his skin was.

His gaze traced over the curve of her neck, she saw, and his lips parted a little. 'You look—' he said. 'You remind me of someone I used to know.'

Katherine. Elena suppressed a grimace. The Stefan of this time was still guilt-stricken over the role he thought he'd played in Katherine's death. She wanted to announce the truth: *She's not dead. Crazy and vicious, but not dead. It's not your fault.*

But she couldn't. There was no way she could know that now, or at least no way she could explain. And so, Elena said nothing. Instead, she reached out a hand, slowly, carefully, as if she was taming some wild creature, and finally touched him. Just for a moment, her fingers brushing across the bare skin of his wrist.

She couldn't have him. But this – a moment of touch – she needed.

It was like a circuit connecting. Warmth flooded through Elena's body and she wobbled for a moment, ready to fall into his arms. Stefan became utterly still, his eyes dilated and dark as he stared at her. She thought he was holding his breath. There was a moment when it seemed like time was suspended, like anything could happen.

And then, with an intense jolt of sorrow, Elena pulled away, letting her hand fall limply to her side.

'Here,' Stefan said abruptly, pulling something from his pocket with the sleeve of his shirt. His voice shook and he was staring at his hands, refusing to meet Elena's eye. He handed her what looked like a handful of scrappy, skinny weeds, a few with small, pale flowers. 'Keep these with you for good luck. You can even make herbal tea out of them.'

Elena accepted the flowers, recognising them as vervain. If she kept it close, it would keep vampires from being able to cloud her mind. But Stefan didn't know yet that Damon was in town, certainly didn't know about Katherine. Who was he protecting her from? Then she got it.

Himself, of course. It was just like Stefan, to be thinking of himself as a danger while he did everything he could to protect her.

'Thank you,' she said, looking down at the wilting weeds as if they were the most precious thing she'd ever touched.

She stared up at him again, holding her gaze until, reluctantly, he let his eyes meet hers again. 'Remember,' she said softly. 'I don't believe in monsters.'

Stefan's face twisted and he turned and walked away, disappearing into the gathering dusk.

Elena sighed and tucked the vervain into her pocket before heading home. She felt safe, despite the dark. Even if she couldn't see him, Stefan would guard her carefully all the way home.

#TVD13StelenaReturns

CHAPTER

10

Ninety-seven. Ninety-eight. Elena brushed her hair with smooth, even strokes, watching herself in the elaborately framed Victorian mirror above her dresser. She met her own reflected gaze levelly, her dark-blue eyes as steady as her hand on the hairbrush. Her golden hair fanned out like silk across her shoulders.

It was odd, she thought, that she looked almost exactly the same here as she did in her own time. Her friends were younger, softer, but Elena's appearance hadn't changed since she had drunk the Water of Eternal Life and Youth back in her freshman year of college. When she had chosen to be with Stefan forever.

She was *not* going to think about Stefan.

Her hand slowed and her eyes dropped.

There was still that instant fire between them. The rest of the world melted away when she was with Stefan. It had felt so right, so perfect, to talk to him and touch him again.

But it didn't matter. She had to stay away from Stefan. It didn't matter how much she yearned to be with him. She couldn't get caught in that trap. Giving in to her love for Stefan led, in the end, to death and despair. There was a reason she was here.

She put the brush down on top of her rosewood dresser, lining it up neatly between her jewellery box and her comb, and reached into the top shelf of the dresser for a lacy white nightgown. The house was silent. Aunt Judith and Margaret were already fast asleep but Elena was buzzing with nervous energy. Still, she should try to rest.

Suddenly there was a rap at the window, a sharp, cracking noise. Elena spun round. Outside, she could just make out a pale face in the darkness, hair and clothes as black as the night around him. *Damon.*

'Let me in.' The low, coaxing voice sent a shiver up Elena's spine. She didn't move. 'Open the window, Elena. You want to let me inside.'

He was trying to *compel* her? A hot flush of anger ran over her. In two quick steps, she crossed the room and flung the window open.

Damon's eyes widened a bit. She knew she wasn't moving in the dreamy way a compelled person usually would, but the corners of his lush mouth tilted and Elena could tell he'd decided to go with it. 'Good,' he said, his tone soothing, 'Now, invite me in, Princess.'

Elena folded her arms in front of her. 'I don't know if I should,' she said slowly. Her heart was pounding. Gratefully, she thought of the withered vervain in her pocket.

Cocking his head to one side, Damon eyed her thoughtfully. Sitting on a branch of the quince tree outside her window, one arm braced on the windowsill, he somehow managed to look as comfortable and graceful as ever. 'You've got vervain,' he said.

'I do.' Elena didn't offer anything else. If she wanted him intrigued by her, it was probably best to leave a little mystery.

Damon's smile sharpened. 'Didn't you say you knew I would never hurt you?'

Elena's mouth went dry, and then she swallowed hard and stepped back from the window. This was *Damon*. She was safe. 'Come in then, Damon,' she said.

Damon hesitated for just a moment, uncertainty flickering over his face, and then he was through the window smoothly and standing in front of her. 'You know my name,' he said warily.

'Yes.' She didn't try to explain. What could she say? All the things that might make Damon trust her were still in the future.

Damon moved closer. There was something hot and

hungry in his gaze, and she had a sudden urge to raise her hand to cover where her pulse beat.

Elena was glad that she was still dressed in the clothes she'd worn to the woods, not the low-necked nightgown in her hand. It would have felt wrong, would have felt *dangerous*, if he had seen her like that right now, her throat so exposed.

'If you're not afraid, come here,' he said coaxingly. 'Let me taste you.' His irises were so dark that she could hardly make out his pupils.

For *her* Damon, the Damon she loved in her own time, Elena would have swept back her hair and bared her throat in an instant, eager for the sweet connection that came with the exchange of blood. Even now, she ached for that feeling.

But no, not yet. *This* Damon wasn't ready to share with her as an equal: he just wanted to take.

Instead, she set her jaw firmly and stared back at him. 'You *won't* hurt me,' she said. 'But I'm not ready for that.'

Again, Damon hesitated for a moment, his brow wrinkling. 'You know my name *and* you have vervain,' he said. He took a step closer to her. 'Someone's been telling tales about me.'

He was very close to her now, near enough that Elena had to tilt her head back to look up at him, exposing the long lines of her throat. The fine hairs rose on the back of her neck, some small, primitive part of her brain recognising: *predator*. His gaze was unfriendly. But Elena held her ground.

'No one's told me a thing about you,' she said honestly. 'I'm just a girl who happens to know a thing or two about vampires. And how to protect myself.'

'And my name?' Slowly, Damon raised his hand and ran a finger lightly along Elena's jaw. His touch was gentle but his gaze was cold, and Elena suppressed a shudder.

'I don't mean you any harm, Damon,' she said, looking straight into his eyes. 'I might know things, but I would never try to hurt you.' She could hear the sincerity in her own voice, and she thought Damon could too, because his hand dropped and he cocked his head, looking at her more closely.

'You look like someone I used to know,' he said. 'But you're not at all like her.'

Elena didn't know what to say to that, so she said nothing. Damon smiled.

'So, you're a girl who knows things,' he said, a faint mocking tone in his voice. 'A girl who hangs out in graveyards at dusk and willingly invites vampires into her boudoir. Are you flirting with the darkness, Princess? Do you want to come with me into the night?'

He reached out for Elena and pulled her against him. His eyes were on her throat again, and his fingers dug into her upper arms.

'That's not what I want at all,' Elena said, trying to

pull away. Her voice sounded startlingly loud to her own ears, and she realised they had been speaking in hushed voices, almost whispering. Damon's gaze flew from her throat to meet her eyes.

'You're wrong,' she said desperately. His fingers were holding her too tightly. 'I don't want the darkness. I want you to come into the light with me.'

Damon laughed, a sudden burst of laughter, and let her go. The laugh warmed his face, made him look more like *her* Damon and less like the predator who'd been standing too close to her a moment before.

'What, are you a missionary come to save my soul?' he asked, smiling in what looked like honest delight.

'Maybe.' Elena could feel her cheeks turning pink, but she held her head high. 'Things are better in the light. I could show you.'

Damon laughed again, a low, silky chuckle this time, and, before Elena realised what he was doing, he leaned towards her and brushed his cool, dry lips against hers, just for a second. 'You'll see me again, Princess,' he whispered, and then, faster than her eyes could follow, he was gone.

Alone in her bedroom, Elena touched her fingers against her lips, her heart pounding wildly.

He wasn't her Damon, not at all. Not yet. He didn't know her, didn't care for her, and that made him dangerous. For her own safety, she would have to remember that.

CHAPTER

11

'**W**ill you take me to the park tomorrow?' Margaret asked. She gazed at Elena across the kitchen table with wide blue eyes, her unbrushed dandelion-fluff hair sticking up in all directions. Behind her, Aunt Judith poured cereal into bowls.

'Sure, Meggie,' Elena said absently, picking at her toast. Margaret squealed and bounced in her seat. Elena smiled at her sister. They'd go Saturday morning, she decided, just the two of them, before she went dress shopping with Meredith and Bonnie.

Mornings like these were an unexpected blessing of her excursion into the past, Elena thought as she watched Margaret blow bubbles in her milk. She hadn't known to treasure these mundane, everyday moments the first time she was alive, because she hadn't known how quickly they would end. After this year, she'd never live at home with Margaret and Aunt Judith again. In one possible future – the first one, the one she couldn't help thinking of as the real one – Elena would be dead before Christmas.

Aunt Judith set down a glass of orange juice in front of Margaret. 'Stop blowing bubbles,' she told her firmly. 'And, Elena, much as I like having you here for breakfast, you're going to be late for school if you don't get going.'

'Oh,' Elena said, looking up at the clock. She stood and reached for her backpack reluctantly. There was a quiver of nervousness deep in her stomach at the idea of seeing Stefan again. Until yesterday she'd almost forgotten the exact shade of Stefan's green eyes. Now she thought she might have been better off forgetting when she couldn't look into those eyes every day.

And then there was Damon. She could connect with him, she was sure of it. Damon would change for her. He *had* changed for her. Without Stefan between them, it would happen faster. She just didn't know if it could happen in time. Halloween was coming soon and she'd only managed two brief and enigmatic conversations with Damon.

'I don't know if I'll be back for dinner,' she said, dropping a kiss on Margaret's head. 'I might go to Bonnie's house after school. Don't wait for me.' Maybe if she went to the cemetery again this evening, Damon would come to her there.

Aunt Judith sighed and handed her an apple. 'You hardly had any breakfast. Eat something healthy at lunch.'

Elena only nodded. She was thinking of Damon's sharp, brilliant smile, and how quickly it faded. How rough his voice had been when he asked if she wanted to come into the darkness.

She opened the front door and there, a dark figure against the bright colours of the day, was Damon, as if her thoughts had summoned him. Elena jerked back, her mouth dropping open.

The corners of Damon's mouth tilted up at her surprise. 'Hello, Princess,' he said lazily, his voice slow and easy. In one hand, he casually held a bouquet of white roses. 'Here I am in the light, just like you wanted.' He held the roses out to her, his smile mocking.

'Thank you, they're beautiful,' Elena said hesitantly.

She stepped back and headed for the kitchen. 'You can come in,' she said over her shoulder. This was technically a different house than she'd invited him into last night. Her bedroom and the living room were the only remains of the original house, the one that had almost completely burned in the Civil War.

Perhaps, she thought, hearing his soft footsteps behind her, she should have kept him out. But he had never hurt Margaret or Aunt Judith. She had to show that she trusted Damon if she expected him to start trusting her.

In the kitchen, Elena reached into a high cupboard to take out a vase and began to fill it with water.

'Elena?' Aunt Judith asked. 'You'll be late—' She stopped in surprise as Damon came through the doorway.

'Look what Damon brought me,' Elena said lightly. Damon turned on his most brilliant smile and held out his hand.

'Damon Salvatore,' he said, introducing himself. 'I'll drive Elena to school today, make sure she gets there on time.'

Flustered, Aunt Judith reached up to smooth her hair before taking Damon's hand. 'Pleased to meet you,' she said, shooting Elena a look that said, as clearly as words, *Who is this? What happened to Matt?*

Elena plopped the flowers into the vase and took a few minutes to arrange them neatly, half listening to Damon and Aunt Judith's conversation behind her.

'At university,' Damon was telling Aunt Judith. 'I'm just here to visit family. Fell's Church is lovely.' His voice was, if anything, a little too polite. And there was a familiar note in it, almost coaxing. Elena's fingers stiffened on the rose stems. Was Damon using his Power on Aunt Judith? Aunt Judith and her fiancé, Robert, had always liked Damon. Was that because Damon had cheated? She hadn't realised he would use his Power so casually. She swung round to stare at him. Damon met her eyes innocently, a bland smile on his lips.

Behind him, Margaret stared at Damon from the kitchen table. 'Aunt Judith?' the little girl asked, her voice quavering. Perhaps she could sense Damon's will working on Aunt Judith, compelling her to welcome him here.

'Let's go,' Elena told Damon sharply.

'Certainly,' he said, still smiling. 'You don't want to be late to class.' He nodded politely to Aunt Judith.

Elena set the vase of roses down on the table, a little harder than she needed to, and kissed her aunt on the cheek. 'See you later.'

Damon followed Elena to the front door. 'Now that you've got the roses, perhaps you should leave those little flowering weeds in your pocket behind,' he said idly.

'Very funny,' Elena said, opening the door and turning to look at him. She was aware of the vervain nestled deep in her pocket, but it was interesting that Damon could sense it as well. Or perhaps he was only guessing. 'The roses are gorgeous though,' she added, and Damon's lips curved into a smile.

The car parked outside was *amazing*: low, sleek and clearly very expensive. Damon opened the door for her.

'Are you sure you want to go to school today, Princess?' he asked. 'There's a whole wide world out there. You could show me around Fell's Church.'

'It's tempting,' Elena admitted, and Damon's smile widened. 'But I should get to school. Aunt Judith will worry if she hears I cut.'

'I could make her forget,' Damon suggested, and held up a hand defensively when Elena glared at him. 'Just teasing you, Princess. School it is.'

Elena settled back in the soft leather of the passenger seat, and Damon shut the door behind her and crossed to the driver's side. She watched as he started the car and pulled out, admiring his strong, graceful hands on the wheel. When he shot her a sidelong smile, she grinned back. This was all so familiar. She knew the way he scanned the road, the way his long legs fit into the footwell of the car. *This is* Damon, she thought, with a sigh of satisfaction. When she was with him, she felt at home.

When they pulled into the parking lot at school, Caroline's head shot up first. All around her, their friends turned as if drawn by a single, invisible thread. Damon parked and got out, coming around the car to open Elena's door with a flourish.

'Who is *that*?' She heard Bonnie's voice rise above the crowd. Meredith shushed her.

She smiled prettily up at Damon as he helped her out of the car, pretending not to notice the spreading whispers all around them.

'They'll be talking about you all day,' Damon said, his voice low. Elena gave him a small, private grin in reply.

'I'll see you later?' Elena asked him, squeezing his cool hand in her warmer one.

'Oh, I'll be around,' he said, and bent his head to press his lips lightly against her cheek. Raising her hand to touch where he had kissed, Elena watched as Damon slid back into his car and drove away. A tendril of affection curled warmly inside her.

Once the black car had turned out of the high school parking lot, an excited babble of voices rose up behind Elena.

'Did you *see* that car?'

'There was a car? I was too busy looking at the *guy*.'

'No wonder Elena didn't care about the new boy.'

Elena smirked a little. Then, turning, she came face to face with Matt. His lips were pursed tightly. Elena flinched. She had told him there wasn't anyone else.

'Matt,' she said quickly, 'it's not what it looks like. When we talked, I didn't . . .'

Tyler Smallwood and Dick Carter swaggered over. Tyler slapped Matt on the back, his big, red face openly amused. 'So someone finally cracked the Ice Princess, huh? Too bad it wasn't you, Honeycutt,' he said loudly. 'You wasted a lot of time there.'

On Tyler's other side, Dick Carter broke into rough laughter. His girlfriend, Vickie Bennett, clung to his arm and tittered uneasily.

Ignoring them, Elena reached out for Matt. 'I wasn't

seeing Damon yet when we talked,' she said. 'I wouldn't lie to you.'

'It's fine,' Matt said shortly, turning away from her and heading for the school doors.

'Matt—' Elena began. She tried to follow him, but Tyler blocked her path, taking a firm hold on her arm.

'Tell you what, gorgeous,' he said, baring his large white teeth in a smile. 'Forget them both and come to Homecoming with me. We'll show you a good time, won't we, Dick? Vickie?'

Dick laughed, a big dumb har-de-har, and Elena squirmed away, pulling her arm out of Tyler's hot grip. 'Forget it,' she said briefly, but by the time she pushed past them, Matt was gone.

Tyler had always been a jerk, Elena thought dismissively. And then she felt her own eyes widen as what he had said hit her. Homecoming night.

Elena had been so *angry* that night. Angry at everyone: Stefan for snubbing her; Caroline for bringing Stefan to Homecoming; Bonnie and Meredith for thinking that perhaps she should give up on Stefan. And so she had drunk bourbon with Tyler and Dick and their friends, and gone with them to the cemetery.

Tyler had tried to rape Elena. Stefan had rescued her – that was the one moment that had torn down the barriers between them. *It doesn't matter*, Elena thought, repressing a shudder. That wasn't going to happen this time.

But Tyler and the others would probably still go to the cemetery. And Dick and Vickie had fooled around on Honoria Fell's tomb. The tomb that hid the entrance to the catacombs in which Katherine was concealed. Offended, Katherine had tormented Vickie for months, nearly driving her over the edge of insanity.

Elena glanced back at Vickie, who was now crossing the parking lot towards the school, still arm in arm with Dick. Vickie's pale-brown hair flowed down her back as she tossed back her head to giggle up at Dick, her nose wrinkling as she laughed.

Elena had to try to protect her.

'Elena?' Bonnie's voice jolted Elena out of her contemplation. She was staring across at Tyler, she realised, frozen. She shook her head quickly, as if to scatter the memories, and turned to her friend.

Meredith was beside Bonnie, looking at Tyler with an expression of disdain. 'Don't let him get to you, Elena,' she said. 'He's a creep.'

'But who was that guy, Elena?' Bonnie demanded, her eyes shining with curiosity. 'He was so – and you— Is *he* what you've been acting so weird about?'

'I'll tell you later,' Elena said absently, watching as Vickie twisted a lock of her pale-brown hair around one finger.

'Oh, come on!' Bonnie groaned, tugging at Elena's arm. 'A beautiful guy like that? Tell me now!'

'I can't,' Elena said, pulling away. 'I promise I'll tell

you everything I can soon. But right now we have to go to class.' She would have to figure out *something* to tell them. Maybe she could pretend Damon was what he had told Aunt Judith, just a college student who Elena had happened to meet.

Bonnie huffed and rolled her eyes, but Meredith nodded. 'Come on then,' she said. 'We're going to be late.'

Elena followed her friends towards the school doors, but her steps slowed as she saw Stefan waiting just outside, his face as grey as a storm cloud.

'I have to talk to you,' he said, grabbing hold of her arm. Elena stared at him and he let go, snatching his hand back. 'Alone. Please.'

Elena hesitated, and Meredith eyed her carefully. 'Do you want us to go ahead without you?' she asked, ignoring Stefan.

'It's fine,' Elena said with a grateful glance. Meredith nodded and tugged Bonnie after her into the school.

'Wait,' Bonnie was saying, outraged. 'I didn't think she even knew Stefan.'

Elena watched her friends walk away before she looked up at Stefan, who had pulled off his sunglasses. His lips were drawn into a tight line.

'Elena,' he said abruptly. 'What do you know about that guy who drove you here?'

She should have realised this would happen. Unthinkingly, Elena raised a hand to touch Stefan, but he flinched back from her. 'It's OK,' she said steadily. 'I know what I'm doing.'

'I know you've got no reason to trust me,' he told her. His eyes were dark, insisting. 'But he's dangerous.' He stepped closer, taking hold of her arm again, and his touch sent a hot spark through her.

'He's not dangerous to me,' Elena said slowly, holding Stefan's eyes with her own.

'Do you remember me telling you that you reminded me of someone?' Stefan asked her. He was gripping Elena's arm so hard that it ached, and she held her breath. 'Well, that girl died. And it was Damon's fault. Damon's and mine. He destroys everything he touches, and he doesn't care. You *have* to stay away from him.' Stefan was breathing hard.

If only Elena could take Stefan in her arms and hold on to him, shut out the world so she could do nothing but bring Stefan comfort.

'I'm sorry, Stefan,' she whispered, pulling her arm from his grip and brushing past him into the school. She could feel his eyes watching her. Elena didn't look back.

CHAPTER

12

'But where did you even meet him?' Bonnie asked, rifling through a rack of dresses. 'Ooh, pink. I think I might do pink for Homecoming this year.' She pulled a fluffy concoction of satin and chiffon off the rack and held it up to herself to admire in the mirror. 'Adorable, right?'

'It's cute,' Elena agreed. 'You should try it on.' The three girls had headed right after school to one of their favourite boutiques to look for dresses for Homecoming.

Even as she flipped through the dresses, a little sore place deep in her chest kept reminding Elena that this might be the end. If she wasn't successful – if she *died*, back in that future – she would never be with her best friends again. And so she wanted, just for one afternoon, to be frivolous and try on dresses and talk about hairstyles.

'Focus, Bonnie,' Meredith said, amused. 'I'd like to know where Elena met him too.'

'At the cemetery, actually,' Elena admitted, and Bonnie gasped, almost dropping the pink dress.

'You went back to the cemetery? Elena, they still haven't found who attacked that old man. It's not safe.'

'I haven't been there since we promised Mary we'd stay away,' Elena said patiently. 'I met Damon before that.'

Meredith's eyes narrowed. 'The day we found you there?' At Elena's nod, she frowned. 'So he was hanging out at the cemetery alone the day the old man was attacked?'

'So was I,' Elena said drily. 'Damon has family buried there.' She wasn't exactly lying, she told herself. Katherine, who had turned Damon into a vampire, was a kind of 'family'. And her lurking underground in the crypt could count as being 'buried'.

Bonnie rolled her eyes. 'I really don't think Elena's gorgeous rich new boyfriend is attacking homeless people in his spare time, Meredith.'

'Even gorgeous rich guys can be psychos,' Meredith pointed out, her voice light.

'That may be true, but Damon's not one of them,' Elena said shortly. She began flipping through the rack of dresses in front of her and hesitated on a long sweep of silver silk. 'This would look great on you, Meredith.'

Meredith looked at it critically. 'You don't think it's too plain? Or too long?'

'You can pull it off.' Elena was sure the colour would bring out her cool grey eyes and olive skin, while her natural elegance could carry off the style.

'So, are you bringing this Damon to the dance?' Bonnie asked.

'I don't think high school dances are really Damon's thing,' Elena said. She had trouble imagining Damon slow dancing to pop songs and bringing her little cups of punch. And Stefan would be taking Caroline to the dance, she assumed. It was better for the Salvatore brothers not to be in the same room, especially not surrounded by humans.

'Who are you going to go with then?' Bonnie asked, taking both the short pink dress and a blue-green gown in a mermaid style off the rack to try on. 'I'm sure Matt would still take you.'

Elena shrugged. 'No one, I guess.'

Silently, Meredith and Bonnie turned to stare at Elena.

'What?' she asked, but she knew. The Elena who *belonged* here wouldn't be caught dead without a date for a school dance. She hadn't cared about any of those dates either, not until Stefan.

'Are you actually going crazy?' Bonnie asked tartly, and then gasped as Meredith elbowed her in the side. 'I mean, fine, great. Who needs a date anyway?'

'It's not a bad idea,' Meredith said casually. 'I was supposed to go with Ed Goff, but it might be more fun for us three to just go together. Not even bother with boys.' There was something tentative to her gaze, and Elena realised what it was. Meredith was worried about her.

'Are you *both* crazy?' Bonnie asked. 'I want to go with a boy. I want to dance all night. I want romance.'

'With Raymond?' Meredith asked, arching an eyebrow. 'There's nothing wrong with Raymond, but you can't pretend you're all that interested in him.'

'I can pretend anything I want,' Bonnie said, crossing her arms, the dresses she held crumpling against her.

'Come on, Bonnie,' Elena said coaxingly. 'If you go with us, you can dance with all the boys. And we'll have more fun together, you know we will.'

'It's our last Homecoming together,' Meredith said, laying her hand on Bonnie's arm. 'It should be the three of us.'

'Oh . . . oh . . . fine,' Bonnie said. 'But there had better be lots of cute boys who want to dance with me.'

'Of course there will be,' Meredith said reassuringly, 'because you're going to look so great in one of these dresses.'

'Obviously,' said Bonnie with a suddenly teasing, crooked grin. She stuck her nose into the air and sailed off to the dressing room.

Meredith searched through the racks of dresses efficiently, pulling out a short jewel-blue dress to add to the growing pile in her arms. Flicking past a green velvet minidress, Elena wished she could be so enthusiastic. Nothing seemed quite right.

'Here,' Meredith said, stopping. 'This is perfect for you.'

The dress was gorgeous. Silk the colour of crystallised violets, which would bring out the gold of her hair and the deep blue of her eyes. Elena would look magical in it, lit from within. *Had* looked magical.

It was what she had worn to the dance the first time. Tyler had torn this dress. Stefan had fallen in love with her, finally taken her in his arms, while she was wearing it.

Elena stuffed her hands in her pockets, unwilling to touch it.

And then she saw something on the other side of the room, just waiting for her. Yes. Elena brushed past Meredith and headed straight for it.

The iced-violet concoction was a beautiful dress. But this? This dress was a revelation.

It was red, the deep vibrant crimson of blood, and it would cling to Elena like a glove. Even hanging on the rack, it spoke of passion and intensity. It was a dress to fall in love in, or to stir up hate. If Damon were a dress, this was the one he would be.

'This is it,' Elena breathed.

Meredith's eyebrows shot up. 'Wow. It's a statement, all right.'

They headed into the dressing room, Meredith with an armload of selections, Elena with only the crimson gown. Pulling it over her head, she called over the wall of the dressing room, 'Want to get dressed for the dance at my place?'

'We always do,' Bonnie called back.

It had been a ritual of theirs from their earliest dances in junior high to get dressed together, gossiping and doing one another's hair. Caroline had always been with them, but Elena didn't think she was going to join them this time.

Elena smoothed the dress down over her hips and admired herself in the mirror. It fit perfectly, and the weight of the material – some kind of satin – made her feel powerful and protected.

'This is it,' she said, stepping out of the fitting room. Meredith and Bonnie came out in dresses of their own.

'Wow,' Bonnie said, looking Elena over. 'I wouldn't have thought red was your colour, but you look great. Older.' She was in the mermaid green dress. 'I don't love this one. I'm going to try on the gold.'

Meredith looked sleek and composed in a black-and-gold dress with a long slit up the side, but she frowned. 'This itches. Next!'

Elena changed back into her own clothes, draping the red dress carefully over her arm. *Caroline would have liked this dress*, she thought.

'Who's Caroline going with?' she asked. She couldn't help it; she had to know if she was going with Stefan again.

'I don't know,' Meredith said. 'She's been avoiding all of us.'

'She never tells me anything any more,' Bonnie said. 'If it weren't for maths and history, I wouldn't see her at all.' She sounded forlorn, and Elena had a pang of regret for the lost friendship. Maybe, now that they weren't competing over Stefan any more, Caroline and Elena could be friends again, someday.

The fitting room doors opened again, and Elena stepped out to see the next set of dresses. An idea was kindling at the back of her mind. Why not replace Caroline in their little pre-dance group? It would be one way to keep the horrors of her first Homecoming night from repeating. She thought of Vickie's innocent face, the way she had giggled at everything Dick said. How the walls of her room had been coated with blood in the future Elena had lived through. Things had to be different.

'Why don't we invite Vickie Bennett?' she said brightly. If Vickie was with them, she wouldn't leave the dance with Dick and Tyler. She wouldn't desecrate the tomb, wouldn't incite Katherine's anger.

Meredith, dressed in the long silver gown, and Bonnie, in black velvet, stared at her. 'You want to invite Vickie Bennett?' Bonnie said slowly.

'Why not?' Elena asked. 'What do you have against Vickie?'

Bonnie exchanged a glance with Meredith. Meredith cleared her throat. 'Neither of us has a problem with Vickie, but *you've* never liked her.'

Nodding, Bonnie added, 'You've always said she was a useless little drip.'

'Oh.' A little twist of self-disgust curdled inside her. 'Well, I was wrong. Let's bring her along.'

After careful comparisons, Meredith chose the long silver gown, which looked like moonlight on her. Bonnie modelled fourteen different dresses and finally settled on the pink chiffon. Elena, of course, bought the red dress.

Leaving the store, she held her head high, feeling like a warrior. Like a hero. Elena wasn't *just* going to save Damon and herself. She would save everyone.

CHAPTER
13

The weather Friday evening couldn't have been more perfect for the Homecoming game. Gold and pink from the setting sun striped the sky. On the field, the marching band stepped in precise formation for their pre-game show, horns blaring and drums thumping. Cheerleaders cartwheeled in their red and black skirts, warming up the crowd for the game.

'The Homecoming game is a real American tradition,' Elena told Damon, leading him up the bleachers. 'You owe it to yourself to experience it at least once. I can't believe you've never been.'

'You'd be amazed at the number of real American traditions I've been able to avoid,' Damon said drily.

'Well,' Elena said, sitting down and wrapping her jacket more closely around her, 'I'm glad I get a chance to introduce you to something.'

Damon reached out and tucked a lock of Elena's hair behind her ear. 'You're going to show me life in the light, right, Princess?' he asked, his voice low and teasing. 'Football games and sock hops?'

'I don't think sock hops are a thing any more, Damon,' Elena told him, letting her voice take on a flirtatious edge. The brush of his fingers made her skin tingle. Sensing her reaction, Damon smiled and ran his hand down her arm, wrapping his fingers around hers.

This wasn't *her* Damon, not yet, but he felt so familiar that she kept forgetting. The weight of his arm across her shoulders, the scent of his leather jacket, the cool skin of his wrist resting casually against her neck, the affection that shone through his mocking smile: it all belonged to her Damon too.

Elena could feel eyes watching them from all around as they sat waiting for the game to begin. Elena Gilbert with a mysterious, shockingly handsome, older man. Gossip would centre on this for days.

No one approached them though. Elena saw Meredith and Bonnie climbing the bleachers, Bonnie's face brightening as she saw them, and sent a silent plea to Meredith with her eyes. Meredith cocked one elegant eyebrow – message received – and shepherded Bonnie towards a group of laughing girls in another row of seats.

As the team ran out on to the field to claps and

cheers, Damon tensed beside her, letting go of Elena's hand. His jaw was tight and his eyes followed one red-and-black jersey across the field. Stefan.

She was surprised to see Stefan on the team. Perhaps she should have realised that, even without her intercession, Matt would have invited Stefan to try out for the team.

'My appreciation for football is fading,' Damon said drily, his eyes still fixed on Stefan. 'Let's go somewhere else, Princess. I can show you all kinds of things better than high school sports.' He turned towards her, his lips twitching up in a wicked smile, and took her hand again, starting to rise.

'No, wait, Damon,' Elena said quickly, tugging him back down. 'I need a favour.'

Damon's eyes narrowed. Slowly, he sat back in his seat, and fixed her with a steady dark gaze. 'So you didn't just want to expand my horizons when you brought me here?' He leaned closer. 'You're quite devious, aren't you, Elena?'

Pulling her eyes away from his, Elena looked back at the field. Their team had won the coin flip and Matt, as quarterback and captain, chose to receive the kick-off. The teams were lining up and Elena gripped Damon's hand harder as she leaned forward to scan the backs of their jerseys. 'See those two guys?' she said, pointing. 'Carter and Smallwood.'

Damon glanced at them, his face taking on the

thoughtful look she associated with his using his Power. 'A couple of all-American meatheads,' he said dismissively. 'Nothing special about them.'

'I know,' Elena said. 'I need them to fight. It has to be bad enough to get them kicked off the team.'

Damon's eyebrows rose. 'You're more bloodthirsty than I'd realised, Princess,' he said.

'I need them to get suspended. They can't be at the dance tomorrow,' Elena told him. The kicker was moving back, his teammates lined up on either side. '*Please*, Damon,' she said.

Damon leaned back and smiled lazily at her. 'Why should I?' His eyes were locked on hers, challenging her. 'What will you give me?'

'Anything you want,' Elena said recklessly. 'I trust you. Just do it.'

Damon's smile widened and he flicked his eyes back towards the field. The kicker's foot made contact with the ball and it flew in a high arc through the air.

With a shout of fury, Tyler Smallwood launched himself across the field and tackled Dick Carter to the ground.

The stands broke out in screaming excitement. Tyler was punching Dick in the stomach, avoiding his pads to reach the flesh beneath. Dick bucked and rolled, and Tyler hit the ground with a thud.

'Good enough?' Damon asked.

Down on the field, the referees were blowing hard

on their whistles and running towards the fight. Both boys had pulled off their helmets and, as Elena watched, Dick punched Tyler hard in the nose. Bright blood gushed out, drops spilling on to the grass of the football field.

'That should do it,' Elena said, feeling a little sick. But this was necessary. If Tyler and Dick went to the dance, if they left the dance and went to the graveyard, terrible things would happen.

This was the better option.

The coaches were shouting as the other players tried unsuccessfully to pull Dick and Tyler apart. Tyler lunged forward and sank his teeth into Dick's arm. There was more blood, running over Tyler's mouth. Damon was watching, his face lit with pleasure.

'Damon!' Elena said sharply. 'That's enough!'

'Killjoy,' Damon muttered, but he glared at the fighting boys, and they stilled, then pulled away from each other. Matt and one of the running backs were holding on to them, tugging them further apart. Both boys looked dazed, and Tyler wiped at his mouth, smearing dark-red blood across his face.

A chill spread through Elena. The pleasure Damon took in watching the guys fight was something she hadn't seen in years. As comfortable as she felt with him, she still needed to be careful.

Down on the field, Stefan was paying no attention to the aftermath of the fight going on all around him.

Instead, he was scanning the stands, his eyes narrowed. He must be looking for Damon, Elena realised. Of course Stefan would suspect Damon was behind the fight.

Before Stefan could spot them, the referees called the teams back into place. Two second-string players ran out to take Tyler's and Dick's places, and the game began at last.

Elena was surprised at how much she enjoyed it. She had been to football games before, of course she had. But usually, what was going on in the stands had interested her more than what might be happening on the field. Even when she was dating Matt, she hadn't really watched him play.

He was really good. Matt and Stefan made an incredible team, but Stefan had the strength, speed and reflexes of a vampire. Matt was managing on pure skill. Calm and confident, he called the plays, his eyes scanning the field. He ran like the wind, and when he passed the ball downfield, it was in a long spiralling arc that landed safely in Stefan's hands. No wonder he had been – was going to be – offered football scholarships.

Damon watched the crowd far more than he did the game, although his eyes regularly flitted back to Stefan. When he looked at his brother, he wore an expression that Elena couldn't quite decipher. Was this hostile face the one Damon had worn all those centuries, as he kept a distant eye on his little brother, his enemy?

At halftime, Damon bought Elena a cup of hot chocolate.

'Thank you,' she said, pleased at his thoughtfulness, and wrapped her fingers around the warmth of the cup. It was getting chilly. Autumn had really set in now.

'May I?' Damon asked politely, after he'd watched her take a sip. She handed over the hot chocolate and he drank slowly, savouring. 'Very nice,' he said. 'Sweet.' His fingers lingered on hers for a moment longer than necessary as he passed the cup back to her. Damon's words were innocent enough, but there was something darkly teasing in his gaze. Attraction hummed between them. Maybe he wasn't her Damon yet, but he *would* be.

When they got back to Elena's house after the game, the driveway was empty.

'Aunt Judith must have taken Margaret somewhere,' Elena told Damon.

Damon tipped his head slightly to one side, clearly sending out his Power to search the house. 'There's no one home.'

'*Mmmhmm.*' Elena unlocked the door and stepped inside. Damon waited on the porch, his hands in his jacket pockets, casual and confident. Elena didn't hesitate. If she wanted Damon to be trustworthy, first she had to trust him. 'You can come in if you want,' she said. 'The invitation still stands.'

'If you want me,' Damon said coolly, but there was a pleased tilt to his mouth as he followed her in.

Elena led Damon through the house. In the hall he paused, running his fingers across the photographs on the side table. 'Your mother?' he asked, picking one up to look at it more closely.

Elena nodded, her throat tight. Damon kept touching things as he followed her through the house, brushing his fingers over the furniture and opening drawers to look inside. Up in her room, he prowled like a cat, inspecting the books on Elena's bookcase, rifling through the clothes in her closet, delicately rearranging the objects on her dresser. It was as if he was trying to figure her out.

Finally he put down her silver comb and turned to look at her. 'Why did you want them to fight?' he asked, his voice dry. 'It's not for love, is it?'

Elena laughed in spite of herself. 'Tyler or Dick? Absolutely not.' Sobering, she added, 'I know something terrible would have happened tomorrow if they hadn't been suspended. I can't explain any more. I'm sorry.'

Damon stepped closer and brought his hands up to frame her face. His eyes, so dark that she couldn't distinguish the iris from the pupil, stared into hers. Electricity shot through her at the careful touch of Damon's hands on her face. He was trying to use his Power to read her, she could tell.

'You're not a witch,' he said confidently. 'Or a psychic.'

Elena reached up and took his cool hands in hers. 'Like I told you, I'm just a girl who knows some things. I'm nothing special.'

'I wouldn't say that,' Damon said, turning his palm so that his fingers were interlaced with hers. His eyes followed the line of the vein in her neck, all the way down to the collar of her shirt. 'You promised me anything I wanted,' he said.

He expected her to pull away, to be afraid, Elena knew. Instead, she brushed her hair back, cocking her head to expose the smooth line of her throat. 'I trust you,' she said simply.

Damon stared for a moment, then pulled her closer, wrapping his arms around her, and kissed her throat. Beneath the softness of his lips, his sharp canines pricked her, and she pressed closer still. *Yes.*

When his teeth slid smoothly beneath her skin, she could feel Damon with her at last: all his anger and loneliness, that lost child she knew hid beneath his cold façade. And, deeper still, passion. Love that never ended, a burning fire that could never be extinguished.

Their minds intertwined and Elena stifled a sob of pure joy. Damon was hers again. They were both going to live.

#TVD13LovingDelena

122

CHAPTER

14

'They were both amazing,' Bonnie said from the window seat. She was already wearing her fluffy pink dress, her bouncy curls perfectly smooth.

'Who?' Elena murmured as Meredith twisted a long strand of her hair and secured it with a bobby pin.

'Matt and Stefan,' Bonnie said. 'When Stefan caught that last pass, I thought I was going to faint. Or throw up.'

'Oh, *please*,' said Meredith.

Vickie Bennett, carefully ringing her eyes with liner in front of the mirror, giggled nervously. She'd been thrilled when Elena invited her to join them in getting ready for the dance, but she seemed hesitant and unsure now that she was there. As Elena watched, Vickie glanced quickly at her, then looked away, her free hand twisting the hem of her dress.

'And Matt – that boy is simply poetry in motion . . .' Bonnie wriggled around on the seat to fix a bright eye on Elena. 'You could have got either of them to take you, you know. Matt's still crazy about you. And he's a sweetheart. Plus, I saw Stefan's face after Damon brought you to school. He practically swallowed his tongue, he was so upset.'

'It doesn't matter,' Elena said. 'I'm with Damon.'

'Then why isn't he bringing you to the dance?' Meredith asked, her talented fingers twining more of Elena's hair into an elegant golden mass. 'Even if he doesn't like dances, he should have come if you wanted him to.'

'But I didn't want him to,' Elena said, laughing and catching Meredith's hand as she tweaked another strand of Elena's hair into place. 'I wanted to go with you guys.'

Bonnie sat up straighter, her small face growing serious. 'I'm glad you did, Elena,' she said. 'Remember how I saw in your palm that you had two loves? I think . . . I think something bad might happen if you aren't careful.'

Meredith huffed out an exasperated breath. 'Bonnie—'

'I just mean,' Bonnie said, 'that if she wants Damon, it doesn't matter that Matt and Stefan like her. That's all. Two loves aren't necessarily better than one.

You need to be careful, Elena.'

'And you should leave some guys for the rest of us,' Meredith said lightly. Bonnie laughed and looked away, but Elena shifted uneasily under Meredith's hands. How much of the future could Bonnie see? And which future was it?

It didn't matter. Elena knew what would happen tonight. Caroline and Stefan would be at the dance together. Elena would leave them alone this time. She wouldn't ask Stefan to dance. Caroline, Elena thought, would have a perfectly nice time. There wasn't going to be a second love for Elena this time. Whatever Bonnie saw, it wasn't going to happen.

'It's fun to go with just girls anyway,' Meredith said. 'You were right, Elena.'

'Sure,' Bonnie said, rolling her eyes. 'Guys: who needs them?'

Vickie turned away from the mirror to face them and said in an awkward rush, 'Thanks for inviting me to come with you. I probably wouldn't have gone at all otherwise.'

'What happened with Dick and Tyler anyway?' Bonnie asked curiously. 'Did Dick tell you what they were fighting about?'

Vickie spread her hands wide, shrugging in amazement. 'All Dick said was that suddenly he was so angry he couldn't even see straight. The next thing he knew, everybody was pulling him and Tyler apart.'

Meredith frowned. 'They don't take steroids, do they?'

'No! I don't think so.' Vickie was shaking her head, but a shadow of doubt crept into her voice.

Again, Elena felt a flicker of guilt. She remembered the way Dick's head had snapped backward when Tyler punched him in the mouth, the dazed expressions on both their faces when the other players had finally pulled them apart.

But worse things would have happened if they had gone to the church that night. Stefan had almost killed Dick and Tyler after Elena drowned. Vickie had been gruesomely murdered. The memory of Vickie's room, painted in blood, made Elena's stomach turn over.

What were a few rumours or a suspension to that?

'There,' Meredith slid the last bobby pin into Elena's hair. 'Gorgeous.'

Elena stood and pulled her friends close so that they could all look in the mirror. Bonnie, her curls falling over her shoulders, was as sweet as candy in her shimmering pink taffeta. Meredith's hair was swept up into an elegant chignon and the long sweep of silver silk falling almost to her feet made her seem a thousand times more sophisticated than she'd ever seemed before. Even Vickie, in a soft green dress that came to her knees and ended in a puff of lace, looked fresh and delicate despite her nervousness.

As for herself, Elena thought, standing straight and

tall in the crimson dress, she looked like a burning flame. She looked like she could set the world on fire.

They walked down the stairs together to where Aunt Judith and her fiancé, Robert, waited, along with pyjama-clad Margaret. Margaret jumped to her feet and came to hug Elena around the waist. Elena bent down and kissed her little sister on the forehead.

Aunt Judith blinked when she saw Elena. 'You girls all look lovely,' she said slowly. 'That's certainly a . . . dramatic dress, dear.'

'You're pretty,' Margaret said, beaming up at Elena, and Elena gave her a squeeze.

'Runs in the family,' she whispered, and her little sister giggled.

Robert was staring at Elena, looking a little dazed.

'What's the matter, Bob?' Aunt Judith asked.

'Oh.' He frowned and passed a hand across his forehead. 'Actually, it just occurred to me that *Elena* is a form of the name *Helen*. And for some reason I was thinking of Helen of Troy.'

'Beautiful and doomed,' said Bonnie. Her eyes met Elena's for a second, before she quickly looked away.

'Well, yes,' said Robert.

A chill went up Elena's spine. She *wasn't* doomed, she told herself fiercely. Not this time. There was nothing to worry about. 'We have to go,' she said quickly, and kissed Aunt Judith goodbye. 'Don't wait up.'

They all rode to the dance together in Meredith's

car, Elena in the front passenger seat, Bonnie and Vickie in the back. Meredith and Vickie were laughing and chattering, and Elena tried to join in.

But Bonnie was oddly quiet, and when Elena looked into the back seat, the other girl's brown eyes were fixed on her thoughtfully. Elena couldn't escape the heavy, anxious feeling that something important, something terrible, was about to happen.

No, she told herself. *It's just a high school dance. I'm only afraid because of what happened the first time. Everything is different now.* But the thoughts didn't lighten the sickening feeling of dread at the bottom of Elena's stomach.

She almost leaned over and asked Meredith to take her home. She could have given some excuse, said she felt ill – it wouldn't even have been a lie. But she was Elena Gilbert, and she did not back down. She would hold her head high and enjoy this last dance. There was nothing to be afraid of.

Music spilled out the open doors of the auditorium as they arrived. Inside, the cavernous room was a swirling mass of people, laughter and voices. The decoration committee had draped the walls in long swathes of sheer fabric that shone gently in the light, transforming the whole auditorium into something from a dream. In the centre of everything, resplendent in gold, was Caroline.

'Look at that dress,' Bonnie said softly. 'What's the front held on with? Superglue?'

The dazzling dress, made of gold lamé and fitting like a second skin, certainly showed a lot of Caroline. She looked beautiful and wild, her glossy auburn hair streaming down her back as she laughed. Her long limbs were smooth and tanned, and her cat-green eyes shone. Caroline was clearly having a wonderful time.

Elena looked for Stefan beside Caroline, but she couldn't spot him. The crowd around Caroline was constantly shifting. People came up to speak to her briefly, admiringly, like courtiers to a queen, and then stepped back to make room for the next in line.

'Born to rule, apparently,' Meredith said, sounding amused.

Elena kept moving towards Caroline, scanning the changing crowd around her. Stefan had to be there somewhere. Elena wouldn't speak to him, wouldn't touch him, but she wanted to see him. She could have that at least, surely?

As a couple of cheerleaders stepped aside, Elena saw Caroline's date at last and stopped short for a second in surprise.

Not Stefan at all. Matt. His hand was resting lightly on Caroline's arm as he stood beside her, prince consort to the queen, but his eyes were fixed on Elena, his jaw set defiantly.

Elena held her head high and started walking

towards them again, fixing a smile on her face. She
didn't own Matt. She'd prepared herself, she thought,
to see Stefan with Caroline. She wasn't ready, though,
for the sharp sense of loss at seeing Matt with her
instead. Elena hadn't quite realised how much she
thought of Matt as *belonging* to her, at least in this time.
Beyond her feeling possessive of him, Caroline couldn't
possibly be good for Matt.

Vickie had wandered off towards the refreshment
table, and Meredith and Bonnie, one after the other,
were asked to dance and went off on to the dance floor.

'Hey, Elena. Want to dance?' It was her lab partner,
a tall, gangly guy with a wicked sense of humour who
normally she'd have enjoyed dancing with. But Elena
just shook her head, barely glancing at him.

'Not yet,' she said shortly. 'I need to talk to somebody.
I'll catch up with you later.'

As Elena reached the outskirts of the group around
her, Caroline looked up and their eyes met. Elena
smiled, but Caroline just gazed at her. And then she
smiled, and, turning towards Matt, tipped her face up to
his and kissed him, a long passionate kiss.

Elena felt her own face drawing into a scowl and
consciously smoothed it over, fixing a neutral, almost
bored expression in its place.

'Hello, Elena,' Caroline drawled as soon as the kiss
ended. 'Don't you look' – her eyes flicked over the
crimson dress – 'nice. It's so original of you to wear that

shade of red with your complexion. A lot of people would worry about looking washed out.'

Elena forced a smile. 'Hello, Caroline. Hello, Matt.'

Up on the stage near them, the principal tapped his finger against the microphone, clearing his throat. 'Can I get the Homecoming Court up on stage, please? It's time to crown your queen!'

The crowd cheered, but Elena was hardly listening. Instead, she was looking beyond Caroline and Matt. She was positive that Stefan was here, somewhere in the crowd. Even if he hadn't brought Caroline, surely he had come.

The crowd was shifting around her as the princesses, Bonnie and Meredith among them, climbed the steps to the stage. Elena turned her back on them for a minute, scanning the faces behind her for Stefan.

Then strong fingers, their pointed nails digging into her arm, dragged Elena back to attention. Caroline, eyes blazing, leaned in close as Elena pulled away.

'How does it feel, Elena?' she whispered, her voice hard. 'How does it feel to know I've taken everything you wanted?' Almost stamping her feet, she swung round in a sweep of gold and auburn, and climbed the steps on to the stage, holding her head high.

Elena cocked a cynical eyebrow at Matt. 'Caroline Forbes? Really?'

Matt's cheeks reddened and he looked away. '*You* broke up with *me*, Elena. I'll date who I want.'

'Oh, Matt,' Elena said, softening. She thought again of Jasmine, of the beautiful, smart, compassionate woman who would fall in love with Matt, who would hold on to him through all the dangers his life threw at them. 'I *know* you can do better. Don't waste yourself on someone who just wants you as a trophy.'

Matt sighed. 'At least she wants me.'

The principal had finished introducing each girl. Now he tore open an envelope. 'And your new Homecoming Queen is Caroline Forbes!' Around them, the crowd cheered.

Elena squeezed Matt's hand. 'I know you, Matt,' she said in a quick, fierce whisper. 'You don't take the easy route. You're not going to be happy unless a relationship is real, unless it's *true*. I'm sorry it's not going to be with me, but you don't have to settle. Promise me you're going to be ready, when that great girl shows up. Don't waste your time on the wrong people.'

The principal lifted the shiny, plastic crown and placed it carefully on Caroline's head.

For the first time, Matt looked up and made real eye contact with Elena. There was a little bit of warmth in his eyes now, and his mouth turned up into a half-smile. 'Yeah, maybe,' he said. 'One of these days.'

Caroline's eyes were shining and she gripped her plastic sceptre as if it were made of pure gold. Elena leaned forward and hugged Matt.

And then, behind Matt, she finally saw Stefan. With

a satisfying sense of something slotting into place at last, her eyes locked with his. *This*, she thought. *All this time, I've been waiting for this.*

They were in a crowd of people, and his eyes were only on her. Just for now, couldn't she at least pretend he was hers?

CHAPTER

15

Stefan looked *perfect*. Under the dim auditorium lights, Stefan seemed so poised and handsome, his black blazer somehow better cut, more sophisticated than the other boys'. Elena couldn't make out the colour of his eyes, not from this far away, but she knew how green they were, and how, with his sunglasses finally stripped away, they must be broadcasting every emotion he felt.

Elena's chest tightened as raw longing shot through her. She suddenly felt like she was suffocating, the noise and heat of people pressing in around her. She sucked in a desperate gasp of air.

Stefan's eyes were fixed on hers as he began to make his way towards her through the crowd. Elena's heart fluttered in her chest. *No*. She wasn't even allowed to pretend. The connection between her and Stefan could kill them both.

'I have to go,' she muttered, and let go of Matt.

'Elena?' Matt called, but she was already turning on her heel and walking away, as fast as she could without actually running. *Stay calm*, she ordered herself, but she was panting, unable to catch her breath. She hit the swinging door hard and found herself out in the brightly lit, almost empty halls of the school.

Elena leaned against the cool metal of the row of lockers across from the door of the auditorium and closed her eyes for a moment.

She was never going to have Stefan again. All those years together, all they'd been through, and she couldn't even talk to him. All their history, wiped out. If she succeeded, it would never happen.

'Elena?' She knew that voice. Her eyes snapped open.

Stefan stood in front of her, his face soft with concern. 'I heard what Caroline said to you,' he said. 'Are you all right?'

Elena couldn't help laughing, a short, almost-sob of a laugh. 'You think I'm upset about *Caroline*?' she asked. It was so far off it was as if Stefan didn't know her at all. *Well, he doesn't, not now*, she thought, and the thought cut off her laugh. Sobering, she snapped, 'Whatever she thinks, I don't want anything Caroline has.'

Stefan touched her cheek, gently drawing her gaze

back to his, and a spark of electricity flew beneath Elena's skin at his touch. 'I know that,' he said. 'I know you don't care about all this. Popularity. Dances. I've watched you, Elena, and I can tell you're not thinking about those things. But I also know that you're *sad*.'

'Oh.' Tears stung the backs of Elena's eyes, and she squeezed them tightly closed again, shaking her head. 'Caroline's wrong about – well, almost everything. But, even if I don't want to be queen or date Matt, it's true that I can't have everything I want. And that hurts.'

'Maybe . . .' Stefan began, but his voice trailed off as Elena shook her head again, her mouth tight. She'd tried having everything, having both of the vampires she loved, more than once. It had taken her years to learn that trying to have both Damon and Stefan led to nothing but misery for all of them. She couldn't start down that road again, no matter how much she wanted to.

Stefan's oak-leaf green eyes were warm with sympathy, and his voice was soft. 'I understand, Elena. I can't have the thing I want most either.'

Elena couldn't help it. She leaned into his body, just a little, and Stefan's arms circled around her. Elena pressed her face against his shoulder. It was *Stefan*, Stefan who she'd missed so much.

Stefan let her cry, holding her while she shook for a few moments. Swallowing hard, Elena straightened up, her face back under control. Stefan's arms were still around her, as if he didn't want to let go.

'Sorry,' she said, sniffing. 'You must think I'm a lunatic.'

'Not at all,' Stefan said. He stroked her back gently, and Elena arched into his touch. 'Shall we dance?'

'What?' Elena blinked in surprise. Music was streaming softly through the closed door from the auditorium. Stefan slowly lifted Elena's arms and twined them around his neck, then wrapped his own arms around her waist.

'We can't have what we want,' he said with a note of longing in his voice. 'But we could dance, just for now. It is a dance, after all.'

They began to sway in time to the music and Elena leaned her head against the delicate fabric of Stefan's blazer. His strong hands were holding her so tenderly, and she knew that he was looking down at her with painful, aching love shining through his face, now that he knew she couldn't see him.

Stefan was drawn to her, had wanted and needed her from the very beginning. This was one thing Elena knew, one thing that had always been true between them. But he would let her go without a word, for her own good. To keep Elena safe.

Elena was swept up in a great wave of emotion, of love and pity and passion, all mixed together. This was *Stefan*. How could she turn away from him, even for Damon?

Winding her arms around Stefan's neck, his soft brown curls brushing against her fingers, Elena pulled back a little and looked up into his face. His eyes were dilated with passion, the black expanding across the green.

What if Elena's plan didn't work? What if, no matter how she tried, Damon was fated to kill Mr Tanner on Halloween night? Or worse, what if she gave up Stefan, undid their love, for *nothing*?

Elena pulled him closer. Stefan's lips parted in surprise and then, with an anguished look of surrender, he bent his head to hers. 'What are you?' he murmured against her lips. 'What is it about you?'

As their lips met, heat rushed through Elena's body. It felt so familiar, so right. Her Stefan. The rest of the world fell away.

Until a door burst open behind them.

'Elena?'

CHAPTER
16

Elena pulled out of Stefan's arms in a panic, stumbling backward as she put distance between them. What had she been *thinking*?

'Damon,' she said as she turned to face him. Her heart was hammering hard and she knew her voice sounded strained. 'This isn't what it looks like.'

Against the deadly pale of his skin, Damon's eyes blazed like black stars. In an instant, his face smoothly fell back into its customary detached irony. If Elena hadn't seen that momentary look of pain, she might have thought that there was a chance he'd listen to what she had to say.

Damon's lips tightened. 'Funnily enough, I think it's exactly what it looks like, Elena,' he said coolly. 'My little brother makes a habit of trespassing on my territory.' His eyes shifted, and then he was looking past Elena, as if she didn't matter, straight at Stefan. Stefan glared back, his jaw set stubbornly.

'As for you? I'll make you suffer,' Damon told him, his voice cold and clear, ringing through the deserted hallway. 'I told you I would kill you one day, and I will, but first I'm going to destroy everything you care about. You'll *beg* for death in the end.' He flashed a brilliant, scornful smile with no humour in it at all. Faster than Elena's eye could follow, he was gone.

'*Damon*!' Elena tried to scream after him, but her voice was thin with shock, and it came out more a squeak than anything else.

She'd been such a fool, giving in to her emotions, and now she had ruined *everything*.

Elena forced herself still and took a deep gulp of air. Maybe there was time to salvage this. If she could find Damon, if she could explain . . . Elena peered down the hall towards the shadowy corridors leading to the rest of the school. Where would Damon have gone? With a pang, she realised that she didn't know where he was living, had never known that sort of detail about this time in his life.

'Elena.' In her moment of panic, she'd almost forgotten about Stefan. He gripped her by the arm, his voice low and urgent. 'You need to get out of here. Find your friends and go somewhere safe, a house where Damon's never been. Take the flowers I gave you. If

Damon comes to you, whatever you do, whatever he says, *don't let him in*.'

Elena grabbed hold of Stefan's hand. 'I just need to talk to Damon.'

'It won't help,' he said grimly. 'Do what I told you, Elena, please.'

And, in the moments between one blink and another, he was gone too.

Elena swore, slamming her hand against a locker. Stefan was the *last* person who should be going after Damon now, and he ought to know that. But maybe he didn't care.

She took a deep breath and let it out slowly, then another, trying to calm her pounding heart.

Maybe Damon would go to Stefan's boarding house, looking for revenge. Or maybe she could figure out where he was staying. Damon liked luxury – she could check the nice hotel downtown and search for upscale, uninhabited houses. Inhabited ones too. He had hidden her in an attic once, Elena remembered. She let out a long, frustrated sigh.

Damon could be anywhere. But maybe, just maybe . . . Elena looked up and down the halls at the banners cheering on the football team, the dented lockers. Damon had never been one to run away from conflict. He could still be in the school.

And if so, Elena needed to find him, fast.

Elena headed back into the auditorium, music and

chatter swelling around her as she passed through the door. She waited for her eyes to adjust to the darkness as she scanned the crowd, trying to spot her friends.

She saw Meredith first, on the dance floor with a boy whose name Elena didn't know. Elena cut straight through the crowd towards them, putting her hand on Meredith's shoulder.

'I need your help. Please,' she said.

Meredith took one glance at her and nodded. 'I'll be back,' she said to her partner with a smile, and tugged Elena to the side of the dance floor, whispering, 'What? What's happened?'

'Let me get Bonnie and Matt first, and then I'll explain.' Elena had spotted Bonnie, deeper in the crowd on the dance floor. She was dancing with Raymond and getting into the music, her eyes closed and her hands up in the air above her head. Elena shouldered her way towards her, ignoring the grumbles as she shoved past people.

'Bonnie. Come with us.'

Bonnie opened her eyes and scowled. 'I'm *dancing*,' she said, without stopping.

'This is important.' Elena tried to put all the anxiety she was feeling into her face.

Bonnie sighed and rolled her eyes at Raymond. 'Girl stuff,' she said. 'I'll catch up with you later.'

'Seriously, what's going on? It couldn't wait?' she hissed at Elena as they reached the edge of the dance floor and the crowd thinned out a little.

Over at the refreshment table, Matt was pouring two cups of punch. Elena headed for him, Bonnie and Meredith trailing behind her. 'I need help finding Damon,' Elena said. 'He's here, and he saw me kissing Stefan.'

Matt's eyebrows shot up his forehead, and Bonnie and Meredith exchanged a confused glance.

'You were kissing *Stefan*?' Bonnie asked, in a tone midway between scandalised and intrigued.

'I'm not sure this qualifies as an emergency,' Meredith said drily. 'Maybe you should let him cool off and call him tomorrow.'

Matt remained quiet, not able to look Elena in the eye.

Elena felt sick. Of course they weren't panicking. As far as the three of them were concerned, Damon was just a guy she was dating, and Stefan was a guy who went to their school. Good-looking, intense, mysterious guys, but, when you came right down to it, only human beings. They didn't understand how dangerous Damon – *this* Damon, the Damon of now – could be.

'This isn't going to be OK!' she said, hearing her own voice wobble wildly.

'Oh, Elena—' At her outburst, Bonnie's eyes widened in sympathy, and she wrapped her arms around Elena. 'We'll help, whatever you need.' She looked fiercely at Meredith and Matt, as if daring them to disagree.

Meredith nodded in agreement, but Matt hesitated.

'I just— Caroline's waiting for me,' he said, gazing down at the two cups of punch he was still clutching.

'Go ahead and take them to her and then come and help us,' Meredith said firmly.

'Caroline will get over it,' Bonnie added, a smirk playing around the edges of her mouth.

Matt looked torn for a moment, and then his face firmed, his mind made up. 'I'll be back,' he said grimly, and marched off.

The three girls watched as he crossed the auditorium to where Caroline stood. At first, she smiled at Matt and accepted the cup of punch gracefully, as poised as a princess. Matt dipped his head to speak in her ear and, as she listened, Caroline's expression grew more and more thunderous. She snapped something back at him, and Matt replied. Then Caroline, clearly incandescent with rage, reared back and slapped Matt hard across the face.

'Oh my God,' Bonnie breathed.

Matt swung round and hurried back to them. 'I guess that's that,' was all he said. There was a red mark high on his cheekbone where Caroline had slapped him.

Elena slipped her hand into his big, warm one and squeezed, just for a second. 'Thank you.' She didn't deserve him; she knew that.

As she let go, Matt looked down at her, shaking his head slightly from side to side. 'I don't know why

I do the things I do for you, Elena Gilbert,' he said, but a rueful smile was beginning to tug at the corners of his mouth.

'Someday I hope to return the favour,' Elena said, then turned to her other friends. 'If we split up, we can search the school more quickly.' They pushed through the auditorium doors into the hall again. 'But if you see Damon, just come and get me; don't try talking to him. He's upset. If you see Stefan, try to get him to come back here.'

'So Stefan went after Damon?' Meredith asked, confused. 'Why? Do they even know each other?'

'They're brothers, but they don't get along very well,' Elena told her.

She dug into the tiny lipstick-red purse she carried. It didn't hold a lot – just essentials – but one thing in here might be crucial. 'Here.' She pulled out the withered bunch of vervain, now looking more like a bunch of wilted, dead weeds than ever, and quickly divided it into four small portions, a few strands of vervain in each.

'Um, why are you giving us dead plants?' Bonnie asked, holding hers doubtfully between her thumb and forefinger, her nose wrinkling.

'They're good luck,' Elena said, aware of how lame she sounded. 'Damon's very superstitious.'

They all stared at her but, with a shrug, Matt put his bunch into his suit jacket, and Meredith into her clutch.

Bonnie, who had no bag with her, tucked them behind her ear.

They split up, Matt and Bonnie heading down the hall towards the cafeteria, Meredith and Elena going the other way towards the office. As they walked, Elena glanced into every dim classroom, checking for Damon or Stefan.

'Maybe you should just let Damon calm down on his own,' Meredith said hesitantly, but Elena shook her head.

'I have to find him.' The longer she and Meredith looked, the more urgently Elena felt that time was running out. She knew Damon was only getting angrier by the minute.

Unease spread inside Elena, the feeling that someone was watching her from the shadows. The skin on the back of her neck crawled. She stopped to listen.

In the distance someone laughed, and quick footsteps ran down a nearby hallway. Probably just another student, someone ducking out of the dance. Elena took a deep breath and pushed open the next classroom door. No one.

'Do you really think—' Meredith began. She broke off as the fire alarm suddenly began to blare, a deafening screech. Despite herself, Elena jumped.

'Some kid always has to set it off and try to ruin everyone's good time,' Meredith half shouted over the alarm, disgusted.

Elena shook her head. She could smell smoke, faint and far away for now, but there. 'I don't think so,' she said. In the distance, she could hear frantic shouts, the principal's voice rising over the loudspeakers, directing everyone out of the building.

It was a real fire, she was sure of it. She was also sure that Damon had started it. Elena looked around wildly, searching for some clue to his whereabouts.

'Over here,' she said, picking a direction and hurrying forward. They hadn't looked in the theatre yet, maybe Damon – or Stefan – was there.

The smoke grew thicker as they made their way deeper into the school. 'Elena, stop!' Meredith called, her heels clicking against the floor as she ran after Elena.

'I'm sure he's down here,' Elena called back. Damon would want to see the chaos he had created. She could picture him, flames reflected in his dark eyes.

Meredith caught up to her, grabbing hold of Elena's arm with strong fingers. 'It's not safe,' she said. 'We have to get out of here.'

Meredith dragged Elena around the corner, but they were faced with a searing wave of heat. Flames licked the ceiling, melting the lockers like they were made of candle wax. Both girls shrieked as the fire crackled and grew.

'I need to find him,' Elena said, sobs beginning to rise in her throat, her eyes stinging from the smoke.

But as Meredith began to pull her towards the fire exit, Elena felt suddenly, horrifyingly sure that she was too late. She'd lost Damon. She'd failed.

CHAPTER
17

The windows of the school glowed red as flames within climbed the walls, reaching for the upper floors. The bricks of its façade were cracking in the heat. As Elena and her friends watched from the parking lot, a window shattered.

'Oh my God,' Bonnie said softly. The reflected flames made her pale face rosy. Next to her, Meredith leaned her head on Matt's shoulder, gazing wide-eyed into the flames.

It seemed like the teachers had got everyone out of the dance, smoke-smeared and dishevelled in the remains of their formal clothes. Near Elena's group, a girl sobbed hysterically, long streaks of soot crossing her face, while further away, one of the football players hacked drily, a casualty of the smoke.

Only a few minutes after Meredith and Elena had reached the parking lot, the fire trucks pulled in, sirens screaming. But by that time, the flames were already leaping high. Elena had heard Mr Landon, the science teacher, muttering about the electrical wiring of the old building, saying it was a deathtrap, but Elena knew better. This had to be Damon's work.

Elena jumped as another window shattered, this time under the blast of water from a fire hose. The firemen were putting up a good fight, dragging hoses across the parking lot, working together quickly and efficiently, and had at least contained the fire to only half of the school.

Elena looked around the circle of firelit faces. There was Caroline, her auburn head held high despite the flakes of black ash falling on the parking lot around her. Next to her, Sue Carson huddled under her boyfriend's suit jacket that she had pulled over her thin dress. Vickie Bennett was with a group of jocks and cheerleaders, all quiet and subdued. Even among the kids who hated the school, there were no cheers, no laughter. Everyone was shocked into silence.

An ambulance pulled into the lot, its blue light revolving. One of the paramedics got out and jogged across the lot towards a group of firefighters, calling, 'Everybody out?'

The firefighter called back in the affirmative, but Elena's breath caught. She swung round, searching desperately.

'Do you see Stefan anywhere?' she asked the others. They looked around too, their faces anxious.

Maybe he was gone before the fire started.

That didn't make sense though. Why would Damon start this fire, if Stefan hadn't been here? That was who he wanted to hurt most.

'We'd better tell the fire chief.' Matt strode off in the direction of the fire trucks.

That won't help.

Fire was one of the few things that could kill a vampire. There wasn't time for the firefighters to find Stefan. And if they did, it wouldn't be safe, for them or for him.

Elena straightened up, squaring her shoulders. There was no way she was standing uselessly by while Stefan died. Not again.

She had to get past the firefighters. They were grouped closest to the front of the building, where the fire was at its worst. Over at the side, the school was darker, deserted.

Elena shifted her feet, considering the best way to sneak around the building from where she stood.

'What are you doing?' Bonnie asked.

'I'm going to look for Stefan,' Elena told them.

'We'll come with you,' Meredith said quickly.

'No,' Elena said. 'You guys stay here and make sure Stefan isn't outside. If you see him, keep him with you.'

'Um, what if we see Damon?' Bonnie asked uneasily. 'Do you want us to tell him anything?'

Elena hesitated. Was there any message she could send through her friends that would lessen Damon's anger? She didn't think so. 'If you see him, just stay out of his way, OK?' she asked. He was probably long gone anyway.

She worked her way across the parking lot, sticking to the shadows. As she reached the edge of the lot, she walked between the trees on one side and the cars on the other, eyes on the corner of the school building.

'Get back, miss,' a fireman told her as he hurried past. She stepped away from the building, watching him until he had forgotten her and disappeared into the mass of men fighting the flames.

There was a puddle of water at her feet, left by one of the fire hoses. Elena knelt, fumbling at the hem of her dress. She felt a twinge of regret for her beautiful dress as she gripped the crimson silk with both hands and tore. A long strip of silk came off the bottom of the dress. She dipped it into the dirty water of the puddle, soaking the fabric thoroughly.

There was a crash from the far side of the building, something inside collapsing, and, in one motion, the crowd and the firefighters turned in that direction.

Elena seized her chance and ran, cold water dripping over her hand from the torn piece of her dress. Close up, the fire was *loud*. The flames roared, and the dry wood of the school building snapped and popped as it burned.

Around the corner, it was darker. The flames hadn't reached here yet. A fire exit gaped open, and Elena braced herself and stepped through.

The heat hit her like a wave. A haze of smoke hung in the air, and Elena pressed the wet silk over her nose and mouth to block it out. Her eyes began to water and ache.

Where would Damon have taken Stefan? Nowhere where the fire was burning yet, Elena thought. He would want Stefan's suffering more drawn out than that, would want him to hear the crackle of the flames, smell the smoke, and know that the deadly fire – one of the few things that *could* kill Stefan – was getting closer and closer, and that he had no hope of escape. Damon had said he wanted Stefan to suffer.

Of course. She cocked her head to look up the staircase ahead of her. It still looked stable enough. He'd be somewhere high enough that the smoke and heat would rise around him, where he'd feel the flames rising to lick against the floor beneath him. Damon would have put Stefan in the bell tower.

Elena climbed. The silk at her mouth filtered out the worst of the smoke but she still choked and gasped, each breath coming with more difficulty than the last. Heavy boots clumped through the halls on the other side of the building. Firefighters, she supposed, but she saw no one, just the heavy haze of smoke.

From somewhere below came the crash of a falling support beam, and the floor underfoot shook. Elena grabbed at the banister to steady herself, then sped up. She wobbled and her feet ached as she ran. High heels were no good for this but bare feet would be worse, so she had to keep going.

On the third floor, the staircase ended. She peered around, trying to spot the entrance to the bell tower through the worsening smoke. Her eyes burned, and she coughed – the wet silk was drying, it wasn't protecting her enough now.

There it was. She crossed the hall and laid her hand against the wood of the small door to the bell tower. It was cool still, no fire behind it. But the knob wouldn't turn.

It was locked; of course it was locked. The school didn't want the students messing around up here. Elena squeezed her eyes shut against the smoke. What was she going to do?

She tugged at the door again and then began to throw herself against it. She had to get through. 'Stefan!' she called. 'Stefan! Can you hear me?'

There was no answer.

The door wasn't made to withstand a continuous assault. Elena threw all her weight against it over and over, ignoring the bruises she could feel blossoming on her shoulder and side. At last, the flimsy lock broke and the door burst open. She tumbled through and fell to her knees, gasping and coughing.

Elena scrambled back to her feet and up the narrow rickety staircase to the top of the tower. Beneath the heavy bronze bell, archways opened on all four sides, and at last she could breathe. She staggered to one of the arches and took a few deep breaths, looking out over the parking lot below. Police cars were pulling in now, their red and blue lights flashing.

Her head was spinning less now that she had taken a few gulps of air, and Elena turned back round to look at the inside of the bell tower.

There was a weak motion, down in the darkest corner of the cupola. A small sound, barely more than a whimper. Elena crossed towards it and fell to her knees. There was a huddled dark shape there, and he shifted to stare up at her. Stefan mumbled something, his voice thick and choked.

'It's all right,' she said automatically, running her fingers soothingly through his hair. He was tied up and there was a band of fabric across his mouth, pulled viciously tight.

He flinched under her hand, scrabbling back towards the wall. He didn't seem to recognise her. She worked her hands beneath the gag, trying to untie its tight knot with her fingers. She couldn't loosen it.

She fumbled around on the floor, feeling in the dark for something sharp. The floor was hot beneath her hands and knees – the fire must be rising below them.

Her fingers closed around a sharp-edged stone, and she worked it against the gag, feeling the cloth's fibres rip. Finally it came loose and she pulled it away from Stefan's mouth.

As she removed the gag, something else spilled over his lips. Elena leaned closer, bracing herself with one hand on the rough brickwork above Stefan's head, squinting to see what was there.

Thin stalks of vervain sputtered out of Stefan's mouth. He gagged and choked as he spit them out. Anger rushed through Elena, as hot and sudden as a bolt of lightning.

'How *dare* he?' she muttered. 'How dare he?' Damon had stuffed his brother's mouth with vervain, muting his powers and muddling his mind. And then he had left him to die, alone, confused and in pain.

Heedless of Stefan's sharp canines this time, she used two fingers to scoop out more of the vervain clogging his mouth. One tooth scraped her finger stingingly but she barely noticed.

As his mouth emptied, she could hear Stefan breathing, long, ragged, hoarse breaths. She pushed her forefinger in again, checking that she had got every piece.

Stefan's tongue dragged slowly against her finger. Elena hesitated, and he latched on, sucking desperately at the cut on her finger.

After a moment, Stefan's eyelashes fluttered and his eyes slowly opened. He stared at Elena for a second before recognition filtered into his gaze. Abruptly, he pulled away.

'Elena,' he said roughly, and panic flashed across his pale face. 'I . . . don't know how to explain this.'

The bricks beneath Elena's knees were getting uncomfortably hot now. The fire must be climbing. 'We have to get out of here,' she said, her pulse pounding.

Stefan's eyes widened, and he strained visibly. The ropes around his wrists snapped first, and then the ones around his ankles. Without the vervain, they couldn't hold him. He began, slowly, to climb to his feet. 'Is the door blocked?' he asked.

'I-I think so,' Elena said. 'The fire was spreading really fast.'

Stefan shook his head as if he was shaking off the last of the vervain's effects. 'Trust me,' he said. Drawing Elena up into his arms, Stefan climbed into the archway.

Holding her tightly, Stefan leaped into the night.

CHAPTER

18

'Who *are* you?' Stefan asked. 'How did you find me tonight?' After their leap from the school, he'd brought her back to his room at Mrs Flowers' boarding house. He leaned against the wall by the window, his finely drawn features so pale they could have been carved out of marble.

Elena clasped her hands in her lap. 'I knew that Damon must have started the fire, and, after what he said to you, I had a feeling that he wouldn't have let you make it out,' she said slowly.

Stefan pinched the bridge of his nose between two fingers, as if his head hurt. 'And how do you know Damon?'

'I met him in the graveyard.' It seemed wise to stick to the simplest answer.

Coming a step closer, Stefan narrowed his eyes. 'You knew what was going on with the vervain. It didn't surprise you or scare you when we leaped from the bell tower, or when I fed from you. You know what Damon and I are.'

There was something threatening about Stefan now as he almost loomed above her. Elena raised her hands in surrender, doing her best to look harmless. 'I'm not your enemy,' she said. 'Yours or Damon's. I only want to help.'

She hoped that her sincerity shone through. All she wanted to do was to save them both.

Stefan leaned back against the wall. Rubbing a hand across his face, he laughed, a miserable, rough laugh. 'There's nothing *to* help, Elena. Damon and I are monsters, and the sooner we get out of this town the better off everyone else will be. If I leave here, he'll follow me. You'll be safe.' Shaking his head, he added, 'I should have known better than to try, to pretend to be human.'

'No, Stefan, please.' Elena was out of her chair without even thinking about it. Reaching out to take Stefan's hands in her own, she squeezed them tightly. 'It wasn't a mistake.' He shook his head and started to pull away, and Elena stepped closer still, looking up into his eyes. 'We can work together. We can keep Damon under control. You don't have to be alone.'

Stefan eyes grew darker as he held Elena's gaze. And

then he bent his head to her lips. For a moment, it was as if the whole world was just the two of them, heat rushing through Elena's body.

It was all so familiar. They were both filthy and stinking of smoke, but it could have been the night of their first Homecoming – when Stefan had rescued her from Tyler in the graveyard and brought her here. Maybe it was destiny after all. They were always going to end up here, tired and drained, secrets stretching the space between them.

At the thought, Elena pulled away, suddenly cold as she stepped out of Stefan's arms.

'I'm sorry,' Elena stammered. 'I didn't mean . . . I can't do this right now.' She felt as if the world was shifting under her feet.

Stefan turned away so she couldn't quite see his face. 'I apologise,' he said. 'I'll take you home.'

Elena followed him down the darkened stairway, brushing her fingers against her lips. *This is all my fault*, she thought as she left the boarding house and crossed the dirt driveway to Stefan's low, black Porsche. If she hadn't kissed Stefan, if Damon hadn't seen her, things between them wouldn't be deteriorating. The school wouldn't have burned down today.

Stefan's car was just as smooth and luxurious a ride as Damon's. The engine's purr was the only sound in the car as Elena and Stefan sat silently, each wrapped in their own thoughts. Stefan's eyes were fixed on the road and his body was stiff with tension. Elena sighed and wrapped her arms around herself.

How could Stefan and Damon hate each other so much? Elena thought of the rueful affection she'd seen grow between the brothers over the past few years in her own life. They played pool together. They fenced and played cards, all the entertainments they'd both learned to pass the time over the centuries. They fought side by side, graceful and deadly.

The brothers always came back together when it mattered most. They'd saved each other's lives more than once.

Elena remembered Damon's fury after Stefan's death. And more, she remembered the pure despair on his face, the way he had looked as he told her that now there was no one, no one at all, who remembered him when he was alive, when he was a human. He'd lost his past.

How had they got from *here* to *there*?

Then, as Stefan's car purred around the corner on to Elena's street, she finally got it. The loneliness in Stefan's eyes, his room carefully designed for one monastic, solitary life. Damon's vicious hatred for his little brother, paired with the fact that, wherever Stefan went, Damon watched him from afar. Even in tonight's fire, Damon had left him far away from the flames. If Stefan hadn't got away, would Damon have come back for him?

They always came back to each other.

Stefan and Damon were each other's *family*, all they had left. And all their love and history might have got tangled up into one big ball of resentment and anger, but that didn't mean it wasn't still there. She knew it was still there. She'd seen it in the future, as strong as ever.

Maybe it wasn't Elena who had changed Damon, back in her own time. Mylea had said that love would save Damon, would save them all. But it wasn't Elena's love that would do it.

From now on, she realised with a blinding flash, she wasn't going to try to make Damon fall in love with her.

Instead, she needed to fix Stefan and Damon. If they could just be *brothers* again, everything else would fall into place.

Stefan pulled up in front of Elena's house and stopped. Her front door flew open, and Aunt Judith and Robert rushed out on to the lawn. No doubt they'd heard about the fire.

Before she opened the car door to reassure them, Elena turned to Stefan and laid her hand over his.

'I know what we have to do now. We can fix everything,' she told him, feeling strong and sure. 'Tomorrow, we're going to look for Damon.'

CHAPTER

19

Dear Diary,

I woke up this morning and I wished I were dead.

Not really, I suppose. If I meant it, I would just let things take their course. Grab at the chance of a brief happiness with Stefan, knowing that it will lead to so much suffering, to the destruction of all three of us.

But Damon was so full of anger. The way he looked at me when he found me in Stefan's arms – he never looked at me that way before, even when things between us were at their worst. Like he hated me.

Elena glanced at the clock. She needed to leave for

school soon. Downstairs she could hear the familiar clatter of Aunt Judith making breakfast. It felt so much like the morning when Damon had driven her to school, when it had seemed like everything was falling into place. She began to write again.

I refuse to believe that I've ruined everything.

If I can just show Damon how much Stefan still loves him, how much they need each other, maybe things will turn out OK after all. I have to believe that. I can't give up on us, not yet.

'One day off,' Bonnie fumed, flicking her red curls over her shoulder as the two girls crossed the parking lot together. 'We go through a completely traumatising event and they can't give us even one day off.'

'It's amazing how quickly they pulled all this together though,' Elena commented. In daylight she could see that the school hadn't *entirely* burned down.

One side of the building, where the office and most of the classrooms were, was charred and half collapsed. Elena couldn't suppress a shudder as she looked at the bell tower. The staircase she had climbed to find Stefan must be entirely gone. But the other side, where the auditorium and cafeteria were, looked mostly solid even though stained a dirty grey by the smoke. The heavy smell of ash hung over everything.

Behind the school now stood a row of temporary white trailers to be used as classrooms for the rest of the year, until the school could be rebuilt. All around the trailers, students gathered in groups, leaning eagerly towards each other to gossip. Harried administrators were trying to shepherd everyone into the right trailers. Everything seemed to be in only slightly controlled chaos.

'See you later,' Bonnie called as she veered off into chemistry, and Elena found the trailer where her trig class was. Meredith was already there, her homework laid out neatly in front of her.

As Elena settled into the desk beside her, Meredith looked up with a worried frown. 'Have you heard the gossip?' she asked. 'Everyone's saying that Stefan started the fire.'

Elena remembered with a twinge of dismay the low, excited, I've-got-a-secret tone to the whispers before class.

They'd been here before. It might start at the high school, but the rumours would spread all over town. Adults would get upset. Stefan would be shunned.

'That's ridiculous,' she said sharply.

Meredith bit her lip. 'There's no real evidence. Everyone used to think the way he keeps to himself was romantic, but now they're saying it's creepy. He disappeared from the dance right before the fire started.'

'So did *we*,' Elena objected.

'We were all together.' Meredith dipped her head, shuffling the papers around on her desk. 'I don't want to believe it, but it is strange how Stefan disappeared. When Matt told the firefighters that Stefan wasn't there, they started searching for him to make sure he wasn't in the building. You said you didn't see him when you looked either.'

Elena winced. It had seemed simpler when she got home just to call Bonnie and Meredith and tell them she had given up and decided to leave. Now it was too late to pretend to have run into Stefan.

'They found him back at his boarding house. When the police questioned him he was *covered* in smoke and ash.' Meredith raised her head, her grey eyes troubled. 'I'm not saying Stefan did anything. And I promise not to tell anyone that Damon was there either. But maybe you should stay away from both of them, Elena.'

'Anybody could have set that fire!' Elena said, her voice a little too loud. The teacher looked up from her desk enquiringly, and Elena lowered her voice. 'It was probably somebody sneaking a cigarette.'

Meredith's forehead creased in concern. 'Elena, you don't even know Stefan. You've been avoiding him since he started school. And then, suddenly, you've kissed him – *once* – and now you won't hear anything against him? I thought you were with Damon.'

'I am, but—' Elena began.

'OK, time to stop the chatter and review your homework assignments,' Ms Halpern said, stepping up to the front of the room. With one more worried glance,

Meredith turned away from Elena to face the teacher.

Elena chewed on her lip. This was worse than the first time she had been here. Then, everyone had started suspecting Stefan of being responsible for Mr Tanner's murder after Halloween. The gossip had spread until, despite the lack of any real evidence, everyone was convinced Stefan was the killer. Aunt Judith had banned Elena from seeing Stefan, and some of the adults in town – Tyler's dad, especially – had been ready to form a lynch mob and attack him.

Now, because of Elena, all the suspicion and hatred for Stefan was starting earlier. And, that time, at least Meredith and Bonnie had been on her side. They hadn't had any more proof of Stefan's innocence then than they did now, but they had believed Elena when she swore he was innocent. They'd believed her because they knew she knew Stefan.

Elena wrapped her arms around herself, suddenly cold. If Fell's Church turned against Stefan earlier, maybe it would all happen earlier. Was Elena doomed to drive off Wickery Bridge and drown, no matter what she did? She could almost feel that icy dark water rising around her.

Was it hopeless for her to try to fight fate? Was Stefan doomed to die? Would Elena end up back in that cold grey in-between place, heading for death?

The rest of the morning, Elena kept an eye out for Stefan whenever she moved from one trailer classroom to another, but she never saw him. Crowds of students gathered on the crumbling black asphalt between the trailers, talking in low, excited voices. Elena hoped Stefan had come to school today. Nothing would fan the flames of the rumour as much as if it seemed Stefan was hiding.

When she got to history class, Stefan's seat was empty. Elena's shoulders slumped. Mr Tanner began to lecture about the English Civil War, and Elena stared down at her notebook, her eyes stinging.

'I see you've decided to grace us with your presence, Mr Salvatore.' Mr Tanner's voice was whip-sharp. Elena lifted her head.

Stefan, grim-faced, hesitated in the doorway. Mr Tanner waved an arm in an exaggerated gesture of courtesy. 'Please, take a seat,' he said. 'We're all so glad you decided to wander in.'

Stefan sat down without glancing at Elena. He bent his head over his desk. His shoulders were stiffly set, betraying his awareness of the gossip and hatred buzzing around him. Elena sighed. He probably thought it was deserved, even though he hadn't started the fire. Stefan, the Stefan of now, thought he was a monster and that people *should* fear and hate him.

Elena sat up straight and glared around the classroom. The girls beside Stefan, who had been nudging each other and whispering, exchanged a glance and turned back to their books with new interest.

Caroline, though, stared straight back at Elena, her lips turning up in a smirk. Tilting her head, she whispered something to the girl next to her, her eyes never leaving Elena's, and her smile widened. She and the other girl both laughed.

At least Dick and Tyler's desks were empty, since they were still suspended. It was Tyler who had whipped up a frenzy against Stefan last time. Tyler was a bully, he always had been. Elena sighed and pressed a hand against her forehead.

Was everything bound to slide towards the same ends, no matter what she did? Were some things inevitable?

No. She couldn't believe that. She pulled back her shoulders and sat up straight, running a cold eye over Caroline, who was still smirking. When the other girl finally looked away, Elena felt a jolt of satisfaction. Elena was still the queen of the school after all.

When class finally ended, Elena shot out of her seat and grabbed Stefan's arm, pulling him aside before he could leave the trailer classroom.

'You're not afraid to be seen with me?' he asked softly, his head down, eyes fixed on the ugly grey carpeting of the trailer. 'They're right not to trust me, Elena.'

'Don't be ridiculous,' she told him, meeting the hostile looks of the other students as they edged past. Bonnie hesitated in the doorway, eyeing Stefan, and

Elena gave her a quick, reassuring smile.

'Call me later,' Bonnie said pleadingly as she left.

Once the trailer was empty, Elena turned back to Stefan. She was still gripping his jacketed arm, so tightly that her fingers ached, but he barely seemed to notice. 'We don't have much time,' she told him. 'We need a game plan. We need to get Damon under control.'

Stefan huffed a short, bitter laugh. 'Damon's never under control.'

'Stefan, look at me,' Letting go of his sleeve, Elena reached up and framed Stefan's face with her hands. His skin was cool and his cheekbones were strong and wide beneath her fingers. She waited for him to bring his eyes up to meet hers, her heart beating hard as the connection between them slid into place, that sense of recognition and almost magnetic attraction. His face cradled in her hands, Stefan blinked as if he was seeing her for the first time.

'Don't give up,' she said, trying to put the weight of all the secret knowledge she had – all the things she couldn't tell him in words – behind what she said. 'You're the only one who can change things with your brother. I believe in you.'

Stefan gently pulled away from her hands, and Elena ached as their contact broke. His face was sorrowful. 'I don't think that Damon can change,' he said. 'But I think I know where he is.'

CHAPTER

20

Unlike the neatly maintained, modern part of the graveyard where Elena's parents lay, the section dating back to the Civil War was overgrown and crumbling. Long creepers draped themselves across worn grey tombstones and the ground was uneven beneath Elena's feet. Half-broken weeping saints and angels loomed overhead, and the dark, iron-barred fronts of the mausoleums gave Elena the sense that anyone could be watching them.

'I don't understand why you think Damon would be *here*,' she said, stumbling over a broken tombstone hidden in the grass. She grabbed Stefan's arm to keep from falling.

'This is exactly the place Damon would be,' Stefan

said, his gaze moving watchfully from the ruined church to a mausoleum half concealed by overgrown yew trees. 'He thinks acting like a creature of the night is funny. He wants death all around him.'

Elena frowned. It didn't really sound like Damon to *her*. The Damon she knew liked clean, modern lines. And he loved luxury. He didn't stay anywhere long, but the houses and apartments she'd seen Damon live in were rich and elegant. He filled them with every possible comfort but almost nothing personal, nothing he wouldn't be willing to leave behind. He didn't court the trimmings of death.

Stefan glanced down at her with a slight, bitter smile. 'How well do you know my brother really, Elena? You see what he wants you to see.'

Elena shook her head, but didn't answer. Stefan had a point. If she really had met Damon just a few weeks ago, how well could she have known him?

Elena's eyes lingered on the ruined church. It was half collapsed, with most of the roof fallen in. Only three of its walls were standing.

Katherine was underneath there, in the old church's crypt. She might be watching them at this very moment. There was no trace of fog, no cold wind, no blue-eyed white kitten prowling in the dead grass around the church. If Katherine was there, she was lying low, content to watch for now.

When Stefan turned towards the church, Elena

nudged him away. 'Let's look in the mausoleums,' she said.

The grim mausoleums made of granite and iron were scattered around the old churchyard. Each housed the bones of a family of original settlers of Fell's Church. They were dark and forbidding now, overgrown with ivy, their flagstone paths pitted by time. One had the Gilbert name – Elena's father's family – but she didn't know much about the people whose bones laid there, except that one had been a young soldier killed in the Civil War.

Elena and Stefan slipped into an easy routine, working their way clockwise from one mausoleum to the next around the churchyard. Elena would stand lookout while Stefan forced each narrow door.

There was no sign of Damon in the Gilbert mausoleum, only three grey stone coffins and a dusty vase, which must have once been used for flowers. The space inside was claustrophobically narrow, its air stale, and Elena was glad to back out again after one quick look.

Surely if Damon were living here, he would have chosen her family's mausoleum, as some sort of elaborate tease. Elena stumbled as they moved on to the next small tomb, and Stefan steadied her. 'Careful,' he said. 'The ground's uneven.'

Elena cast a glance across to the newer part of the graveyard. 'I'm more worried about someone catching us vandalising graves than I am about tripping,' she said.

Stefan cocked his head, sending Power out around the graveyard. 'There's no one here,' he said. He looked drawn and tired. He probably hadn't fed recently enough to be able to Influence anyone into forgetting about them if they were caught breaking into the tombs.

Elena stood by the next mausoleum and looked up at the ruins of the church as she listened to the grating noise of Stefan forcing the tomb's door. At least she had the rest of the vervain in her pocket. If Katherine came out of the catacombs, she wouldn't be able to Influence Elena.

'There,' Stefan said with satisfaction. Elena stopped staring at the church and jostled her way in beside him.

It was as grey and dusty as the others had been, but the tops of the two tombs inside had been swept clean. On one sat a pile of neatly folded dark clothing. Elena rifled through it: all black, all designer, all clearly expensive. Some of them she had seen Damon wearing. The other tomb held a folded blanket and a thin leather-bound book.

Elena picked up the book. It was in Italian, and seemed to be a book of verse. 'Stefan, what—' she began. A loud groan of rusted metal interrupted her and, before she could move, the door to the tomb slammed shut. A huge thud followed, something terribly heavy slamming into the outside of the mausoleum. The small building shook and Elena screamed, a high, thin noise.

Then there was silence. With the door closed, it was pitch-black inside the tomb. For a moment, Elena could hear nothing but the pounding of her own heart. From the other side of the tomb, Stefan swore.

'Stefan?' Elena asked, her voice rising.

Starting towards Stefan and the tomb's door, she banged her elbow hard against something in the dark. 'Ouch,' she said, and rubbed at it, tears prickling at the back of her eyes.

'Keep still,' Stefan said. She didn't even hear him coming towards her, but suddenly he was touching her gently, running his hands over her arm.

'I don't think anything's broken,' he told her. 'You'll have a bruise though.'

'Are we stuck in here?' Elena's voice wavered, despite herself. She was suddenly, terrifyingly aware of the dead all around her. The tomb she stood beside was full of mouldering bones.

There was a short pause and then Stefan spoke, sounding grimmer than before. 'Damon's shut us in. I tried the door, but I can't force it. There must be something jammed up against it, holding it closed.'

'Oh.' For the first time, Elena noticed how cold it was inside the mausoleum, the cold of a stone place that never felt the sun. She shivered.

'We'll find a way out of here,' Stefan said, his voice

lightening. 'Or someone will come.' Suddenly his hands were around her waist and he lifted her gently. In a second, she was sitting on the cold top of the tomb, and Stefan was beside her, wrapping his jacket around her shoulders.

For a while, they sat in silence. Stefan was reassuringly solid beside her and, after a while, Elena let herself lean slightly against him.

Who would come for them? It was rare that someone came into this part of the cemetery, even rarer after dark, and night was coming. Elena felt a clutch of panic in her chest, and her breath got shorter. She didn't want to stay here.

'Stefan,' she said. She turned her head towards his.

'What is it, Elena?'

'There is a way for you to get us out of here.' She brushed her hair away from her neck, dipping her head in a clear invitation.

Stefan's breath caught and he shifted away, his slight warmth disappearing from her side. When he spoke again, he sounded choked. 'I can't.'

'You can. If you're going to save us, you need the strength my blood will give you.'

'Elena.' Stefan sounded panicked, and she automatically reached for his hand in the dark to reassure him. 'I haven't fed from a human being for a long time. I tried once, not long ago' – *The man under the bridge*, Elena's mind supplied – 'and I couldn't control myself. I don't want to hurt you.'

'You won't,' Elena told him, hanging on to his cold hand. 'I trust you.' He still hesitated, and she added, 'It's the only way out of here, Stefan.'

With a small, soft sigh of surrender, Stefan bent his head to her throat.

It had been so *long* since she had been with Stefan like this. Elena's eyes filled with tears of joy and sorrow at the familiar twin pricks of pain as his canines slid beneath her skin. His lips were gentle against her throat, and his pulse was speeding to pound in time with hers.

Elena tried to hold back the memories that were tumbling through her mind: the night she had pledged to be Stefan's for ever – *sleek and elegant in his best suit, his eyes wide and wondering, greener than ever*; the first night they had kissed, after Homecoming in that other world – *the look of helpless desire as he bent his head to hers* – the incredulity and horror in his face when she was reborn as a vampire and at first forgot who they were to each other – *the pure defeat on his face as he let her claw at him*. The life they'd built together. The warmth and comfort she'd found in his arms as he'd held Elena close.

Even though she kept the memories from him, Elena couldn't help some of her emotions pouring through the careful wall they'd constructed between them. Love and tenderness and regret. Pain and joy. Guilt. Passion.

It was enough that, as he slowly withdrew his canines from her throat, Stefan cupped her face for a moment, his fingers cool against her skin. She could see nothing through the darkness, but Elena thought he was staring into her eyes. 'Who *are* you?' he whispered, just as he had the night of the fire.

'Someone who cares about you,' Elena whispered. *Please*, she thought desperately, *please let me save him*.

Stefan's hand lingered on Elena's face for a moment, just a gentle brush of skin on skin, and then he was gone.

Over at the door, Elena heard a great, creaking crash, and then light appeared, flooding through the crack as Stefan forced the door open. There was a rustling, the sound of breaking branches, and finally a huge thud.

'You can come out now,' Stefan said, a dark shape against the light of the doorway.

Elena came through, squinting. It was brisk outside, although not with the heavy bone-chilling cold of the tomb, and the sun was setting. It was almost dark, really; it just seemed bright after the pitch blackness.

A huge oak tree lay across the churchyard, its branches brushing the door of the mausoleum where they had been trapped. It had been ripped out of the ground; Elena could see the great pit in the earth left by its roots.

'It was jammed up against the door,' Stefan told her.

Now that Elena's eyes had adjusted to the evening light, she noticed the long, already healing scrapes on his arms from the tree's branches. Stefan gazed past her and Elena turned, following his eyes to the dent in the mausoleum's stone façade, where the tree had slammed against it.

There was so much rage in the way the tree had been torn out of the earth and thrown against the stone tomb. Elena's stomach twisted nervously. She might love Damon, but he had no love left for them.

CHAPTER

21

It was fully dark by the time Elena slipped through her front door. She could feel her whole body relax at being home at last. The tall Victorian house where she'd lived since she was born felt clean and bright and warm, its heavy curtains shutting out the darkness. From the kitchen, she could hear the clatter of pans and smell a chicken roasting.

'Dinner in twenty minutes,' Aunt Judith called cheerfully. Elena called back an acknowledgement, staring at herself in the mirror by the door. She looked tired and dishevelled, her hair matted and a streak of dirt across her forehead. There was a purpling bruise on her throat where Stefan had bitten her, twin dots of dried blood in its centre, and she pulled her shirt collar up to cover it.

'You're home!' Margaret thudded down the stairs and leaped towards Elena, catching her around the waist in a bear hug. 'I missed you.'

'I missed you too,' Elena said, laughing. 'All day long.' She bent to press her cheek against her little sister's soft hair and breathed in the Play-Doh and baby shampoo scent of her.

Pulling away, Margaret grinned up at her. 'Your friend came over looking for you,' she said. 'He gave me this.' She pulled a lollipop out of her pocket and waved it in triumph.

Elena examined the candy. It was a pink rose made out of thin slivers of almost-translucent hard candy. 'Pretty,' she said. 'Matt gave you this?' Matt had a soft spot for Margaret and he was always bringing her little treats.

'No, your friend Damon gave it to me,' Margaret said, and tried to take the lollipop back.

A wave of panic washed over Elena, and her fingers tightened automatically on the candy. Elena had invited him into her home. How could she have been so stupid?

'Give it,' Margaret said, pulling on the candy.

'No, wait,' Elena said, but Margaret yanked the lollipop out of her hand, pulled it out of the wrapper and defiantly stuck it into her mouth before Elena could snatch it back.

It was wrapped, Elena reassured herself as she watched her baby sister eat the candy with evident enjoyment.

Poison wasn't really Damon's style. If he had wanted to hurt Margaret or Aunt Judith, he would have done it more directly. No, this had just been a warning. Damon was letting Elena know that he could get to her family whenever he wanted.

'Listen to me, Margaret,' she said, squatting so that she was eye to eye with her little sister. 'Damon's not my friend, OK? If he comes here again, stay away from him.'

Margaret frowned. 'He was really nice,' she said. 'I don't know why you don't want to be friends with him.'

Was it Margaret saying this, or was it something Damon had told her to say, Elena wondered. What if Damon had used his Power to Influence her little sister? She looked into Margaret's sky-blue eyes, trying to see if there was anything off about her, any sign that her words were not her own.

The Damon that Elena loved wouldn't have used his Power on a child, Elena thought. He would have considered it ungentlemanly and beneath him. With a heavy, sick feeling, she admitted to herself that she didn't know exactly what the Damon of this time was capable of.

'Meggie, can you come and put the napkins on the table for me, please?' Aunt Judith called from the kitchen, and Margaret twisted out of Elena's hands and was gone without a word.

Elena headed up the stairs, her steps slow and heavy. She had to think. There must be some way to get Aunt Judith and Margaret away from here. She couldn't let them get hurt, and she couldn't let Damon use them as pawns to hurt Elena.

By the time she reached the top of the stairs, Elena had made up her mind. She went into the bathroom and grabbed a towel. Pulling off one of her shoes, she wrapped the towel around it and then opened the hall window. Outside, the branches of the quince tree almost brushed the window frame. It was close enough that someone could conceivably climb inside, although it would be a dangerous stretch.

Bracing herself, she slammed the heel of the shoe against the window's catch. The towel muffled the sound of the blow, but not as much as Elena had hoped. She paused and listened. Aunt Judith was running water downstairs, and under the noise of the water Elena could hear both the television and Margaret singing to herself. Trusting in the noise downstairs to cover the thuds, Elena slammed the heel of her shoe against the window catch again and again until it finally bent and twisted, breaking.

With a sharp crack, the pane of glass below the catch shattered, broken glass falling in shards on to the hall carpet. Elena froze. She hadn't expected that. Still, maybe it made the whole scene more convincing.

Quickly and quietly, Elena picked up a silver

candlestick from the windowsill. She took a carved jade box from a little table in the hall and a small marble figure of an angel that her parents had once brought home from Italy from another. Hurrying into her room, she slipped her shoe back on, wrapped the objects in the towel and shoved the bundled towel deep into her closet.

After one last glance around to make sure everything was concealed, she went back to stand in front of the broken hall window, took a deep breath and screamed.

There was a sudden, shocked silence downstairs, followed by a flurry of movement. 'Elena?' Aunt Judith called worriedly, running up the stairs. 'What happened? Are you all right?'

Elena turned to meet her as she reached the top of the stairs. 'I think someone broke in,' she said. She was so full of dread that it was easy to infuse the words with fear.

As Elena pointed them out, Aunt Judith examined the broken catch, the smashed windowpane, and the spots where knickknacks were missing from the hall. Looking in her own room and Elena's, she saw that nothing else seemed to be missing.

'I don't know,' she said finally, doubtfully. 'A branch could have blown against the window and broken it. It seems strange to me that a thief would take just three little objects, and nothing else. All my jewellery's still here, and I had some money on my dresser that's completely untouched.'

Elena wanted to scream with frustration. She didn't have to try hard at all to bring tears to her eyes or a waver to her voice.

'Please, Aunt Judith,' she said. 'I really don't think any of us should sleep here tonight. Can't you and Margaret go to Robert's, at least until we can get someone to fix the window? Anyone could come in.'

Aunt Judith hesitated. 'What about you, Elena?' she asked. 'I'm certainly not going to leave you here all alone.'

'I can go to Meredith's,' Elena said quickly. 'It's closer to school, and her parents won't mind.'

Convincing Aunt Judith was agonising. A hundred times, her aunt wondered if they were just being hysterical and almost changed her mind about leaving the house. Once she *had* finally agreed to leave, she insisted on them all sitting down and eating dinner together first.

Elena could barely nibble the juicy roast chicken even though she recognised that it was delicious. Her eyes kept straying to the darkness beyond the dining-room windows. Was Damon out there? She could imagine him in his crow form, huddled on a branch and watching her with bright, malicious eyes.

By the time Robert's grey Volvo turned into the drive, Elena felt like she was almost bursting out of her skin with anxious, restless energy. They had to *go*. They had to get away, before it was too late.

Grabbing her sister with one hand and both their bags with the other, Elena hustled Margaret out to the car, ignoring her protests, and buckled her securely into her booster seat.

'Do you want me to check the window?' Robert said, politely getting out of the car to take Aunt Judith's bag and open the passenger's side door for her.

'No!' said Elena sharply before Aunt Judith could answer. When they both looked at her in surprise, she gave them a small, weak smile. 'Sorry. I'm just so nervous. Can't we get out of here?'

As they pulled out of the driveway, Elena settled watchfully in the back seat next to Margaret, her overnight bag clutched in her lap. She felt sure that nothing would happen to them on the drive over to Meredith's. And then, after they dropped her off, she could only hope that Damon would lose interest in them. At least he'd never been invited into Robert's house. Getting Aunt Judith and Margaret as far away from her as she could seemed like the only way to protect them.

'This is the best part,' Bonnie said as she rolled on to her stomach on Meredith's bed, her eyes fixed on the TV screen a few feet away. 'After he kisses her, you know they're going to get past all the stuff that came between them.'

'I still think she should have ended up with her friend instead,' Meredith said critically from where she leaned against the headboard. 'That was the first ending, you know, and the test audiences hated it so much that they reshot it.'

'And rightly so,' Bonnie said. 'Bleah.'

Elena laughed and jostled against her. 'There's nothing wrong with him. I think he's cute.'

'Bleah,' Bonnie said again, wrinkling her nose.

The sick, dread-filled feeling in the pit of Elena's stomach hadn't gone away for a moment. But, despite all of that, it was good to be here once more. When Bonnie had heard that Elena was spending the night, she had invited herself over too. The warm smell of baking cookies rose comfortingly from the kitchen downstairs.

'Hey, would you plait my hair?' Bonnie asked, as the couple on screen finally kissed.

'Sure,' Elena said, and Bonnie wiggled around so that her back was to Elena.

'Do you want a French plait?' Elena asked. Bonnie nodded, and Elena began separating the curling strands of Bonnie's hair just as the oven timer went off downstairs.

'I've got it,' Meredith said, hopping up.

'Wait, I'll come with you,' Elena told her, letting go of Bonnie's curls.

'I think I can handle it,' Meredith said wryly.

After a moment of hesitation, Elena took hold of Bonnie's hair again. This was Meredith's house and Damon wasn't invited in. She would be fine.

'So . . .' Bonnie said playfully as Meredith left the room. 'Who's the better kisser, Stefan or Damon?'

Elena winced. 'It's not that easy.'

'Easy or not, I bet they're both pretty good, aren't they?' Bonnie asked. Elena could hear the cheeky grin in her voice.

Heat flooded Elena's cheeks. She thought of the nostalgic emotions that had washed through her as Stefan had kissed her, and, darker and more intimate, the way it had felt when Damon had drunk her blood. 'Yeah,' she admitted in a tiny voice.

'Uh-huh,' Bonnie said smugly. Then she twisted round to look at Elena, her brown eyes bright with sincerity. 'If you say Stefan didn't start the fire, I believe you, Elena.'

'I know he didn't,' Elena said.

'*Mmm*. He's much too cute to be a psycho.'

Elena laughed despite herself. 'I'm not sure that's the best way to tell.'

She busied herself twining Bonnie's hair into an elegant plait. 'There,' she said, after a few minutes. 'Gorgeous.'

Bonnie bounced to her feet. Going to the full-length mirror hanging on the back of Meredith's closet door, she turned her head from side to side, admiring herself.

'Nice. Thank you.'

As she watched Bonnie, Elena became aware of a niggling sense of something not quite right.

'Does it seem to you like Meredith's taking a really long time?' she asked.

Eyes still on her own reflection, Bonnie lifted one shoulder in a shrug. 'I know, right?' she said. 'How long does it take to put some cookies on a plate? I'm starving.'

'That's not what I mean,' Elena began, and then the door opened and her shoulders sagged with relief. Meredith was back.

'About time,' Bonnie said cheerfully, and grabbed a cookie.

'Careful, they're hot,' Meredith said, smiling. Then she caught Elena's eye and her smile faded. 'What's wrong?'

Elena felt like she was frozen in place. Looped around Meredith's neck was a deep-red scarf that she certainly hadn't been wearing when she went downstairs.

'Why are you wearing that?' she said, her voice cracking. 'Take it off.'

Bonnie and Meredith looked at each other, their eyebrows lifting. 'Um . . . Elena?' Bonnie asked. 'What are you talking about?'

'The scarf!' Elena insisted. 'Take it off right now!' She should have gone downstairs with Meredith. It had been stupid of her to think they would be safe, just because Damon hadn't yet been invited into Meredith's house. Even if he hadn't had his Power, Damon would have been able to charm and talk his way into almost anywhere. *With* all the Power at his command, all he would have to do was ask. And Meredith was defenceless: she didn't even know that Damon was someone to be afraid of.

'I don't know what your problem is, Elena,' Meredith grumbled, slowly unwrapping the scarf from around her throat. 'I was cold, OK? It's freezing downstairs. And I think this looks nice.'

Elena stared. Unwilling to trust her eyes, she went closer and, ignoring Meredith's startled objections, brushed the other girl's hair aside and inspected her neck. It was smooth and unmarked. No vampire had touched her.

'Hey!' Meredith finally said, stepping back and staring at Elena. 'Personal space! Please.'

'Sorry, sorry. I thought there was something on your throat.' Elena felt ridiculous.

'Like a mole or something?' Meredith said uneasily, rubbing the side of her neck.

'I don't know. Like a shadow, I guess.'

Elena felt sick. Damon could get to them easily here if he wanted to. Was she putting Bonnie and Meredith in danger by staying here?

The other girls picked up on Elena's change in mood and after only a little while, Bonnie stretched and said, with forced brightness, 'Well, I'm wiped out.'

'We should get to bed,' Meredith agreed. 'I've got a French test tomorrow.'

Bonnie shared Meredith's double bed, and the loveseat in the corner of the bedroom unfolded into a narrow single bed for Elena. After they had all climbed into bed and Meredith had switched out the light, Elena thought of something.

'Hey,' she called softly across the divide between their beds. 'Do you still have the vervain I gave you?'

'The *what*?' Bonnie asked sleepily.

'The vervain. The plants I gave you after Homecoming. Do you still have them?'

'The weeds?' Bonnie's voice was puzzled. 'I don't know what happened to them. They probably fell out of my hair. There was a fire going on, remember?'

'Meredith?'

'No,' Meredith said, sounding exasperated. She sat up and turned on the light. 'I don't remember what happened to the dried-out weeds you gave me at Homecoming.'

For a moment, Elena thought of telling them everything. They were her friends. And they were smart and brave; they'd been her allies through thick and thin. If they knew what was going on, they could help her. And they would be better able to protect themselves.

She licked her suddenly dry lips and took a quick breath. But it was that knowledge that had ruined their lives. She couldn't do that to them, not again.

'I . . . I'm sorry, you guys,' she said. 'I know I'm acting weird. Just promise me you'll be careful.' She would have to get more vervain and give it to them, hide it in their rooms and backpacks.

There was usually almost no physical resemblance between tiny, pale, redheaded Bonnie and tall, olive-skinned, raven-haired Meredith, but at that moment the suspicious, exasperated, yet affectionate expressions on their faces were almost identical.

'We promise we'll be careful,' Meredith said gently, and Bonnie nodded. 'But we're worried about you.'

'I know,' Elena said in a small voice. Silence stretched out between them and finally Meredith turned the light out again.

'We're here for you,' Bonnie said in the darkness. 'When you're ready.'

'I know,' Elena whispered again.

As she lay in the dark and listened to her friends' breathing gradually even out into the sounds of sleep, Elena turned and twisted from one side to the other, unable to get comfortable.

In Elena's own time, Meredith was miserable. She tried to cope, and she had Alaric helping her, and she almost never complained. But that didn't change the fact that Meredith had become a vampire, the one thing she never wanted to be.

Elena had to keep her out of this. Meredith deserved

a chance at a normal life.

Knowing she had made the right decision, Elena finally dozed off into an uneasy sleep. When she woke, sunlight was shining brightly in the windows, and Meredith was standing at the foot of Elena's bed.

'Come on, sleepyhead,' Meredith said lightly, jingling her car keys. 'We've got to get to school.'

'OK, OK,' Elena grumbled, sitting up and rubbing at her eyes. 'I hardly slept, I couldn't—' She broke off in dismay, her words drying up.

Around her neck, Meredith was wearing the same deep-red scarf she had worn last night. But something had changed while Elena slept. Below the scarf, she could see the edge of a deep purple-blue bruise. Elena knew exactly what it was, she had seen enough of them: a vampire bite.

Damon Influenced her, once we were all asleep, she thought, feeling dazed and nauseous. *Nowhere is safe.*

CHAPTER
22

'We have to stop him,' Elena insisted. 'He's hurting the people I care about.' She could hear her own voice rising hysterically and she took a deep, shuddering breath, trying to calm down. The seemingly endless school day was finally over, but there were plenty of students still milling around. Enough people at their school already thought Stefan was an arsonist, no need to feed the rumours by making it sound like he was fighting with the queen of the school.

The *former* queen of the school, Elena amended mentally, noting another pair of eyes sliding over her suspiciously as two girls from her chemistry class walked by, heading between the trailers towards the parking lot. Everyone had noticed how different Elena was this year, and being seen arguing intensely in corners with

Stefan was only pounding the nails in the coffin of her popularity.

Elena couldn't bring herself to care.

'Damon is coming after my friends,' she said to Stefan, gripping his sleeve even more tightly. 'It's all because of me. We have to protect them.'

'I know,' Stefan said. His leaf-green gaze was steady and reassuring. 'Come back to the boarding house with me. We'll figure something out.'

On the drive to the boarding house, Elena noticed how vividly red and yellow the leaves of the trees at the side of the road were getting. The long winding drive up to Mrs Flowers' boarding house was lined with graceful birch trees whose golden leaves glowed like candles. Elena shivered. Halloween was coming soon. They were running out of time.

The old redbrick boarding house was dark and silent. Stefan unlocked one of the oak double doors and led Elena up the flight of stairs ahead of them. On the second-floor landing, Elena turned automatically to the right, putting a hand on the knob of the door to the bedroom there.

Stefan went still as he stared at Elena. 'How did you know which way to go?' he asked.

Oops. When Stefan had brought her here after Homecoming, they had gone in to his room via the balcony. Elena had never been up these stairs before. Not in this version of her life, anyway. 'Just guessing,' she said tentatively, and stood back to let him pass.

Stefan's lips thinned suspiciously, but he didn't say anything else. Elena meekly followed him through the bedroom and stood by as he opened what looked like a closet, revealing the flight of stairs that led up to his room.

Elena and Stefan stepped out of the stairway and into his dimly lit room. Stefan stopped dead, horror on his face. His room was destroyed. The heavy trunks that had stood between the windows were overturned, their lids smashed. Books cascaded from a broken bookcase, their covers dirty and torn as if they'd been stamped on. The blankets that had lain on Stefan's narrow bed were shredded. A cold breeze blew through the room from a smashed window at the far end.

'My God,' Elena whispered. Damon must have done this.

The heavy mahogany dresser by the window was the only piece of furniture still standing, seemingly undamaged. Centred on its top stood a simple black iron box with a curving lid.

Stefan brushed past Elena and flung open the box. And then he froze, staring down into it.

'Stefan?' asked Elena softly after a moment. He didn't move or answer, and she wasn't sure if he had heard her. Stepping up beside him, she looked first at his face. It was even paler than usual, set in grim lines as if carved out of stone. His eyes, dark and stormy, stared unblinkingly down into the iron coffer, and Elena followed his gaze.

The box was empty.

Elena instantly understood. The iron box was where Stefan had kept his most precious things, the objects that recorded all his long, lonely history. His father's watch, carried by Stefan since the fifteenth century. The ivory dagger he had been given for his thirteenth birthday. Golden coins from his homeland. An agate-and-silver cup his mother, dead at Stefan's birth, had once treasured. Katherine's lapis lazuli ring. In a different time, a silk ribbon from Elena's hair.

All his treasures, gone. Elena looked back up at Stefan, but the words of sympathy she was about to offer died on her lips. Stefan's face was no longer blank and cold. Instead, it was twisted in silent fury, his lips drawn back in a snarl.

He didn't look human, not any more.

'I'll kill him,' Stefan growled, his canines lengthening. 'Damon destroys everything. For the *fun* of it.'

Elena turned on her heel and raced down the stairs. 'Mrs Flowers!' she called as she hit the first floor. 'Mrs Flowers, where are you?' She stopped and listened, frustrated. Despite the many times she'd been in this house, she had never quite got a mental map of Mrs Flowers' quarters, and the old witch woman wasn't especially likely to come when she was called.

'What is it, girl?' The voice was cold and clear, and

Elena whipped round, her heart pounding. Stefan's landlady stood at the far end of the hall, a small, stooped figure, all in black.

'Mrs Flowers,' Elena said desperately, going towards her. 'Someone was in Stefan's room. Did you see anyone?'

Mrs Flowers was wise, and her magic was incredibly strong. But now the frail old lady looked at her warily, with no sign of recognition, and Elena remembered with dismay that, in this time, they had never met before.

'The message is for Stefan,' Mrs Flowers said clearly, in a slightly singsong voice, as if she was reciting from memory. Elena's heart sank further. Damon must have compelled her to let him in and deliver his message.

'I'm here,' Stefan said from behind Elena. 'Give me the message.' He looked furious still, but intensely weary. It was as if all the years, all the centuries, were catching up with him all at once.

'Damon says that you've taken something of his, and so he will take everything you have,' Mrs Flowers said, her face impassive. 'Your precious things are his now.'

'I never belonged to him,' Elena said indignantly. 'And I don't belong to Stefan. I'm not a *thing*.'

But Mrs Flowers, her message delivered, was already drifting back into her private part of the house, her long black shawl fluttering behind her.

Stefan's jaw was clenched tight, his fists balled and his green eyes dark. Elena didn't think she had ever seen him so angry, not in all the years she had known and loved him.

If, as Elena thought, Stefan and Damon carried each other's humanity . . . if it was the love between the brothers that was the key to Elena being able to change Damon and save them all . . .

If all these things were true, Elena couldn't help feeling like she might have already lost.

CHAPTER

23

The next day, Elena hurried out of class and was the first one at her lunch table. The fire department had just declared this wing of the school safe, and this was the first day they could eat in the cafeteria instead of outside. A smell of smoke still lingered here though, and there were streaky grey stains of smoke on the walls and ceiling.

The morning had passed in a haze as she obediently went through the motions of being a high school student without hearing a word that was said. She thought that she might have taken a test in one of her classes, but she wasn't sure which class or what the test had asked. She couldn't think of anything that mattered less at this point in her life.

Maybe, she thought, staring down at her own

nervously tapping fingers, her friends would be able to help after all. Elena was still determined not to tell them the truth about what Stefan and Damon were. They had all, Matt and Meredith especially, given up so much in Elena's real world. But, even without knowing all the facts, perhaps her friends could be her eyes and ears in Fell's Church. They could help her find Damon.

If she could just speak to Damon face-to-face, maybe Elena could talk some sense into him. She couldn't believe that he wouldn't come round. Deep down, Damon loved his brother. Elena was sure of it.

Caroline paused by the table. 'All alone, Elena?' she asked, poisonously sweet.

Elena glanced up and a sarcastic reply died on her lips. Around Caroline's pretty bronzed throat was wrapped a gauzy green scarf. Below it peeked out the edge of a telltale purpling bruise.

'What happened to your neck, Caroline?' she asked, her mouth dry.

Caroline sneered. 'I don't know what you're talking about. Everything's wonderful.' Turning on her heel, she walked away from Elena's table, her head held high.

Elena pressed a hand to her chest, trying to calm her pounding heart. First Meredith, then Caroline. Damon wanted Elena to know that he knew who the people around her were, that he could get to anyone that mattered to her.

'You OK, Elena?' Matt had stopped at her table. He grinned at her, solid and reassuring in his letterman's jacket.

Elena flinched. Beneath the collar of Matt's jacket, she could see a bite, angry purple with two darker marks in the centre.

'What's that?' she asked dazedly.

Matt raised his hand, brushing his fingers lightly across his neck just where the top of his shirt ended. For a moment, his face clouded, faintly puzzled, and then it cleared. 'Everything's wonderful,' he said slowly, then turned his back on Elena and walked away.

The same thing Caroline had said: *Everything's wonderful*. Damon had compelled them to say exactly those words and walk away. A hot flush of anger spread through Elena.

'It's only October, and I'm already so sick of school I could scream,' Bonnie said, clattering her tray down on the table. 'When am I really going to use Spanish anyway?'

'When you go to Mexico? Or talk to someone who speaks Spanish?' Meredith suggested drily. 'It might actually be one of the more useful subjects you take.'

Bonnie clicked her tongue irritably as they sat down, but didn't argue. 'Hey, Elena.'

Elena greeted them distractedly. Meredith had another scarf looped around her neck, this one white with threads of sparkling silver woven through it. It covered the bite mark Elena had seen earlier, but she knew it was there.

Bonnie . . . Bonnie was fine. She was wearing a V-necked sweater, her slender white throat fully visible and completely unmarked. Elena looked carefully at Bonnie's wrists to see if Damon had fed from her veins there instead, but there was nothing to see but a plaited bracelet and a thin gold watch.

'Elena, are you hearing a thing I say?' Meredith asked sharply. As Elena looked up, Meredith's expression of irritation softened to concern. 'What's wrong?'

Elena straightened up and gave her a reassuring smile. 'Nothing. I'm just distracted. What are we talking about?'

'We need to go to the warehouse at the lumber yard and finish planning out the Haunted House this afternoon,' Meredith said patiently. 'I know we still have the plans from last year, but this is our senior year. We should make it really special.'

'Doing it there like we've always done will make things much easier. It would have been a huge hassle if we had to do it in the gym instead like the school board was talking about,' Bonnie said. 'It's, like, five hundred feet shorter. Yay for the fire, I guess.'

The first time around – when Elena had been chairman of the decorating committee, instead of Meredith – the school board *had* made them set up the

Haunted House in the gym. They'd been worried by the attack on the homeless man under Wickery Bridge and thought everyone would be safer at school instead of at the lumber yard.

It was good that would be changing this time, she thought. If it were in a different place, were things less likely to happen the same way? Maybe.

Meredith pulled out her planning notebook, and she and Bonnie were quickly absorbed in the pictures and sketches from the previous year's Haunted House. Elena's eyes wandered back to Bonnie's unmarked throat.

It just didn't make *sense*, she thought. If Damon was being thorough enough to go after everyone important to Elena – and Caroline was important to her, Elena admitted to herself, even if they didn't like each other – then why hadn't he fed from Bonnie?

Maybe he just hadn't got around to it yet.

'I think we should have druids,' Bonnie was saying.

'Actually, that's not a bad idea—' Meredith said, and Elena interrupted.

'Bonnie, have you seen Damon lately?' she asked abruptly. 'The guy who brought me to school that day?' *Why* had he not bitten Bonnie?

'The one who saw her kissing Stefan,' Meredith said unhelpfully.

Bonnie flushed right up to her hairline and shifted uncomfortably in her seat. 'I meant to tell you,' she blurted. 'Only it was really weird, and I didn't want you to feel bad.'

'What do you mean?'

'I was at the grocery store the other night picking up milk for my mom, and he came up and started talking to me.' Bonnie looked down, pushing her hair shyly behind her ear. 'He was looking into my eyes and saying, just, really weird stuff. Like that I *wanted to be close to him*. I didn't want to tell you because it felt like he was hitting on me.' She glanced up at Elena, looking guilty. 'I didn't do anything, I swear.'

'I believe you,' Elena said soothingly, trying to think. Why would Damon have let Bonnie go? It certainly sounded like he had started to compel her; why would he have changed his mind?

Bonnie and Damon had always had a special bond. He called her his redbird, and was protective, treating her almost like a little sister. But, no, that wasn't true *here*. Damon didn't know Bonnie well enough to care about her, not yet.

Elena looked at Bonnie's white throat again, at her slender wrists, checking once more for bites and bruises she knew she wasn't going to find.

Bonnie's wrists . . . Elena leaned forward, frowning. The narrow woven bracelet around Bonnie's left wrist was made of thin strips of leather and bits of coloured thread and small silver beads. And strands of some kind of plant. Was it *vervain*?

'Where'd you get that bracelet?' Elena asked her.

Bonnie stretched her left arm out to look at it. 'I know, it's kind of ugly, isn't it? My grandmother gave it to me this summer though, and she told me never to take it off. It's supposed to protect me against all kinds of things.'

'Because she and your cousin and you are all psychic.' Meredith said teasingly.

Bonnie shrugged. 'It's all about the druids. Which is why we should have them in the Haunted House. For one thing, they did human sacrifice, and we could have, like, a standing stone and a big knife . . . Elena? Where are you going?'

Elena wasn't listening any more. Without even thinking about it, she stood up from the table and walked out, first through the cafeteria doors and then the doors of the school. No one stopped her as she strode between the temporary trailer classrooms and through the parking lot.

She felt hot and angry, fuming as she stamped down the sidewalk away from the school. Damon had attacked Meredith. Matt. Even Caroline. And he'd tried to feed on Bonnie as well.

Bonnie was safe. For now. As long as she didn't take that bracelet off and Damon didn't decide that just grabbing her and feeding off her without first compelling her was just as good.

Elena had kissed Stefan *once*. Once. And her friends

had had nothing to do with it.

She was tired of playing games.

When she reached the graveyard, Elena hesitated for a moment, staring through the fence. The day was cloudy, and the cemetery looked grey and gloomy. Beyond the ruined church, she could see the branches of the uprooted tree, pointing skyward.

As she passed through the gate, a cold wind began to blow, whistling in Elena's ears and whipping her hair against her face. She turned towards the well-kept, modern part of the cemetery with its neat rows of granite and marble tombstones. For this confrontation, Elena instinctively felt that it would be comforting to have her parents nearby.

The cemetery was empty and still. As Elena crossed it, the wind came with her, piles of dry leaves rising up into the air as she passed. She stopped by her parents' grave and rested a hand on the cool grey granite of their stone, gathering her strength. 'Help me, Mom and Dad,' she murmured. Anger was still simmering inside her, black and hot.

Elena spun round, searching between the headstones. She knew he was there, somewhere, watching her. It didn't matter that the bond between them had been severed, she could *feel* him.

She gathered her breath and shouted, into the wind. '*Damon*!'

Nothing. A memory of doing this once before had

her turning on the spot, looking over her own shoulder, only to see no one there.

'Damon!' she shouted again. 'I know you're there!'

Icy wind blew straight into Elena's face, making her flinch. When she opened her eyes, she found herself staring across the graveyard at a grove of beech trees, their leaves bright yellow and red against the greyness of the sky. Something dark moved in the shadows between their trunks.

Elena blinked. The blackness was coming closer, its shape resolving into a black-clad figure. Golden leaves blew around him, parting as he stepped forward to the edge of the grove, and his pale features became clearer.

Damon, of course.

He stayed where he was, watching Elena calmly as she hurried towards him. She almost slipped in the grass, catching herself against a tombstone, and heat rose in her cheeks. She didn't want to seem vulnerable in front of Damon. Whatever game he was playing, she would need all the advantages she could get.

'What do you think you're doing?' she snapped when she reached him, slightly out of breath.

Damon flashed her a bright, insincere smile. 'I came when you called, Princess,' he said. 'I could ask you the same thing. Everything's wonderful.' He hissed the words, his lips curling into a cruel smile, the same words he'd primed Matt and Caroline and probably Meredith with, and her anger flared up, hot inside her.

Elena's hand flew out and she slapped Damon hard across the face.

Her hand stung with the force of the blow, and Damon's cheek reddened, but he was still smiling. 'Don't push me too hard, Elena,' he said softly. 'I've been kinder than you deserve.'

'You've been feeding on my friends,' she said, her voice shaking.

Damon's eyes glittered, so black she couldn't tell the iris from the pupil. 'Not just feeding on them, Elena. I've got big plans.'

Elena went cold inside. 'What do you mean?'

Damon's smile disappeared. 'The way I fell for you so quickly . . . It made me realise how lonely I must be.'

Elena's heart thumped hard. Damon didn't do vulnerable, didn't admit to having emotions. Could this be a *good* thing?

But Damon went on, lightly. 'And so, I decided what I needed were some protégés.'

'You can't do that,' Elena said. Damon had never turned anyone into a vampire, never, to her knowledge, even offered to turn anyone except Elena herself. He wasn't looking for companionship; this was pure spite.

'Oh, I can,' Damon said. 'I think Halloween will be an appropriate day to do it, don't you? It's a very American holiday, of course, but I've always liked costumes. Ghosts and ghasts and all sorts of ghoulies.'

'Damon,' Elena said. '*Don't.*'

She could hear the pleading tone in her own voice, and so could Damon. His smile reappeared, flashing sharp and bright and quickly disappearing again.

'They'll thank me,' he said softly, 'when they realise they'll be young and beautiful for ever.' His eyes ran over her, pausing on the bite mark Stefan had left low on her throat. When he spoke again, his voice was laced with bitterness. 'I'd invite you to join us, Elena, but you'll have Stefan for that.'

Elena stepped closer. 'I'm not with Stefan,' she said, her words tumbling over one another. 'I was never with Stefan, Damon. We kissed *once*, that's it, and that was a mistake. The only reason he fed on me was so that we could get out of the tomb *you* locked us into.'

Damon's mouth tightened. He looked as disturbingly handsome as ever, but there was something bitter and distrustful in his face. 'I'll see you on Halloween, Elena,' he said, and then he was gone.

Elena stood alone in the cemetery, surrounded by strangers' graves.

She swallowed once, hard, and pressed the heels of her hands against her eyes for a moment.

Damon wanted to change Matt, Meredith and Caroline – and who knew who else – into vampires at Halloween. Elena had to stop him. And she needed to stop him from killing Mr Tanner that same night. She didn't know how she was going to do it alone.

Stefan was clever and strong. If he drank her blood,

he'd have more Power, maybe enough to stop Damon.

But no. Elena discarded the idea as swiftly as it had come to her. Stefan had been so angry at Damon when he realised Damon had stolen his treasures. All the conflict, all the resentment that had lain between the brothers since the days of Katherine, five hundred years before, had simmered behind Stefan's green eyes, ready to boil over. If she brought him up against Damon now, Stefan might lose his head and attack. And then there was a good chance that Damon might kill him.

But thinking of the brothers' shared past had given Elena an idea. Straightening her sweater and squaring her shoulders, she turned and began walking back towards school, leaves crunching beneath her feet.

She needed magic.

Despite all that had happened since she left the cafeteria, Elena was only a few minutes late for history class. Murmuring an apology to the teacher, she ignored the curious gazes of her classmates. Pulling a sheet of loose-leaf paper out of her backpack, she bent her head over her desk and wrote a note.

> *SOS. I need your help. Meet me at your house after school. TELL NO ONE!!!*

Folding the note and passing it to a girl to her right, Elena jerked her head towards Bonnie's front-row seat, and the girl obediently passed it forward. Elena watched as Bonnie glanced up to make sure Mr Tanner's eyes were elsewhere, unfolded the note, read it and then scribbled a reply.

When it came back to Elena, Bonnie's rounded handwriting read,

> *Can't! We have to go to the warehouse to plan the Haunted House, remember? Meredith would kill us!!!*

Mr Tanner's attention was fixed on a boy answering a question on the other side of the room, and Elena took the chance to grimace appealingly at Bonnie, trying to express urgency in her face. Bonnie, twisted round in her seat, shook her head.

Elena quickly wrote another note and passed it back up to Bonnie.

> *You have to meet me. I have so much to tell you.*

> *Bonnie, you're a witch.*

CHAPTER
24

'**A**re you serious about all this?' Bonnie asked. 'I'm not going to be mad if you were kidding, Elena.' She hefted one of the bags Mrs Flowers had given them over her shoulder and stepped carefully over a broken gravestone.

Elena had told Bonnie everything. About Stefan and Damon, about coming here from a possible future. About how Bonnie would grow into one of the most powerful witches Elena had ever met. How much Elena needed her help.

Telling Bonnie was the only thing she could think of to do. Matt and Meredith had been hurt too much by their association with the supernatural to bring them into this. Stefan would have been the worst person imaginable to pit against Damon right now.

But Bonnie? In the future, Bonnie was happy. And she was amazingly full of Power. If only they could tap into that Power now, use Bonnie's magic even though she was completely untrained, Bonnie could be a true asset.

It hadn't been easy. At first, Bonnie had shaken her head, her large brown eyes wide, and backed away from Elena nervously. The step from saying she was psychic and could read palms to being told she was a budding witch had almost been too much for her. Even now, she was sneaking dubious, worried glances out of the corner of her eye at Elena. But she was here. She wasn't running away.

Mrs Flowers had been a surprisingly huge help. She had stood in the doorway of her big old house, listening silently as Elena stumbled through an explanation that really explained nothing. It boiled down to the fact that they knew Mrs Flowers was a witch, and that they needed help opening something.

'And protecting ourselves,' Elena had tossed in, almost as an afterthought.

Mrs Flowers' sharp eyes examined first Elena, then Bonnie. After a while, she had simply turned and walked away.

'Uh,' Bonnie had said, peering down the dark hall after the old woman. 'Are we supposed to follow her?'

Despite everything, Elena could feel a smile curling at the edges of her lips. 'It's just the way she is. She'll come back.'

They'd waited what felt like for ever at Mrs Flowers' door, long enough that Bonnie began casting dubious looks at Elena again and Elena began to worry about what she would do if Stefan came home and saw them there.

But Mrs Flowers had returned eventually, carrying two duffle bags, and spoke for the first time since Elena had asked her for help. 'You'll find things labelled in there, dear. And good luck getting back where you belong.'

'Thank you—' Elena began to say, but the heavy doors were already swinging shut, leaving Elena and Bonnie on the doorstep. She frowned, confused. How had Mrs Flowers known this wasn't where Elena belonged?

'Pretty weird,' Bonnie had said, shaking her head. But she had actually seemed slightly less freaked out after that, as if she found it comforting that Elena wasn't the only possibly crazy person around.

Now they crossed the older part of the graveyard, staggering a little under the weight of the duffle bags Mrs Flowers had given them. Bonnie hesitated in the empty hole that had once been the doorway of the ruined church.

'Are we allowed in here?' she asked. 'Is it safe?'

'Probably not,' Elena told her, 'but we have to go in. Please, Bonnie.'

Most of the roof had fallen in and late afternoon sunlight streamed through the holes above them, illuminating piles of rubble. Three walls still stood, but the fourth was knee-high, and Elena could see the far end of the graveyard through it. The uprooted tree, its branches brushing the walls of the small mausoleum Damon had trapped her and Stefan in, still lay there in ruins.

At the side of the church was the tomb of Thomas and Honoria Fell, a large stone box, heavy marble figures carved on its lid. Elena walked over to gaze down on the founders of Fell's Church, lying with hands folded across their chests, their eyes closed. Elena brushed her fingers across Honoria's cold marble cheek, taking comfort from the face of the lady who had guarded Fell's Church for so long. Her ghost hadn't appeared this time. Did that mean she trusted Elena to handle the situation? Or was something preventing her from coming?

'OK,' Elena said, all business, as she swung round to face Bonnie. 'We have to get the tomb open.'

Bonnie's eyes rounded. 'Are you kidding me?' she asked. 'That's what you want to open? Elena, it's got to weigh about a thousand pounds. We can't open that with herbs and candles. You need a bulldozer or something.'

'We can,' Elena said steadily. 'You have the Power, Bonnie.'

'Even if we could' – Bonnie's voice wobbled – 'what would be the point? Elena, there are *dead people* in that thing.'

'No,' Elena said, her eyes fixed thoughtfully on the grey stone box. 'It's not really a grave. It's a passageway.'

They rummaged through the duffle bags. 'Here,' Elena said, pulling out two little red silk bags, each on a long loop of cord. 'Mrs Flowers gave us sachets for protection. Put it around your neck.' The tiny bag was round and fat with herbs, fitting comfortably in the palm of Elena's hand.

'What's in them?' At Elena's shrug, Bonnie sniffed the sachet before stringing it around her neck. 'Smells good, anyway.'

There were small jars of herbs, labelled in Mrs Flowers' crabbed, almost illegible handwriting. 'It says these are cowslips,' Elena said, making out the label on a jar of small dried yellow flowers, several blossoms on each stem. 'According to the label, they're good for unlocking.'

Bonnie leaned against her and looked down at the jar in Elena's hand. 'OK. So what do we do with them?'

Elena stared at her. *What would Bonnie, my Bonnie, do?* She tried to think.

'Well, when you're doing a spell that uses herbs, you usually scatter them around what you're working on,' she said. 'Or you burn them.'

'Right. Well, I'd rather not set the church on fire, so

let's try scattering them,' Bonnie said drily.

As well as the cowslips, there were jars of prickly dried evergreen needles and dried berries labelled JUNIPER – FOR SPELLCASTING and a herb Elena recognised as rosemary, the label of which claimed it was used for luck and power. Mrs Flowers had given them several small jars of each, so there was more than enough to strew thoroughly over the lid of the tomb and in a circle around it.

Help us, Elena thought fervently as she sprinkled rosemary over Honoria Fell's grave. *If this works, we'll be protecting Fell's Church. Just like you wanted.*

'Now what?' Bonnie asked when they'd scattered all the herbs. 'There are candles in the other bag, and matches. And a torch. And, yikes, a knife.'

There were twelve candles, four each of black, white and red. Mrs Flowers hadn't included any kind of note to tell them what the colours meant or what exactly to do with them, so Elena, hoping she was doing the right thing, decided to put them in a circle, colours alternating, around the tomb, outside the circle of herbs.

'And what do we do next?' Bonnie asked, watching as Elena lit the last candle.

'I'm not sure,' Elena told her, dripping a pool of candle wax on the floor and carefully sticking the candle upright in it. 'Usually you say something, maybe just saying what you want to happen, and it looks like you're concentrating.'

Bonnie's eyebrows shot up. 'So the next step is that I say "open" and think really hard? Elena, I'm not sure this is going to work.'

'Try it,' Elena said hopefully.

Bonnie frowned at the tomb. The flames of the candles danced, reflected in her eyes. 'Open,' she said firmly.

Nothing happened.

'Open. I command you to open,' Bonnie said more doubtfully, and closed her eyes, scrunching her forehead in concentration. Still nothing changed.

Bonnie's eyes opened and she huffed in frustration. 'This is ridiculous.'

'Wait.' Elena thought of the knife, still in the bag. 'Sometimes you use blood. You say it's important, that it's one of the strongest ingredients you can use in a spell. Because it's vitality, it's life in its most basic form.' She hurried towards the bag and felt inside. The knife was more like a small dagger, its blade pure silver and its handle some kind of bone.

Bonnie hesitated, biting her lip, and then nodded. She came to stand beside Elena, her eyes fixed on the knife.

'I'll go first, OK?' Elena said. She made a short, shallow cut on the inside of her own arm, hissing a little at the stinging pain. Turning her arm, she let the blood drip across Honoria and Thomas Fell's effigies. Splotches of her blood stained their lips, the lids of their closed eyes. Blood dripped on Honoria's neck and trickled down, making it look as if she'd been a vampire's feast.

Please, Elena thought, breathing hard. *Please let us in*. She wasn't sure who she was begging: Honoria Fell; the mysterious Powers that filled the universe; the Celestial Guardians; or Katherine, down below the church. Whoever was listening, she supposed. Whoever would help her.

Bonnie, white-faced but resolute, held out her own arm, and Elena ran the blade quickly across it, watching the blood spill out and over Bonnie's porcelain-white skin. More blood spattered over Honoria's and Thomas's stone torsos and their folded hands.

'Draw on your Power, Bonnie,' Elena said softly. 'It's there. I've seen it. Pull it out of the earth under your feet and the plants growing all around us. Take it from the dead; they're right here with us.'

Bonnie's face tightened with concentration, her fine bones becoming more defined beneath her skin. The candle flames flickered all at once, as if a wind had passed through the ruined church.

Elena wasn't a Guardian here, and she didn't have those Powers any more. But she could remember what it had felt like when she and Bonnie worked together, their auras combining, feeding her Power into Bonnie's. She tried to find that feeling, pushing out, trying to let Bonnie take whatever might help her. Her hand found Bonnie's smaller one, and Bonnie twined their fingers together and squeezed hard.

All at once, the candles all went out. With a huge, grating, cracking noise, the top of the stone tomb split in half, one side falling heavily to the flagstones of the floor.

Elena peered down. As she had expected, there was no grave beneath the stone. Instead of bones, she was looking down into the dark opening of a vault. In the stone wall below her were driven iron rungs, like a ladder.

'Wow,' Bonnie said next to her. She was pale but her eyes were shining with excitement. 'I can't believe that worked. *I can't . . .*' She closed her mouth, then cleared her throat and lifted her chin bravely. 'What now?'

'Now you go home,' Elena said. She looked nervously out through the broken wall of the church. It was still daylight but the sun was sinking low. She pulled the torch out of the bag and tucked it into her back pocket. 'I'm sorry, Bonnie, and *thank you*, thank you so much. But the next part I have to do by myself. And I'm not sure if it's safe for you up here. Please go home before it gets dark.'

'If it's not safe for me, it's not safe for you,' Bonnie said stubbornly. 'At least I can watch your back.'

Elena squeezed her friend's hand. 'Please, Bonnie,' she begged again. 'I can't do what I have to do if I'm worrying about you. I promise I'll be OK.'

She knew she had no way of guaranteeing that, but Bonnie's shoulders slumped in acceptance. 'Be careful, Elena,' she said. 'Call me as soon as you get home.'

'OK.' Elena watched as Bonnie picked up the duffle bags with their depleted jars of herbs and left the church, casting worried glances back at Elena over her shoulder.

Once Bonnie's small, upright figure was out of sight, Elena took a deep breath. There was an icy breeze coming from the opening in the tomb, and it smelled like earth and cold stone that never saw the light.

Steeling herself, she swung her legs over the edge of the tomb, took hold of an iron rung and began to climb down into the vault beneath the church.

CHAPTER

25

Elena climbed down into darkness, the iron rungs cold in her hands. By the time her feet hit the stone floor at the bottom of the ladder, she was in total blackness. Pulling the torch from her back pocket, she flicked it on and ran the beam of light over her surroundings.

The opening of the crypt was just as Elena remembered it. Smooth stone walls held heavy carved candelabras, some with the remains of candles still in them. Near Elena was an ornate wrought-iron gate. Pushing the gate open, Elena walked forward with a slow, steady tread, trying to calm her hammering heart.

The last time she had been here, she'd been a vampire, and she'd had Damon and Stefan both with her, as well as her human friends. More important, that time she hadn't known what she was getting into. Only that she had been led down here, and that something terrible lurked, just out of sight.

Now Elena knew exactly what was down here.

Her steady footsteps echoed against the stone floor, their sounds only emphasising how silent it was. Elena could easily believe that no one else had been down here for more than a hundred years. No one else alive, anyway.

Beyond the gate, the beam of the torch caught on pale, familiar marble features. A tomb, the twin of the one up in the church. The stone lid here had been broken in two also, and the pieces flung across the crypt. Fragile human bones were splintered and strewn stick-like across the floor. One crunched beneath Elena's feet as she approached, making her wince guiltily.

She had hoped that, since Katherine hadn't appeared in Fell's Church, hadn't sent disturbing dreams to torment Elena, it meant she wasn't so filled with rage in this time. But the violence with which the tomb had been desecrated seemed to prove that Katherine was as furious and destructive as she had ever been.

Elena turned the thin wavering beam of the torch to the wall beyond the Fells' tomb. There, as she'd known there would be, lay a gaping hole in the stone wall, as if the stones had been ripped away. From it, a long black tunnel led deep into the earth beyond.

Elena licked her lips nervously. Resting her hands on

the cold moist dirt at the edge of the tunnel, she peered into it. 'Katherine?' she said questioningly. Her voice came out softer and shakier than she had meant it to, and she cleared her throat and called again. *'Katherine!'*

Straining her eyes to see into the darkness, Elena waited.

Nothing. No sound of footfalls, nothing white coming swiftly towards her. No sense of something huge and dangerous rushing at her.

'Katherine!' she called again. 'I have secrets to tell you!' That might bring her if anything would; Katherine von Swartzchild, first love of Damon and Stefan, the one who had made them vampires and turned them against each other was nothing if not curious and eager for information. That was why she had followed Stefan and Damon here, why she had spied on Elena.

Elena waited, watching and listening. Still nothing. She felt her shoulders sag. Without Katherine, she didn't have a plan at all.

How long should she wait? Elena pictured herself sitting against the wall, surrounded by the Fell's broken bones, waiting for Katherine, growing colder and colder as the light of the torch dimmed. Elena shuddered. No, she wouldn't stay here.

She turned to go, and the beam of the torch landed on Katherine, standing only a few feet behind her. Elena jumped backward with a strained yelp, her light skittering wildly across the crypt.

Katherine looked so much like Elena that it knocked Elena breathless, even now. Her golden hair was perhaps a shade lighter and a few inches longer, her eyes a slightly different blue. Her figure was thinner and more fragile than Elena's: girls of her time and class had been expected to sit and embroider, not run and play.

But the delicate curve of Katherine's brow, her long golden lashes, her pale skin, the shape of her features – they were all as familiar to Elena as looking in a mirror. Unlike Elena, who was dressed in jeans and a sweater, Katherine wore a long, gauzy white dress. It would have made her look innocent if it weren't for the brownish-red streaks across the front, as if Katherine had absent-mindedly wiped bloody hands on it.

'Hello, pretty little girl, my sweet reflection,' Katherine said, almost crooning.

Elena swallowed nervously. 'I need your help.'

Katherine came closer, touching Elena's hair, running cold fingers across her face. 'You're a nasty, greedy girl,' she said sharply. 'You want both my boys.'

'You wanted them too,' Elena snapped, not bothering to deny it. Katherine smiled, her teeth disturbingly sharp.

'Of course I did,' she said. 'But they're mine. They've always been mine. You should have left them alone.'

'I *am* going to leave them alone from now on,' Elena said. 'I promise. I just want them to be brothers. I want them to be happy. You did too, once.'

Katherine had, Elena knew, let both brothers drink her blood, promised them each eternal life with the secret idea that they would love each other, that the three of them could be a happy family, together for ever. When they had rejected the idea of sharing her, she faked her own death, sure their mutual grief would bring them together.

She'd been a fool. Damon and Stefan had loathed each other already, distanced by their competition for their father's love, by their roles as the good and bad sons. Jealousy over Katherine had only heightened their dislike, and their anger and grief at her death had ripened it into hatred.

Katherine had expected Stefan and Damon to turn to each other, but instead they had turned *on* each other, swords in hand. Each murdered at his brother's hand, they'd died with Katherine's blood in their systems and risen again, vampires, cursed for ever.

'They don't want to be happy.' Katherine's eyes widened with remembered hurt, and for a moment Elena saw the fragile, naive girl who had destroyed Damon and Stefan with a mistaken idea of romance. 'I gave them a gift. I gave them life for ever, and they didn't care. I told them to take care of each other, in my memory, but they wouldn't listen. They threw everything I'd given them away.'

'But maybe it's not too late,' Elena said. 'Maybe if

they knew you were alive, they could forgive each other.'

Katherine's eyes narrowed angrily, her lips curling into a sulky pout. 'I don't want them to forgive each other,' she said in a childish voice. Then she began to smile, an unpleasant, hungry smile. 'You, on the other hand . . .' She stroked Elena's cheeks. Her hands were terribly cold, and they smelled of the earth around them. Elena shivered. 'We look so much alike,' Katherine said musingly. 'I should make you like me. We could travel together. It would be such fun. Everyone would think we were sisters.'

There was something wistful in Katherine's eyes as her hand shifted to run through Elena's hair, pulling a little at the long strands. Maybe family was what Katherine needed. She'd lost her father when she'd lost the Salvatores and fled Italy. Would knowing she had other family make a difference to Katherine?

'We are sisters,' she said, and Katherine's hand pulled away.

'I don't know what you mean, little one,' Katherine said. 'You're no sister of mine.'

Elena swallowed, feeling the dry click of her throat. 'We really are. My mother – your mother – was an immortal. A Celestial Guardian. She left you to keep you safe. And when, hundreds of years later, she tried to keep me safe, the other Guardians killed her.'

Katherine's mouth tightened into an angry line.

'That doesn't make any sense. My mother died when I was a baby.'

'No, it's true,' Elena said simply. There was nothing but hostility in Katherine's face, but Elena pushed on. 'I ask you, as your own flesh and blood, to help me. You wanted to be the one to bring Stefan and Damon together, and you still can be. They need you, Katherine. Five hundred years and they've never stopped loving you. It's torn them apart.'

Katherine's face was blank and cold. 'They deserve to suffer.' She squeezed her fists tightly, slamming her arms down at her sides. 'They'll suffer if I kill you. Or if I take you with me.'

'No.' Elena took Katherine's cold, muddy arm, her heart pounding. 'They've suffered all along. You can *save* them this time. You're the only one who can.'

Hissing, Katherine pulled away. With a rattling noise, the crypt began to shake around them. Despite herself, Elena shrieked as the lid to the tomb fell to the floor with a crash, Honoria Fell's face cracking. Another tremor had Elena stumbling and grabbing on to the stone wall to keep from falling.

'Stop it!' she demanded, glaring at Katherine. The other girl stood stock-still, her pale face tilted up as if she could see through the dirt and stone to the ruined church above. From high above, Elena heard a heavy thud, and Katherine's lips curled in a joyless smile.

Elena ran. Her heart hammering, she shoved through

the half-open gate and down the long dark corridor, her torch swinging wildly. She didn't look back but her nerves were on edge, listening for a footstep, waiting for Katherine's inhumanly strong hands to clamp down upon her shoulders and drag Elena back.

Katherine could kill her, could turn Elena into a vampire if she wanted to, and there was nothing Elena would be able to do about it. Why had Elena tried to reason with her?

Grabbing hold of the iron rungs set in the wall, Elena began to pull herself up as fast as she could, her breath coming fast and anxious. The crypt had stopped shaking for now, but her hands, sweaty with nerves, still slipped as she climbed. Partway up, she lost her grip on the torch and it fell, crashing into the stones below and going out, leaving Elena in darkness. Far above was the faintly lit rectangle of the tomb in the church, and Elena kept climbing towards it as fast as she could, holding tightly on to the rungs.

At last Elena reached the top and scrambled out through the Fells' tomb, gulping deep breaths of the cold fresh air. Once she was standing on the floor of the old church, she dared to glance down into the crypt below.

There was nothing there, no white-clad figure following her. But that proved nothing. Katherine could take many forms, and she was much, much faster than Elena. Elena's best chance, she thought, would be to cross Wickery Bridge and head home as quickly as she could. Katherine was powerful enough that she had trouble crossing running water.

The sun had set and night had fallen while Elena was down in the crypt. *Terrific*, she thought, *a cemetery after dark without a torch and a vampire on my heels. This was a truly genius idea, Elena Gilbert.*

She stumbled over what seemed to be every tombstone in the long grass of the older part of the graveyard, once falling hard enough to skin the palms of her hands. Elena scrambled up and hurried on, finding her way by the light of the half-moon above her.

Once she reached the road outside the cemetery, the tight ball of anxiety in Elena's chest relaxed a little. Not much further until she could cross the bridge and then head back home. She'd have to go back to her own house. Aunt Judith had called someone to fix the window and insisted on moving back home. At least it was closer than Meredith's, but Elena didn't know how to keep them safe from Damon. Perhaps now that he was focusing on her friends, he would leave Elena's family alone.

Just before the bridge, a white-clad figure barred Elena's path. Katherine's pale-gold hair whipped around her in the wind.

Elena glanced back over her shoulder. There was no point in running. Katherine was a thousand times faster than Elena, and the only thing that would hinder her – running water – was on the *other* side of her.

For a moment, Elena thought of begging for mercy. But she knew Katherine well enough to know that wouldn't do any good. Whatever Katherine decided to do, she would do.

Might as well go out fighting. Elena tossed her head back and marched straight up to Katherine. 'What do you want?' she asked.

Katherine's cold blue eyes regarded Elena for a long moment. Finally she spoke. 'You think that I can save them? I'll do as you ask, little mirror. I will let Damon and Stefan know that I still live.'

'Oh.' Maybe Elena's pleading had done some good after all. 'Thank you.'

Katherine frowned at her crossly. For a moment her voice sounded young, a hurt child's, but her eyes seemed terribly old. 'There's no happy ending in this for either of us. I hope you know that,' she said. 'I've lived this once already. I know what it's like to love them both, and to lose them.'

CHAPTER

26

Heavy clouds loomed overhead and the air seemed ominously electric, on the verge of a storm. Outside the Haunted House appeared a devilishly masked mannequin, its black clothing flapping in the wind and giving an appropriately nightmarish ambiance to this Halloween night.

Stefan and Elena stopped outside the Haunted House. Stefan's face was drawn tight, and Elena felt sick and anxious. Pulling up the hood of her Red Riding Hood costume, she carefully covered her distinctive golden hair.

'This is the night Damon said he was going to turn Meredith and Matt and Caroline into vampires,' she whispered to Stefan. 'He has to be here. They're all here, and there's so much confusion, it will be easy for him.'

Stefan nodded grimly. Looking up at him, Elena couldn't help the little clench her heart gave. He looked so good in his tuxedo and cape, elegant and completely natural. A debonair vampire costume, what else? And people thought Stefan didn't have a sense of humour.

She hadn't been completely honest with him. For her plan to work, for the brothers to forgive each other, Katherine's revelation that they hadn't caused her death had to come as a surprise. So she had told him only that they needed to protect her friends from Damon.

'We'll mingle with the crowd and keep an eye out for him,' she said as they approached the Haunted House entrance. 'If you hang out in the Torture Room, that might be a good place. It shouldn't be too crowded; it's off the main path and it's mostly dummies, not people in costume. It's the kind of place Damon would be likely to take someone if he wanted to be alone.'

Despite Elena's defection from the Haunted House committee – which Meredith had only reluctantly forgiven her for – and Bonnie's missing most of the all-important planning stage, Meredith and the rest of her decorating committee had done an amazing job on the Haunted House. It looked nightmarishly creepy, the entrance enthusiastically draped in spiders' webs and handprints made with fake blood.

Now everything was in chaos as the seniors rushed to get the last pieces in place before the paying public was allowed in. Elena and Stefan ducked through the crowd and made their way along the twisting route of the tour.

Outside the Torture Chamber, Elena squeezed Stefan's hand. 'This is it,' she said. 'Good luck.'

'I will protect them if I can, Elena,' Stefan told her, and slipped through the doorway to hide inside among the torture implements.

Elena went on, glancing in at the different sets as she passed. The Alien Encounter Room was already dark, lit only with phosphorescent paint, and zombies milled around the Living Dead Room, adjusting one another's make-up.

The Druid Room was near the back of the warehouse, and Elena frowned. If she'd had time to really participate in the committee, maybe she could have made it more central, so that it would be more difficult for Damon to feed from – and kill – Mr Tanner.

Love is powerful, Mylea had said, but should Elena have paid more attention to logistics and less to changing Damon's heart? She should have made it *impossible* for Damon to kill Mr Tanner instead of hoping she could make him not want to.

She swallowed hard. This was the right way to go. If she couldn't change the relationship between the brothers, surely it was only a matter of time before Damon killed again. She could only hope that Katherine would pull through, for all their sakes. If it didn't work, maybe there was never any hope for Elena's mission.

And there Mr Tanner was, upright and indignant, arguing with white-robed Bonnie in front of a cardboard Stonehenge. 'But you've *got* to wear the blood,' she was saying pleadingly. 'It's part of the scene; you're a sacrifice.'

'Wearing these ridiculous robes is bad enough,' Mr Tanner told her. 'No one informed me I was going to have to smear syrup all over myself.'

'It doesn't really get on *you*,' Bonnie argued, but Elena had heard enough for now. She remembered this argument. She'd joined in the first time, trying to convince Mr Tanner to cooperate, and then Stefan had finally compelled him. But Meredith, a witch in a tight black dress, was already approaching, and Elena realised she had faith that Meredith's logic and persistence would be just as effective as Stefan's Power had been.

Both Bonnie and Meredith were focused on Mr Tanner, not even noticing Elena, and she hesitated, watching them. Meredith was talking softly and reasonably to Mr Tanner while Bonnie looked harried but amused, a smile lurking at the edges of her mouth.

Elena's heart ached with how much she loved them. Memories came rushing back to her: Meredith telling ghost stories at their junior high sleepovers, Bonnie's face bright over her ninth birthday cake, the focused frown Meredith wore as she studied, the shine of Bonnie's eyes on her wedding day. Damon wanted to *change* them, destroy their lives, make them unageing killers. She had to stop him.

It was almost time for the Haunted House to open. Time to look for Damon.

The Haunted House was like a maze this time, Elena realised. The warehouse was bigger than the school gym had been, and Meredith had filled the space with many more horrors than they'd been able to fit in the school gym the first time this Halloween had happened, when Elena had been in charge. Elena cut through the Séance Room and the Deaths from History Room, where she spotted Caroline, a nubile Egyptian priestess in a linen shift that left very little to the imagination, talking to Tyler in his werewolf costume. *One potential victim*, she thought, and looked for the others. She would have to keep them all safe.

Slipping between the temporary partitions, Elena cut through the Spider Room, where she had to push her way through dangling rubber spiders. She found Meredith and Bonnie again, and followed as they hurried back towards the entrance, ready to lead customers through the house. Outside the entrance to the Fun House she finally identified Matt, who had taken the head of his own werewolf costume off. *Everyone in place*, she thought, and glanced automatically towards the Torture Chamber.

The last of the seniors were getting in position. The doors were about to open. 'Bonnie,' Elena said softly, coming up next to her.

Bonnie jumped a little. 'Elena,' she said. She looked curiously at Elena's costume. 'I thought you were going to wear that Renaissance dress your aunt had made for you.'

'No, I lent that to someone else,' Elena told her. 'Bonnie, can you do me a favour? Damon's going to come here, dressed as the Grim Reaper. Be nice to him, OK? Don't let on that you recognise him if you can help it, and steer him towards the Torture Chamber. I'll take it from there.'

Bonnie paled, but she nodded. 'I'll try,' she said, and lowered her voice to a whisper. 'What if he tries to bite me, Elena?'

Elena slipped an arm around her friend's shoulders. 'I don't think he will, at least not here,' she said comfortingly. 'You've got your bracelet and Mrs Flowers' sachet, so he can't Influence you, and I don't think he'll try anything with this many people around. If he does, just scream as loudly as you can.'

Bonnie didn't seem terribly comforted, but she nodded again and squared her shoulders. For a moment, she looked to Elena like a young soldier heading into battle. Frightened, but firmly determined to face down death if necessary. Suddenly filled with affection, Elena hugged her friend tightly. 'It'll be all right,' she breathed in Bonnie's ear. 'I promise.' Something twisted inside her, and she hoped, fervently, that she would be able to keep the promise.

A voice sounded through the warehouse. 'OK, they're about to let in the line. Cut the lights, Ed!' Gloom fell, and with an audible click somebody started the recorded sounds of groans and maniacal laughter, so that they resounded through the Haunted House. Letting go of Bonnie, Elena headed for her own chosen spot as the doors opened to let in the crowd.

It took a long time for Damon to appear. From her hiding place behind a particularly gruesome-looking plastic apparatus and agonised dummy in the Torture Room, Elena listened to the shrieks of kids going through the Haunted House and itched with impatience and anxiety.

Stefan paced from one side of the room to the other and hesitated in the doorway, listening carefully. The red light that illuminated the room turned his skin a ghastly shade. Things were coming to a crisis, Elena could see that. Stefan's jaw was set and he was kneading the bridge of his nose between his finger and thumb. He was worried that Damon might be feeding on humans while he and Elena waited in the wrong place. Finally he straightened, making up his mind, and stepped towards the entrance once more.

Just then, a hooded figure came through the door, black robes sweeping around him. The Grim Reaper regarded Stefan silently for a moment, scythe clutched in front of him, and then he swept back his hood.

'Hello, little brother,' Damon said, showing his teeth in what looked more like a snarl than a smile.

Stefan looked at him gravely. 'I've been waiting for you, Damon,' he said.

Damon cocked a cynical eyebrow. 'Saint Stefan,' he said mockingly. 'Does the lovely Elena want you to make peace? Stop me from making a new family?' He moved closer, resting a hand lightly on Stefan's shoulder, and Elena saw Stefan flinch. Stefan was, she realised, afraid.

When he spoke, though, his voice was steady. 'It's been a long time since I thought talking to you would do any good, Damon. If you want family, I'm here. All I can do is try to stop you from doing your worst, from doing something you'll regret.'

Damon's smile widened. 'You stop me, baby brother? All you do is ruin everything, without even trying to.' He pulled Stefan closer, his hand clamping down on Stefan's shoulder like a vice.

Moving so fast that Elena had no time to react, not even to gasp, he spun Stefan round and slammed him into the wall, sinking his teeth deep into Stefan's throat. Stefan gave a small choked moan of pain, and Elena flinched. Damon hadn't taken care, hadn't bothered to soothe Stefan the way he would have a human. He wanted to this to hurt.

A terrible ripping noise came from the grappling brothers – Damon's teeth tearing something in Stefan's throat – and Elena clenched her fists. *This was a stupid plan*, she realised. *Damon's angry enough to kill Stefan.*

Just as she began to step forward out of her hiding place, a new voice, cool and arrogant, rang out.

'Stop it.' Katherine, her head held high and her mouth thin and angry, was suddenly beside them. Damon lifted his head, his mouth dripping with blood from his brother's throat, and they both stared at her.

She was wearing the Renaissance dress Aunt Judith had made for Elena's Halloween costume and she looked lovely, as delicate and ornate as an expensive doll, just the way she must have looked five hundred years before. The red lighting changed the ice blue of the dress to a pale violet and threw pink shadows on Katherine's pale face and golden hair.

Elena had thought that Stefan and Damon might mistake Katherine for Elena, just for a second, but it was clear that neither of them had the least doubt about who she was.

'Katherine,' Stefan said. His face was full of mixed emotions. Shock, disbelief, dawning joy and relief. Fear. 'But that's impossible. It can't be. You're dead . . .'

Katherine laughed, a brittle, desperately unhappy laugh. 'I wanted you to believe that. Your little human toy, the one who looks so much like me, *she* figured it out, but you never did.'

'Elena?' Damon asked, his eyes narrowing suspiciously.

Katherine circled them, head held high. Her long skirts swept the floor with a quiet susurration and Damon turned slowly, so that he was always facing her, tense and wary. 'Your Elena convinced me to tell you the truth.'

'Tell us then,' Stefan said steadily.

'I wanted us all to be happy,' Katherine said, looking back and forth between Stefan and Damon. Under the red lights, tears glistened on her cheeks. 'I loved you. But it wasn't good enough for you. I wanted you to love each other, but you wouldn't. I thought if I died, you *would* love each other.'

Elena had heard Katherine's story before. She let the words wash over her and concentrated on Stefan's and Damon's faces as Katherine unfolded her tale: how she had another talisman against the sun made and given her maid her ring. How the maid had burned fat in the fireplace and filled Katherine's best dress with it, left it in the sun along with Katherine's note telling Stefan and Damon she couldn't bear to be the cause of strife between them. That she hoped that, once she was gone, they would come together.

Katherine's face was paler than ever, her eyes huge, tears running down her cheeks. The story had taken her back, and it was in the hurt, puzzled voice of the young girl she had been that she exclaimed, 'You didn't listen, and you ran and got swords. You killed each other. *Why?* You made your deaths my fault.'

Stefan's face was wet with tears too, and he was as caught up in the memory as she was. 'It was my fault, Katherine, not yours. I attacked first,' he said in a choked voice. 'You don't know how sorry I've been, how many times I've prayed to take it all back. I murdered my own brother . . .'

Damon was watching him intently, his eyes dark and opaque. Elena couldn't tell what he was thinking. Surely this was what he needed? To know their centuries of enmity had been pointless, that his brother regretted striking that blow and dooming them both?

Stefan turned to him. 'Please, Damon,' Stefan said, his voice cracking. 'I'm sorry. What we've fought about for so long, hated each other over' – he gestured to Katherine – 'none of it was real.'

Trembling, Stefan reached a hand towards his brother, and something snapped shut in Damon's expression. He stepped away as quickly as a cat.

'Well, it's lovely to know that you've survived,' he said, turning to Katherine. His voice sharpened. 'But don't flatter yourself that I've spent the last five hundred years pining over you. It's not about you any more, Katherine. It hasn't been for a long time.'

As he spoke, his eyes fixed on the spot where Elena was hiding. *He's known I'm here all along*, she realised. She stepped out from behind the dummy. 'Please, Damon,' she began.

But Damon's face was a mask of fury. 'You think this

changes anything, Elena? I'm not going to forgive you so you can live happily ever after with my whining weakling of a baby brother. The world is *nothing* but suffering, and the fact that one girl lived when we thought she was dead doesn't make any difference. This doesn't change my plans.'

Moving too quickly for their eyes to follow, Damon was gone.

CHAPTER

27

'He's beautiful,' Katherine said, 'but he's always had that rage inside him. When he was human, I thought it was romantic.'

'We have to stop him,' Elena said to Stefan. 'In this mood, he'll kill anyone who gets in his way.'

'You promised me I would save them,' Katherine said. Her face began to crumble with disappointment. 'You said I'd be a hero.'

There was a glimmer of violence in Katherine's eyes. Elena remembered the white tiger Katherine could become, the cruelty of the Katherine she'd met the first time she'd gone through this. Elena's lips parted. She had to say something to defuse the situation.

'I want what you wanted for us, Katherine,' Stefan cut in. His face was more open than Elena had seen it in this time. 'You sacrificed everything for us and I won't forget that. But we have to find Damon before it's too late. Before your sacrifice was for nothing.'

In a moment of sympathy and understanding, Katherine approached Stefan. Elena saw in Katherine what she'd been feeling for the past few weeks – loss of true love. Katherine pressed her lips to Stefan's cheek, as gently as a human would. And then in the blink of an eye, Katherine was gone.

'Come on,' Elena said, gripping Stefan by the hand and pulling him out of the door of the Torture Chamber. 'We have to find him.'

A giggling group of girls pushed past them into the Torture Chamber, and Elena hesitated in the passageway, looking both ways. The Haunted House was teeming with people. Which way would Damon have gone?

Stefan pushed her gently towards her left. 'You go that way,' he said grimly. 'I'll work my way back towards the entrance. There are only so many places he could be.'

'Check on the Druid Room first,' Elena said. They needed to make sure he wasn't anywhere near Mr Tanner. 'We'll find him, Stefan.'

Of course, we don't know what we'll be able to do if we find him, a nagging voice remarked in the back of Elena's mind. Still, she headed through the maze of rooms, her eyes raking the shadows, looking for the Grim Reaper.

There were a lot of people in black-robed costumes but none of them were Damon.

An engine revved behind her and Elena was shoved sideways by a shrieking group as a chainsaw-wielding masked man chased them down the hall. She took a turn between two partitions and found herself suddenly alone.

'On your way to Grandma's, Little Red?' someone whispered throatily behind her.

Elena turned to see a werewolf, its mask's muzzle dripping with gruesomely realistic blood. 'Matt?' she asked uncertainly.

'Didn't they tell you to stay on the path?' The werewolf's voice got a little louder as he leered at her.

Tyler, Elena realised with disappointment. 'Have you seen Matt?' she asked, her voice flat.

'There's more than one wolf in these woods, Little Red,' Tyler told her, laying a large, hairy paw on her shoulder.

Elena shrugged it off. 'Look, Tyler, I really need to find Matt. Or Meredith,' she added. If she knew where they were, maybe she could hide them from Damon.

Tyler scowled. 'No, I don't know where they are.' He leaned against her, his breath hot on her neck. 'Come play with me instead, pretty girl. I'll show you the way to Grandma's house.'

'If you see them – or Caroline or Bonnie – tell them I'm looking for them, OK?'

He huffed a sigh. 'Whatever.' Two girls Elena didn't know turned the corner into the other end of the hall and Tyler lost interest in Elena. 'Full moon, ladies,' he shouted, walking towards them, and tipped his head back in a throaty howl as they giggled.

Elena passed through the Spider Room next but there was no one there but a bunch of rowdy junior high boys, batting the rubber spiders at each other. The Living Dead Room was teeming with people, one of whom, moaning, '*Braaaaains,*' pretended to take a bite out of Elena's face. But there was no black-clad Meredith in a witch costume, no werewolf Matt, no Egyptian Caroline.

Dread settled in the pit of Elena's stomach. Could Damon have trapped them all in the fated Druid Room? Could Stefan be outnumbered? Bonnie ought to be there too, playing a priestess sacrificing Mr Tanner. At least she knew where Bonnie was supposed to be.

I told her it was going to be all right, Elena remembered. Half running, she headed for the Druid Room.

Bonnie wasn't there. There was no one poised above the altar, although Elena could hear shrieks and laughter coming from not far away. Strobe lights flashed, giving the whole room a dizzying, dreamlike quality. Beneath the cardboard Stonehenge, Mr Tanner was stretched out across the sacrificial stone altar, his robes heavily stained with blood, his eyes blankly staring up at the ceiling. Beside him lay the ritual knife in a pool of blood.

The chill in Elena's centre hardened into a frightened little ball. She rushed towards him, trying to see if Mr Tanner was breathing. His eyes were rolled back in his head, showing little more than the whites.

She bent over the still figure, working up the nerve to touch him. 'Mr Tanner?' she said softly. *Too late, too late*, the little voice in the back of her head mourned. If Damon had managed to kill Mr Tanner, then Elena was dead, Damon was dead, Stefan was dead.

Elena extended a shaking hand, her heart hammering, to touch Mr Tanner's neck, to feel for a pulse.

Just before her hand made contact, Mr Tanner sat up. 'AAAAARRRGGGGGHHHH!' he shrieked into her face.

Elena screamed, a thin, high sound of shock, and back-pedalled away from him, banging her hip hard against the wall. Stiffly, Mr Tanner lay back down in the same position, his eyes rolling back into his head again. A small, pleased smile tugged at the corners of his mouth.

Pressing a hand against her chest, Elena tried to calm her wildly pounding heart. She took a deep breath as it started to sink in: Mr Tanner was still alive. She hadn't failed. She could still save herself, save them all.

CHAPTER
28

Elena rushed from room to room, looking for the others. She was panting, but she couldn't stop to catch her breath. She had to stop Damon before it was too late.

'Elena.' Outside the Mad Slasher Room, Stefan came towards her, his dark clothes and hair blending into the shadows of the hall, only his pale face and white shirt front standing out clearly. Elena stopped, eager for news. 'I found Meredith,' he said. 'She's up at the front with a lot of other people, taking money.'

'She should be safe there,' Elena said. 'As long as she doesn't head out alone.' Meredith was in charge of the whole Haunted House; she could be called into the more isolated recesses of the warehouse at any moment.

Stefan glanced away, a touch of colour rising in his

cheeks. 'I, er, Influenced her to stick with the group instead of wandering off by herself.'

'Good thinking,' Elena said. 'Now we just need to find everyone else.'

The Mad Slasher Room was packed and full of noise. A boy with a chainsaw was enthusiastically revving it, chasing screaming victims around the room. Fake blood was grotesquely sprayed across the walls, and less noisy maniacs strangled and hacked at anyone who came close. Elena jumped and shuddered as the laughing, shrieking victims shoved past her.

They were playing at blood and death, and Damon could be anywhere, watching, ready to tear them apart. She felt sick as she tried to make out individual faces and costumes in the crowd.

There was no Grim Reaper, no Egyptian priestess, no werewolf, no Druid.

In contrast, the Alien Encounter Room was quiet when they passed through. Bright beams of light flashed on and off overhead, while a girl stretched out on a table below was poked and prodded by grey alien-looking figures. The girl glanced up and winked at Elena, and Elena realised it was Sue Carson.

No one Elena and Stefan were looking for.

Caroline should have been in the Deaths from History Room, playing with a rubber snake, but she wasn't.

Turning to leave, Elena caught sight of red curls

peeking out from under the black hood of a rather short executioner wielding a plastic axe over Anne Boleyn's head. Grabbing hold of the executioner's axe arm, she asked, 'Bonnie? What are you doing here?'

'Ray had to go to the bathroom,' Bonnie explained, pulling off the hood. Underneath, she looked a little sweaty and dishevelled, strands of hair sticking to her forehead. 'I said I'd take over for a few minutes.'

'Bonnie, Damon's here somewhere,' Elena said. 'Have you seen Matt or Caroline?'

Bonnie sobered. 'Caroline ought to be here,' she said. 'Everyone's been wondering where she is. The last time I saw Matt was in the Fun House. I'll come with you.' She propped the plastic axe against the wall and led the way, Stefan and Elena hurrying after her.

The entrance to the Fun House was concealed behind a long black curtain. As Elena reached to twitch it aside, a hooded figure stepped out, black clothes swirling all around it. Elena jerked backward, her breath catching in her throat.

But the dark figure was too short to be Damon.

'Vickie?' Elena said, peering beneath the hood. 'Have you seen Matt or Caroline?'

Vickie frowned, thinking hard. 'I can't say,' she said.

Beside her, Elena felt Stefan stiffen, turning his full focus on to Vickie. 'You can't say?' he asked slowly. 'Vickie, can we come into the Fun House?'

'The Fun House is closed,' Vickie told them.

'What? No, it's not,' Bonnie said, and tried to dodge past her, but Vickie shoved her backward.

'You can't go in there,' she said. There was something flat behind Vickie's usually timid brown eyes, and Elena finally figured out what was going on: Damon had compelled Vickie to keep them out.

Stefan wouldn't be able to compel Vickie to let them in – his Power wasn't as strong as Damon's – but he was stronger than any human. Her eyes met Stefan's green ones, and she knew they were in perfect agreement. He would have to overpower Vickie.

'Hang on,' Bonnie said. Her small hand gripped Elena's and she pulled on Stefan's arm with her other hand. She tugged them down the hall with her, looking back to smile over her shoulder at Vickie.

'Damon's compelled her,' Stefan said, pulling out of Bonnie's grasp as soon as they turned the corner away from Vickie's gaze. 'Caroline or Matt – maybe both of them – must be in the Fun House. There isn't much time.'

'I know,' Bonnie said. 'But there's another way into the Fun House.'

Crooking a finger for Elena and Stefan to follow, Bonnie led them to a narrow opening between two partitions and pulled aside a swathe of black cloth. 'Duck under here,' she said softly, 'and we'll come out at the other end of the Fun House.'

'You're the best, Bonnie,' Elena whispered, and

ducked under the cloth.

When Elena straightened up, she had to blink and shield her eyes for a moment. Strobe lights were flashing here too, but far faster and brighter than in the Druid Room, as if they had been turned up to their maximum settings.

In one bright flash of light, Elena saw a twisted face, pale and staring. A corpse. They were too late, she realised with numb horror. Everything was lost.

'Elena?' Stefan asked. He must have been able to hear the panicked change in her breathing. The lights flashed again and she realised there was no corpse, just her own reflection, distorted by a Fun House mirror.

The mirrors were everywhere. An image of Elena and Bonnie stretched out like elastic bands stood by a reflection of Stefan with an enormous head. Loud carnival music blared all around them.

The whole effect was dizzying, and Elena wanted to shut her eyes, but there was no time. They had to find Damon.

The hall of mirrors curved in front of them and they couldn't see the other end. Cocking her head to indicate the direction, Elena led Bonnie and Stefan up the hall, stumbling as the lights dimmed, then flashed again.

As they rounded the bend, she saw Damon and Caroline, reflected over and over. There were a hundred Damons and Carolines in the flashes of light, all around her, squashed and bulbous, long and thin, bulging oddly.

In the centre, two perfectly beautiful people, one human and one vampire, were locked in what was almost an embrace.

Damon had thrown off his cloak and wore jeans and a black shirt. His head was bent back, exposing his long white throat to Caroline. In one hand he clasped a dagger loosely – Stefan's dagger, Elena realised, one of his stolen treasures – and Elena could see that he had made a cut along his breastbone for Caroline to feed from. Her face was pressed against Damon's chest and, with a shudder of disgust, Elena realised Caroline was swallowing his blood eagerly.

When Caroline raised her head for a moment, her mouth was red and slick with blood. It dripped down her chin and marked her pure-white shift. Elena recoiled. The girl's cat-green eyes seemed dazed, and as she gazed up at Damon adoringly, Elena was quite sure he'd put Caroline heavily under his Power.

'Stay back, Elena,' Stefan said softly.

At the sound of Stefan's voice, Damon looked up and threw him a dazzling, brief smile. Turning Caroline gently round so that she faced them, he raised his dagger and laid it against her throat. Caroline hung in his grasp, blinking slowly, not seeming to even see them.

'No,' Stefan said. Elena could feel him tensing himself for one desperate run at Damon. And she knew, as surely as if she had seen it, that if Stefan made a move towards him, Damon would cut Caroline's throat.

'Stop,' she said, her voice breaking. 'Everybody, just stop.' She pushed back her own red hood so that she and Damon could see each other more clearly. His eyes held hers, wide and dark, and his lips tipped up in a mocking smile.

'You *need* each other, you and Stefan,' she said. 'Why are you trying to make another family when your family is here?'

Damon sneered. 'Family. Stefan hasn't been my family since he stuck a sword through my heart.'

Beside her, Elena felt Stefan stiffen. Then he stepped forward. 'There is *nothing* I regret more than that. I killed you. My only brother.' His green eyes were full of tears. 'Even if I lived for ever, I could never make it up to you.'

Damon stared at him, his handsome face blank.

'Remember how Stefan followed you when you were a child?' Elena asked. 'He'd take a beating from your father rather than ever betray your secrets. He *worshipped* you.' She felt Stefan glance at her curiously, wondering how Elena could know that, but it didn't matter now. She kept her attention firmly fixed on Damon.

Was his grip on the dagger pressed to Caroline's throat loosening? Elena wasn't sure.

'Remember Incognita, the beautiful black mare you

won playing cards, when you were just sixteen?' Stefan said hoarsely. 'That morning when you brought her home, you let me ride behind you, and we went so fast, her hooves hardly touched the ground. We were invincible then. Happy.'

Surely the taut line of Damon's mouth was softening, Elena thought. The dagger had slipped a little, resting gently against Caroline's throat as she sagged, half conscious, in Damon's arms. But then Damon tensed again.

'Sentimental tales from the nursery,' he scoffed. 'Those children have been dead for centuries.' He took a fresh grip on the knife.

'It still matters,' Elena said desperately. 'You're both still *here*. There are only two people left in the world who remember you when you were alive, Damon. Once Stefan is gone, only Katherine will remember, and she's the one who changed you. No one else knows anything but the monster. It's not too late to change that.'

Damon hesitated for a split second. 'Again with these promises you can't keep. If you want the good brother, you already have him.'

Elena shook her head. 'No,' she said. 'This isn't about that. I never had either of you, not in this world.'

Damon's forehead creased in a puzzled frown, but Stefan held out his hands to his brother beseechingly, walking slowly towards him. 'I never meant to kill you,' he said, as softly and soothingly as he would have spoken to a wild animal. 'I would spend the rest of my days trying to right that wrong, if you would be my brother again.'

There was a long, tense moment. The cheerful, hectic carnival music was at odds with the mood of the room.

In a quick motion, Damon pushed Caroline forward so that she fell on to the floor, landing hard and lying motionless. Bonnie gasped and rushed to her.

Looking past Stefan, Damon's black eyes met Elena's. 'I won't turn your friends,' he said shortly. His gaze shifted back to Stefan's. 'I won't kill you either, I suppose. Not now at least.'

There was no embrace between Stefan and Damon, no show of catharsis. But Elena caught a hint of a smile on Damon's face – a small, private smile Elena had seen before, in the future she left behind. It was a smile Damon only ever gave to his brother.

Joy flooded through her, as if she was filling with sunlight. Mr Tanner had survived. Bonnie and Meredith and Matt and Caroline – who Bonnie was fussing over now – were still human. Halloween night was almost over.

She was going to have a future. They were all going to live.

CHAPTER
29

'It went really well, don't you think?' Meredith said, tucking a long lock of dark hair behind her ear and looking up at the closed entrance to the Haunted House.

It was late, but they'd only managed to clear out all the customers about half an hour before. Across the parking lot, the last of the costumed workers were climbing into their cars, laughing and calling goodbyes to one another. The heavy clouds that had hung overhead at the beginning of the evening had cleared and now stars shone brightly in the sky.

Elena linked her arms through Bonnie's and Meredith's, pulling her best friends close, and smiled at Matt beside them. 'I thought it was amazing.'

Stefan and Damon had disappeared somewhere

together shortly after their reconciliation, but that was all right with Elena. She was happy, for now, to have this last time with her oldest, dearest friends.

And it was the last time, she was suddenly sure of it. The Guardians hadn't sent Elena to start over; they had only sent her to change things. There would probably be an Elena here tomorrow, she thought, but she was pretty sure it wouldn't be her, it wouldn't be the Elena who had lived this more than once.

She was going to wake up in that Elena's future, whatever future she had made. And she hoped that Matt, Meredith and Bonnie would be part of that future somehow, but they wouldn't be the ones she knew now.

This was goodbye.

'You did such a good job planning the whole thing, Meredith,' Elena said. 'It seems like you can do anything you put your mind to. You're *wonderful*.'

Meredith's olive cheeks flushed pink. 'Thanks,' she said, dipping her head shyly.

They'd reached Matt's car, and Meredith opened the passenger door and climbed in. As Matt crossed to the driver's side, Elena hugged him. 'You're one of the best people I know, you know that?' she said. She was choking up a little. 'I *promise* everything will be OK. Remember that.'

Kissing her on the cheek, Matt drew back with a little rueful half-smile. 'You still have to help us clean up the Haunted House tomorrow,' he told her. Elena just laughed.

As Matt closed the car door behind him, Elena turned to see Bonnie watching her with an affectionate, knowing gaze. 'This is it, huh?' she said. She was smiling, but her lips were quivering a little.

'I guess so,' Elena told her.

With a sniff, Bonnie threw herself into Elena's arms and held her tightly.

'Oh, Scarecrow,' Elena murmured into her friend's bright curls. 'I think I'll miss you most of all.'

After one tight hug, Bonnie pulled back, swiping a hand quickly under her eyes. 'Seven years in the future isn't that long. You'll see me then.'

'I hope so,' Elena said. She reached out and took Bonnie's hand for a moment, squeezing it tightly. She tried to memorise the feeling of Bonnie's small, strong hand gripping hers.

She would remember this, just in case. She would remember Matt's open, honest face and Meredith's wry smile. Whatever happened, she wouldn't forget them.

For now, there was one more thing she had to tell Bonnie. 'You should go and talk to Mrs Flowers. You saw how much Power you have, and she'll be able to teach you how to use it. I expect you to be crazy-powerful seven years from now.'

'Aye aye, Captain,' Bonnie said, saluting ridiculously.

Then her gaze slipped past Elena and Elena turned to follow it.

Stefan was crossing the parking lot towards them. Elena and Bonnie exchanged a glance.

'I'll tell the others to wait. Take your time,' Bonnie said, and slipped into the car.

Elena walked slowly towards Stefan. As she reached him, he looked down into Elena's eyes. There were no words worthy of expressing what either of them felt.

Elena wanted to take him in her arms and hold on tight, but she didn't. He wasn't hers now.

She might never see him again. The thought filled her with an almost painful sorrow, but not with the angry bewilderment she'd felt at his death. Now she had the chance to say goodbye.

Stefan's green eyes searched hers, as if he was looking for answers. 'I wanted to say thank you,' he said finally. 'Damon and I are leaving. We've decided to go back to Italy for now. I wanted – we wanted – to see what's left of the Florence we remember.' His lips quirked up in a half-smile. 'We'll see if we can find more of our humanity there, I suppose.'

Elena nodded. 'I'm glad,' she said.

He reached out and took her hands, so gently and carefully that Elena's heart ached with longing. 'What can I do to thank you?' he said slowly.

Elena squeezed his hand once, fiercely, and then pulled away. 'You don't need to thank me,' she said, hearing the roughness of almost-tears in her own voice. 'Just take care of Damon. And of yourself.'

She turned towards the car where her friends were waiting, and Stefan touched her on the shoulder. 'Will I see you again?' he asked.

'I don't know,' she said honestly. 'I don't think so. But just . . . keep going, OK? For yourself, and for Damon. Remember that there's someone out there who cares about you, the real you.'

'You are a mysterious one, Elena Gilbert,' Stefan said. With one last nod of appreciation, Stefan turned to go.

Hot tears were running down her cheeks as Elena watched Stefan walk out of her life for ever. But Elena wasn't sad, or not only sad. This Stefan might live. And that made it all worthwhile.

CHAPTER

30

As Elena rode home in the back seat of Matt's car, her thoughts drifted to the one person she hadn't had a chance to say goodbye to. Maybe it was for the best. She didn't know how she'd say goodbye to Damon.

In the front seat, Matt and Meredith were laughing, talking about the Haunted House. They'd missed *everything*. With luck, they'd never know about vampires, never be touched by the darkness all around them. They'd be normal. Happy.

Bonnie jostled Elena gently. 'Are you OK?' she whispered.

Elena sighed and laid her head on her friend's shoulder, just for a moment.

Bonnie wrapped an arm around her shoulders. 'You helped them. From what you told me, I think you've saved a lot of people.'

'Yeah,' Elena said, her voice small. She blinked back the sting of tears in her eyes. She'd saved herself too. Stefan. Damon.

In the big picture, it didn't matter if she never got to say goodbye to Damon, if she never saw either Salvatore brother again. Not if they all got to live.

When they pulled up to her house, Elena hugged all three of her friends again, fast and hard, before climbing out of the car and waving goodbye.

Aunt Judith had left the porch light on for her but the windows of the house were dark. They must already be in bed.

As Elena crossed the lawn, a dark shape detached itself from the shadows beneath the quince tree and came towards her.

'Damon,' she said, happiness flaring up inside her, hot and sudden.

Damon came close and looked at Elena for a few moments without speaking, his black eyes unreadable. 'I suppose I should say thank you,' he said at last.

'You're welcome,' Elena said, holding his gaze steadily.

'You're no coward.' Damon gave her his quick, devastating smile.

Elena smiled back, and Damon took her by the arm and led her to her front porch. 'More comfortable here,' he said, sitting down on the porch steps, and Elena sat beside him. She was still wearing the Red Riding Hood cloak, and she was glad of its warmth.

Damon tilted his head back to look at the stars. 'I suppose Stefan told you we've decided to go back to Italy,' he said conversationally. 'He seems to think that things might get sticky here, with the fire and the graveyard desecration and all that.' Damon lifted one shoulder in a graceful shrug.

'I can imagine,' Elena said. She let herself lean into him a little bit. She felt as if her heart was, very quietly, breaking.

'Come with us,' Damon said suddenly. 'I have this strange feeling that it would be a terrible mistake to leave you behind.'

He was still looking up at the stars, as intensely as if he could read the future written in the sky. The moonlight and the porch light combined threw shadows across his face, softening Damon's aristocratic features and the stubborn set of his mouth.

'Oh, Damon,' Elena said. Tears started to pool in her eyes.

Damon tore his gaze away from the sky and looked at her, his eyes dark and more open than she had ever seen them in this time. 'Come,' he said again. 'Please.'

'I can't,' Elena said. Damon flinched and, on an impulse, she put out one hand and covered his heart. 'You're good,' she told him furiously. 'In here.

You can be so good, so *wonderful* if you decide to be. Don't forget that.'

Tears ran down Elena's face, hot on her cold skin. She scrambled to her feet and backed away towards the front door.

'Goodbye, Damon,' she said quickly, longingly. His face was full of confusion and he started to rise, but she was already closing the door behind her.

Elena leaned against the door and just let the tears fall. Every part of her yearned to go with Stefan and Damon.

What if she did? Would she wake up in a future where she and Damon and Stefan had been travelling Europe together, a happy triumvirate, for the last seven years?

No. Elena shook her head. She wasn't going to be selfish like that, not the way she'd always been selfish with the Salvatore brothers. She'd seen where it led. She wasn't going to make Katherine's mistakes. Not again.

Wiping her eyes, Elena peered out the window by the front door, but Damon was gone.

Her shoulders slumped and Elena started up the stairs, feeling unutterably exhausted.

Margaret's trick-or-treat bag was in the hall outside her door, stuffed with candy, and Elena smiled a little.

Turning into her own bedroom, Elena kicked off her shoes and lay down on the bed, not bothering

VAMPIRE DIARIES

to change into her nightgown.

A tear slipped out from under her eyelids and ran slowly down her cheek. But a certain peace settled over Elena, and as she fell into a slumber, she knew without a doubt that, as much as it hurt, she'd done the right thing.

CHAPTER
31

Elena woke up in a room flooded with light. The white ceiling above her was unfamiliar, outlined with ornate crown moulding. Sitting up, she looked around. She was in a big bed heaped with soft pillows and a thick duvet. Sunlight streamed in through full-length windows at one end of the room, which opened on to a tiny balcony she could just see from the bed.

Hopping out of bed, Elena wiggled her toes against the thick pale carpet and padded out barefoot to examine the rest of the apartment. She wasn't in the clothes she'd fallen asleep in any more, she realised, but in crisp, white cotton pyjamas. Elena ran a hand across them wonderingly.

It wasn't a big apartment: bedroom, bathroom, a kitchen with a small dining alcove at one end, a little living room with a large, cushy pale-green sofa. Everything looked peaceful and comfortable in light, neutral shades, accented with forest green or jewel blue. Paintings hung on the walls – not posters, but real paintings, a couple of them abstract, one an intricate landscape, another a charcoal sketch of a young girl's face. The apartment felt like a nest, a retreat made just for one. Just for her.

It felt like home, she realised, even though she'd never seen it before.

She rummaged through the kitchen, finding coffee and figuring out the intimidatingly complicated brushed-steel coffee maker. While it brewed, she went back into the bedroom to get dressed. Everything in the closet seemed simple and chic, more sophisticated than the old Elena had been used to, and she pulled on a pair of close-fitting black trousers and a light-blue top made of impossibly soft fabric.

Picking up a hairbrush, she looked into the mirror and froze. For a moment she held her breath, examining the almost-stranger in the mirror.

She looked older. Not too old, but like she was in her mid-twenties. Her hair was shorter, falling just past her chin, and there were a few tiny lines beginning at the corners of her eyes, as if she'd been squinting in the sun. Elena tilted her head, watching the swing of her hair against her cheek. She looked good, she thought.

In the life she'd lived with Stefan, Elena had drunk

the Waters of Eternal Life and Youth at age eighteen, and stopped getting older. Stopped changing. She hadn't wanted to age while Stefan stayed young, had wanted to be by his side for eternity.

It had been the right choice when they had been together. After Stefan had been killed, it had seemed like living death to go on without him for ever, to never grow old or have the possibility of having children. Now she would get to change. She had grown up, and she would keep ageing.

As she turned away from the mirror, Elena's gaze fell upon something on her bedside table that she hadn't seen before: a golden ball, just the right size to fit comfortably in her palm. Picking it up, Elena pressed the catch and watched the ball unfold into a small golden hummingbird set with gems.

The music box Damon had given her.

Was it possible? Had they found each other again, somewhere in the intervening years between Fell's Church and now? Her heart began to pound wildly, full of hope.

Carefully, she put the music box back on the table. There was a crisply folded note next to where it had stood. Elena picked the note up with shaking hands and unfolded it.

> *Well done, Elena. Here is a small souvenir of your past life, as a token of our regard. Enjoy your*

humanity – you've earned it. I hope you find your true destiny. Mylea

The Celestial Guardians had given her a piece of the life she had lost. It was a kind gesture, she knew, but it pierced a hole in her heart. A token could never replace the love she had sacrificed. No home could be home without someone to share it with.

Stepping out on to the balcony, Elena gazed over the city before her and felt her mouth drop open. Far away, over the rooftops, she could just glimpse the Eiffel Tower.

'Hideous,' she suddenly remembered Damon saying, that last day together in Paris. 'A truly tragic streetlamp.'

Elena stifled a giggle. *She* thought it was beautiful anyway.

Wow. She lived in *Paris*.

Energised, Elena turned to the task of figuring out just who Elena Gilbert was in this new future. She rifled through her drawers, read her own papers, sorted through the mail. Rummaging through the cupboards and refrigerator, she devoured the chewy bread, soft cheese and crisp fruit she found inside.

By the time a couple of hours had passed, she knew that she worked at an art gallery. She had an undergraduate degree in art history, from the Université de Paris. Apparently, Elena had come to Paris for a junior year abroad from the University of Virginia – not

Dalcrest College – and never left, finishing her education here.

She had lived alone in this apartment for two years, according to her lease. There were notes from friends in both English and French – and it was a relief to realise that she could read French much more fluently than she had been able to in her old life. Elena smiled over a gossipy birthday card from Aunt Judith that made it clear she and Robert and Margaret were just as happy in this life as in Elena's previous one.

There was no sign of any romance. Elena's heart ached a little at that. But who could she have loved after the Salvatore brothers?

Just as Elena was sweeping papers back into her desk drawers, there was a tapping at her front door.

Leaping up, Elena rushed towards it. It was Bonnie, she was sure of it, or Meredith. She could picture them here. Meredith probably had helped Elena pick out the chic outfits. Bonnie must have cast a protection spell over the whole apartment.

She flung open the door.

'Elena!' said the dark-haired girl on the other side, her arms full of shopping bags. Elena had never seen her before. She kissed Elena enthusiastically on each cheek in greeting. 'Can I leave these here? Come on, we'll be late.'

She said it all in French, very fast, and Elena was relieved to realise she spoke and understood French as well as she read it.

A name popped into Elena's head, along with a remembered warm affection. 'Veronique,' she greeted her friend. 'Where are we going?'

Veronique made a little moue of pretended offence. 'You forgot our Sunday lunch?' she asked. 'The others are probably already there.'

The restaurant at which they had lunch was as stylish and tasteful as the rest of Elena's new life. The two friends waiting for them there were as lovely as Veronique was. They jumped to their feet and kissed Veronique and Elena on both cheeks, laughing. Elena laughed with them, knowing beyond a shadow of a doubt that these were people she loved.

She just wished she could remember them properly.

After a few minutes she got them all straight. Veronique was talkative and bossy, with a quick, good-humoured smile. She was a stockbroker, and she and Elena had been roommates in college. Elena had a flash of memory: Veronique, softer and younger, her hair tied up in a sloppy bun, hollow-eyed from staying up late studying for exams.

Lina was quieter and more soft-spoken, with huge dreamy eyes and long light-brown hair. She worked at the gallery with Elena and was the niece of the owner.

And Manon, sharp-witted and sarcastic with very short, very pale-blonde hair, was a graduate student at the Sorbonne, doing a joint degree in art history and law. She had gone to university with Elena and Veronique.

'If you want to get further with art history,' she was advising Elena, 'you should come back to school. The museums will never hire someone with only an undergraduate degree.'

'Perhaps,' Elena said, sipping her wine. She hadn't found school particularly interesting back in the life she remembered. There had been too much else to do: monsters to fight, the ongoing drama of her love life to manage.

Maybe here, studying something she loved, with the idea that it would actually help her get a particular job . . . She felt excitement blossom in her chest. She could tell from the way Manon was talking that the Elena these girls knew was serious about her career.

Lina began to describe a show she and Elena were organising at the gallery to the other girls, and Elena listened, eyes wide.

'It was Elena who suggested arranging the pieces by the models instead of chronologically,' Lina said. 'A very interesting effect. He used the same models over and over, for years, and you can see the women growing older, just as his art developed.'

Elena felt a flush of pride. Even though she didn't remember it, apparently she was good at her job.

'Let's talk about something more interesting than art,' Veronique said eventually. 'Elena. Are you going to go out with Hugo again?'

Hugo? Elena tried to prompt the memory that had given her the names of her friends, but came up blank. 'I don't know,' she said slowly.

In unison, all three girls sighed.

'He's such a nice man,' Lina said, tucking a long lock of hair behind her ear. 'And he's crazy about you.'

'I will take him off your hands if you don't want him,' Manon said. 'That lovely man, just going to waste.' She rolled her eyes exaggeratedly, laughing.

'Obviously you shouldn't date anyone you don't want,' Veronique added, 'but it seems like you're never even open to the *idea* of love.'

Elena didn't know what to say. Even without memories of this time, she knew why she wasn't looking for love, why she wasn't falling for the lovely man they were talking about. How could she? She had left her heart with Damon and Stefan, wherever they were. Finally she shrugged. 'Sometimes it's not meant to be, I guess.'

'We worry about you,' Veronique said flatly. 'It's like you're waiting for something, and we don't want you to let life pass you by.'

Looking back at her Parisian friends, Elena was hit by a sudden rush of homesickness. Meredith and Bonnie would have fussed over her and nudged her in just the same way. Where were they now? Had the vow they had sworn in the churchyard, to be friends for ever, come true? *I hope so*, she thought. *I hope I haven't lost everyone from my old life, even if I've lost . . . even if I can't have . . .*

'Oh, we didn't mean to make you sad,' Lina said softly, laying a warm soft hand over hers. 'It will all come right in the end.'

When she came back from lunch, the apartment seemed entirely too quiet. Elena wandered through the flat, touching the sleek, pale furniture, rearranging the books and ornaments.

It was exactly the kind of place she'd always dreamed of. And yet, she felt terribly wistful.

She was reminding herself of Damon, she realised. How he had brushed his fingers across her possessions, opened drawers to peer inside, inspected her photographs. Like him, she was trying to figure out the person who lived here.

Elena laughed a little and wiped her eyes. The person who lived here had a wonderful life. Elena just wasn't sure if it was really hers.

In the kitchen she found an invitation held by a magnet to the refrigerator, something she'd somehow managed to overlook on her first rummage through the apartment.

Elena read: '. . . invite you to the wedding of their daughter Bonnie Mae McCullough to Zander—' She stopped.

Zander? She could feel a smile beginning on her face. Some things must be destined after all.

CHAPTER

32

Amazing. Despite everything that had changed, Bonnie was not only marrying the same guy, she'd chosen the same bridesmaids' dresses. As she waited to walk down the aisle behind Bonnie's two older sisters, Elena carefully straightened the long rose-pink gown and held her bouquet – pale lilies and bright roses – at waist level.

This time, though, the wedding was in the church Bonnie's parents attended, and there seemed to be a lot more people in attendance. Elena looked over the crowd, picking out faces she recognised: Sue Carson, Bonnie's dad's business partner, Mrs Flowers. Apparently, when Bonnie's mom and sisters had time to get involved, things got a lot more elaborate.

Someone struck up the wedding march and the

bridesmaids began to file in, first Bonnie's sisters; then Shay, Zander's second-in-command in the pack; then a girl Elena didn't know who had been Bonnie's roommate at Dalcrest College; then Meredith, head held high, stepped down the aisle.

Meredith looked terrific. Confident and elegant, her beautiful thick dark hair piled on top of her head. And she was *human*. Elena let the spreading joy of that fact run through her. The changes Elena had made back during those fateful few months in high school had saved Meredith.

When it was Elena's turn, she raised her head high, held her flowers low and stepped carefully and slowly, just the way she'd been told. At the front of the church, she took her place next to Meredith and looked over at the guys' side of the aisle.

It was all werewolves – Matt and Zander must not be good friends here – jostling one another rowdily, but they stilled and came to attention as Zander lifted his head, pushing his pale-blond hair out of his eyes, and saw Bonnie.

She looked beautiful. She came down the aisle on her father's arm, draped in creamy lace. Pink rosebuds were twined in her hair. Bonnie and Zander gazed at each other, and they both looked so incredibly happy that Elena's breath caught in her throat.

'Dearly beloved,' the minister said, and Elena listened with only half an ear as she watched Bonnie and Zander take each other's hands and smile at each other, a warm, private smile.

Elena had had a chance to talk to Bonnie last night after the rehearsal dinner. She and Meredith and Bonnie had sat up half the night in Bonnie's room, talking things over, just like old times. When Meredith had stepped out for a minute, Elena had turned to Bonnie and breathed, 'Bonnie, the last thing I remember before two weeks ago was Halloween night in Fell's Church.'

Bonnie had squealed and leaped up to hug Elena. It was such a relief to have just one person to share this huge secret with, Elena thought, watching as Bonnie began to speak her vows, promising to have and to hold.

Things hadn't changed that much for Bonnie in this life. She was a witch, she had gone to Dalcrest, she taught kindergarten, she loved Zander, she lived in Colorado. She was happy. Perhaps a little softer and gentler than the Bonnie Elena had known in the future she'd left behind. This Bonnie hadn't been through so much, hadn't seen her friends die.

Meredith, on the other hand, had changed. Elena cast a sideways glance at her grey-eyed friend. Meredith was so much happier here. She didn't know anything about the supernatural, Bonnie had quietly confirmed. Well, she knew Bonnie said she was psychic, and was sort of New Agey with candles and herbs, but Meredith thought it was all a game. It was, Bonnie and Elena agreed, better that way.

Meredith had graduated from Harvard Law School. She was going to take the bar next month, and she wanted to work for the public defender's office in Boston. She wasn't a hunter. She wasn't a vampire.

Last night, when they'd been sharing gossip and updating one another on their lives, Meredith, eyes shining, had told them about the work she'd done with some of her classmates and professors, researching the cases of prisoners on death row that hadn't been handled properly, trying to prove the innocence of people who had been wrongly convicted.

'You're saving people,' Elena had said, impressed. 'Like a warrior.' Meredith had blushed with pleasure. It didn't matter if she hunted monsters or not, Elena realised. Meredith was always going to find a way to be a hero.

'You may kiss the bride,' the minister said, and Bonnie leaned up as Zander leaned down and they wrapped their arms around each other and kissed tenderly.

Unexpectedly, tears welled up in Elena's eyes and she bit her lip, hard, to force them away.

She was so happy for Bonnie, she told herself fiercely. And her own life was wonderful, everything she would have dreamed of in a world where she didn't have to hunt monsters, didn't have to be a Guardian.

It was just that the last time she'd been at Bonnie's wedding, she'd felt the brush of Damon's admiring regard from his seat in the audience.

Bonnie and Zander were heading down the aisle, leaving the church, and it was time to follow them. Elena took the arm of her werewolf groomsman – Spencer, the preppy one – and laughed politely at his joke without really hearing it.

Outside it was early evening and the leaves were just beginning to change. There was a briskness in the air, the beginning of autumn. Autumn, again. The last time she'd been in Fell's Church in the autumn was seven years ago, although it only felt like a few weeks, the night she'd said goodbye to Stefan and Damon.

They were out there somewhere – probably – and she should be glad of it, was glad of it, fiercely glad that they were still alive.

She felt that wistfulness again, stronger still, at the beginning of the reception, when Jared, Zander's best man, started his toast.

'Uh . . .' the shaggy-haired werewolf began, 'when Zander started dating Bonnie, we all thought she was awesome, but we were like, "Really?" because she wasn't, uh, the same kind of person we were.' Looking around the circle of faces smiling at him, Jared's eyes went wide and panicky.

This was the same toast Jared had given in that other world, so Elena knew he'd be able to pull it together. But that time, Damon's eyes had met Elena's, and she had felt Damon's rich amusement coming straight through the bond between them. They'd both laughed at the same time, quiet laughter at an inside joke.

At this wedding without that bond, without Damon, Elena felt slightly adrift.

After the toast, she and Meredith picked up their place cards and found their tables at the reception. There was someone already sitting there, and Elena grinned with delight. 'Matt!'

Matt – bigger and broader than the last time she'd seen him, but with the same open, friendly face – got to his feet and hugged them both. Beside him, a tiny woman, almost as tiny as Bonnie, jumped to her feet and hugged them too, blond curls bouncing over her shoulders.

'This is Jeannette,' Matt said proudly.

'I've heard so much about you!' she said excitedly to Elena. 'Matt and I keep saying we're going to come to Europe and see everything you've been emailing him about since college. The gallery and all.'

Sue Carson and her husband and a couple of Bonnie's college friends came to join them at the table, and the next few minutes were full of greetings and introductions.

'I'm going to get another drink,' Jeannette said brightly after a few minutes, hopping up from the table.

'I know you want a beer, honey, and can I get anyone else anything?'

Matt watched her walk away with a fond, proud smile. 'She's great, isn't she?' he asked. 'Did I tell you she's finishing up vet school? And not just poodles and things. She's going to be a large-animal vet. As little as she is, she can handle a bull or a wild horse.'

'She seems terrific,' Elena said, sipping her wine. She was happy for Matt, but she couldn't help missing Jasmine, the girlfriend he'd had for so long in the world she remembered. Maybe not everyone had a soul mate.

A thick band across one of Matt's fingers caught her eye and she leaned forward suddenly, shocked. 'Matt Honeycutt! Is that a *Super Bowl* ring?'

Matt blushed, and Meredith stared at her in disbelief. 'Honestly, Elena,' Meredith said. 'I know you live in France, but don't you even hear who wins the Super Bowl?'

Elena was momentarily dumbfounded, but Matt just rubbed at the back of his neck, embarrassed. 'It's not a big deal,' he said. 'I'm not first string, I only played for a little while.'

'Are you kidding?' Elena said, and got up to hug him. 'It's a huge deal.' She held on to him tightly for a moment. He was happy and successful. Even without Jasmine. *Maybe this is his true destiny*.

Time passed and Elena drank wine and talked to familiar faces. Dinner was served, salmon or steak, and the DJ began to play. Bonnie and Zander came out on to the dance floor for their first dance, gazing up into each other's eyes. Elena was watching their dance from the half-empty table when she looked up and saw a familiar face. *Alaric*.

He was listening to Meredith, his sandy head inclined politely as she talked, a smile on his handsome, boyish face.

Alaric Saltzman had been called in by some of the citizens of Fell's Church to investigate Mr Tanner's death. He had taken over as their history teacher to investigate the possibility of vampires being behind Tanner's murder.

In a world where Mr Tanner had survived, Alaric had never come to Fell's Church. They had never met him.

So why was he at Bonnie's wedding? Why was he talking to Meredith?

'Who's that with Meredith?' she asked, leaning across the table towards Matt and interrupting his conversation with Sue Carson. They both looked.

'I don't know,' Matt said, and Sue shook her head. 'One of Zander's friends, probably.'

As they watched, Meredith took Alaric's hand and pulled him out on to the dance floor.

'He's cute,' Sue said. 'They look good together.'

'Excuse me,' Elena said, pushing back her chair and getting up.

When she found Bonnie flitting about happily between tables, the redheaded girl hugged her enthusiastically. 'Was that not the best wedding?' she asked.

Zander's smile widened. 'She's been saying that to everyone,' he said affectionately. 'I totally agree, of course, but I might be biased.'

'It was a wonderful wedding,' Elena agreed, 'but actually I wanted to ask you, how do you know Alaric Saltzman?' On the dance floor, Alaric said something softly in Meredith's ear, and she tossed her head back and laughed.

'Alaric? Oh, the High Wolf Council called him in to consult on some problem they had a while ago,' Bonnie said vaguely. 'He and Zander got to be friends.'

Zander added, 'He's a really good guy. Meredith's OK with him.'

'How do *you* know Alaric Saltzman?' Bonnie asked curiously.

'Oh.' Elena shifted uncomfortably. It was way too much to explain, especially in a crowded reception hall. 'It's complicated. I'm sure he won't know who I am.'

'Huh. *Oh*,' Bonnie said, getting it. 'One of that kind of friend. Out of the past. Or a different time, anyway.' Zander frowned, looking slightly bemused, but he didn't say anything.

'Yes,' Elena said. 'Exactly.'

A few minutes later the photographer came over to ask Bonnie and Zander to pose with a table of Bonnie's cousins, and Elena went back to her own table. From across the room, Elena watched as Alaric and Meredith danced, and then got a drink at the bar together, laughing and leaning towards each other, Meredith reaching up unconsciously to twirl a falling tendril of her hair around her finger as she smiled up at him. When they went out on the dance floor again, Alaric was holding Meredith's hand firmly in his.

Elena took another sip of wine but it suddenly tasted bitter.

She was happy for her friends. She truly was. They deserved every happiness, both of them, and Zander and Alaric were perfect partners.

But, despite that, Elena felt like the walls she'd built up inside herself were breaking, cracking, letting a flood of misery spill through her, one small stream at a time. She put down her wine glass and clenched her hands together, willing back the tears. She wasn't going to make a scene at Bonnie's wedding.

But she would grow old and die, and she would never know what had happened to Damon and Stefan. If they'd stuck together.

She might love each of them. Did love them, had a thousand memories of love, but they were only hers. They wouldn't remember.

A lump was rising up in her throat and she knew

with sudden, devastating certainty that she was about to cry after all.

'Hey,' Matt said, leaning towards her. 'Elena. Are you OK?'

'Of course,' Elena said, her voice brittle and cracking. 'I always cry at weddings.'

'Sure,' Matt said. 'Come and dance with me then. You don't mind, do you, Jeannette?'

'Of course not,' Jeannette said lightly, looking at Elena with sympathetic, intelligent eyes. 'I'm going to see if I can track down a waiter to bring me more of those tiny crab cakes.'

His big hand securely holding hers, Matt led Elena to a distant corner of the dance floor and wrapped his arms around her. Elena pressed her face against his shoulder, glad of the warm, reassuring bulk of him.

'Do you want to talk about it?' Matt asked softly, and Elena shook her head, not looking up.

Matt held on to Elena tightly and she let the tears flow, her face buried in his shoulder where no one could see.

At least I still have this, she thought, sniffling. *At least I still have my friends.*

CHAPTER

33

Dear Diary,

The last four days in Virginia were wonderful ones. I went up and stayed with Aunt Judith and Robert in Richmond and spent some time with my baby sister. It's so hard to believe that Margaret's in middle school now. When I think about her, I still imagine that four-year-old with the big blue eyes, but she hasn't been that little girl for a long time. We went with Aunt Judith and got our nails done together, and Meggie even told me about a boy she likes! How can she have grown up so fast?

Elena glanced up from her diary and out of the tiny, rounded window as the wheels of her plane jolted as they landed on the runway. The sky at Charles de Gaulle airport was grey and drizzly, and just suited her mood. Elena sighed drearily and turned back to the diary.

> I was thinking about moving back to Virginia. I'd get to see my baby sister grow up. Aunt Judith would be happy, and even Robert would be pleased.
>
> I've got a life in Paris, of course. Friends. A job I love.
>
> And none of it feels like mine.

The plane was taxiing to the gate, and Elena looked absently out of the window again, watching the hubbub of the airport – catering trucks, baggage handlers, other planes shining wet with rain – without really seeing them.

I decided I ought to give it a chance though, she wrote slowly.

> That last night, Damon called me brave. Running back home would be just about the furthest thing from brave I can imagine.
>
> I chose *this* life, even if I can't remember it.
>
> And wherever I live, I'll have to try to figure out how to be normal. Wasn't that something I longed for, all those years?
>
> It's not the only thing I ever wanted. Not by a long shot.

But it's the only one I've got.

Up at the front of the plane, the door opened and the other passengers climbed to their feet, surging towards the exit. Elena closed her diary and tucked it in her purse, then stood up and pulled her carry-on out of the overhead bin and, squaring her shoulders, followed the other passengers out of the plane. She was going to be brave.

The airport was crowded with hurrying passengers and, despite being in Paris, managed to have the same soul-deadening atmosphere as any big airport. Fluorescent lighting hummed overhead and the smell of disinfectant was everywhere. There was a headache building up behind Elena's eyes. Maybe she was getting sick. Elena sniffed experimentally, feeling sorry for herself.

Heading for the baggage claim, all at once she saw him, and her whole inside jolted in instant, eager recognition.

No. It was impossible.

But there he was, standing by a magazine rack, looking just the way she remembered him. Strong and graceful and so beautiful, one of the most beautiful people she'd ever seen. He was wearing a beautifully cut black jacket, and he held himself like the aristocrat he'd been born as. Elena couldn't breathe. If she moved, this might be snatched away from her.

Elena knew the exact moment when he saw her too, and his whole body stiffened in shock. His eyes were wide and his lips were slowly turning up into a smile of amazement.

And then she was in motion, moving straight towards him, her high-heeled boots clacking on the tiled floor, her carry-on rattling along behind her on its little wheels.

He was coming towards her too, his gaze fixed unwaveringly on her.

This is it, Elena realised, stopping stock-still in front of him and staring dumbly up into his face. *This is who I'm meant to be with. My destiny caught up with me after all.*

'Hello, Elena.' Damon's mouth twisted into its telltale smirk, and Elena knew she was home.

#TVD13TheEnd

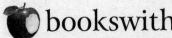

The Secret Circle

THE DIVIDE

The bewitching saga continues as the bonds of the Secret Circle are weakening...

Cassie's evil half-sister has surfaced and won't rest until she has taken Cassie's place in the Secret Circle. And a band of powerful witch-hunters are targeting the group, determined to destroy them.

Will the circle remain intact despite the powerfully evil magic that has infiltrated their ring?

And will Cassie survive this ultimate battle between good and evil?

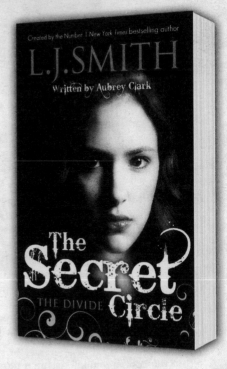

Created by the Number 1 New York Times bestselling author

L.J. SMITH

Written by Aubrey Clark

The Secret Circle
THE DIVIDE

www.hodderchildrens.co.uk

Hodder Children's Books

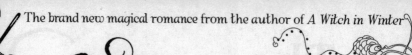

The brand new magical romance from the author of *A Witch in Winter*

WITCH FINDER

Sworn to a loveless marriage.
Sworn to avenge the death of a parent.
Sworn to kill the one you love.

Jan 2014

London 1880.

Witches killed Luke Lexton's parents and he is determined to
avenge their death by becoming a Witch Hunter. But first he must
prove his loyalty and pick a name from the Book of Witches to
track down and kill within a month or face death himself...

ISBN: 9781444914467

www.hodderchildrens.co.uk

Hodder
Children's
Books